Robert Lowell's Shifting Colors

THE POETICS
OF THE PUBLIC AND
THE PERSONAL

William Doreski

OHIO UNIVERSITY PRESS ■ *Athens*

Ohio University Press, Athens, Ohio 45701
© 1999 by William Doreski
Printed in the United States of America
All rights reserved

Ohio University Press books are printed on acid-free paper ∞ ™

03 02 01 00 99   5 4 3 2 1

Library of Congress Cataloging-in-Publication Data

Doreski, William.
    Robert Lowell's shifting colors : the poetics of the public and
    the personal / William Doreski.
        p.   cm.
    Includes bibliographical references and index.
    ISBN 0-8214-1279-5 (cloth : alk. paper)
    1. Lowell, Robert, 1917–1977—Criticism and interpretation.
I. Title.
PS3523.089Z649   199
811'.52—de21   99-13112
                                                                     CIP

Frontispiece photograph:
By permission of the Houghton Library, Harvard University

For Carole

Contents

Preface

For a brief scholarly book, *Robert Lowell's Shifting Colors* has had a long incubation, dating back to a memorable lunch with Robert Lowell in October 1969 at the Café Iruña in Harvard Square, coincidentally two days after the death of Jack Kerouac. Lowell generously entrusted a budding would-be poet with manuscript drafts of some of his unrhymed sonnets. I was flattered at being asked for my opinion and impressed by the detailed revisions already penciled on those flimsy typescripts. Then and there I decided to make a thorough study of Lowell's work. It has become something of a lifetime's effort. Along the way, the example of other scholars, the dedication of Lowell's many friends, and the support of my wife Carole have meant a great deal to me. Richard Tillinghast and Frank Bidart deserve special mention here both for their encouragement and for the efforts they have made in promoting Lowell's work and honoring his memory.

My thanks for other help appear in the acknowledgments.

Acknowledgments

Permission to quote from materials listed below is gratefully acknowledged.

Excerpts from uncollected material from the Robert Lowell Papers, reprinted by permission of Houghton Library, Harvard University, and the estate of Robert Lowell.

Excerpts from *Land of Unlikeness,* by Robert Lowell, reprinted by permission of Cummington Press.

Excerpts from *Lord Weary's Castle,* by Robert Lowell, copyright © 1946 and renewed 1974 by Robert Lowell, reprinted by permission of Harcourt Brace & Company.

Excerpts from *Life Studies,* by Robert Lowell, copyright © 1959 by Robert Lowell, copyright renewed © 1987 by Harriet Lowell, Sheridan Lowell, and Caroline Lowell; *For the Union Dead,* by Robert Lowell, © 1964 by Robert Lowell, copyright renewed © 1992 by Harriet Lowell, Sheridan Lowell, and Caroline Lowell; *Near the Ocean,* by Robert Lowell, copyright © 1967 by Robert Lowell; *Notebook 1967–68,* by Robert Lowell, copyright © 1967, 1968, 1969 by Robert Lowell; *History,* by Robert Lowell, copyright © 1973 by Robert Lowell; *Day by Day,* by Robert Lowell, copyright © 1977 by Robert Lowell; *Collected Prose,* by Robert Lowell, edited by Robert Giroux, copyright © 1987 by Harriet Lowell, Sheridan Lowell, and Caroline Lowell. Reprinted by permission of Farrar, Straus, & Giroux.

Several of these chapters, in part or in somewhat different form, have appeared in scholarly journals. I am grateful to editors and readers for commentary and editorial help: in the *New England Quarterly,* "'One Gallant Rush': The Writing of Robert Lowell's 'For the Union Dead'" (67, no. 1 [1994]: 30–45); in *Modern Philology,* "'The Sudden Bridegroom': The

Dialectics of *Lord Weary's Castle*" (93, no. 3 [1996]: 352–70); in *Southern Humanities Review,* "War and Redemption in *Land of Unlikeness*" (28, no. 1 [1994]: 1–14); in *Prospects: An Annual of American Cultural Studies,* "'Cut Off from Words': Robert Lowell's 'Tranquilized *Fifties*'" (21 [1996]: 149–68).

Introduction

On June 2, 1967, *Time* magazine ran a cover story on Robert Lowell headlined "Poetry in an Age of Prose." The cover painting, by Sidney Nolan, depicted a laurel-wreathed Lowell as a bodiless iconic head, heavy-browed, bespectacled, brooding. This formalized poet also appears on the first page of the story (buried deep in the magazine, in the Books section), where his photograph is flanked by those of a visibly crazed septuagenarian Ezra Pound and a flaccid, vest-wearing T. S. Eliot. Lowell, their presumptive heir, sports a tuxedo, the bow tie firmly tied, long hair carefully combed over his balding dome. The story eulogizes poets as those whose "heads being in the clouds" manage to see and communicate more than mortal folks: "They are aware of hard, sharp words that can clobber the emotions, that communicate one-to-one, man-to-man."[1] Not only the sexist language but the whole issue feels out of date. The sternly male ads for Old Crow blended whiskey, Smirnov vodka, and Seagram gin, the articles on bikinis and teen magazines, the minimal coverage of the Vietnam War, which was then approaching maximum intensity, suggest a worldview that, even allowing for its translation into *Time*-speak, seems aged beyond recovery. The subsequent discussion of a poetry world dominated by Lowell's stony iconic head delineates a white-male cultural construct few now wish to enshrine as a definitive version of literary history.

Yet Lowell was far more than the presiding figure of an outmoded literary era. His work and his public presence reached beyond the parochial world of modern poetry into the political and social worlds of protest, unease, dissent, and racial agony. As Richard Tillinghast has noted, "This poet's public gestures were consistent with an attitude he maintained throughout his life, not a stance or a consciously assumed position, but something that was simply part of his character, one that struck those around him as *sui generis,* that drew people to him and made them love him."[2] Lowell spoke to and for a generation younger than he—spoke not just to creative writing students and budding professors of English but to a larger critical mass of educated readers. In 1970, with Lowell still famous and the Vietnam War raging, Monroe Spears emphasized the importance of Lowell's political presence to his reputation as a poet: "Certainly the wide and rapid acceptance of Lowell as the leading poet of his generation resulted in part from his commitment to the obligation of taking a public stand on politico-moral issues."[3] That his political views vacillated between conservative and radical, that he was intermittently drawn to the vilest totalitarian authority figures, was not widely known and would have puzzled his audiences. But the fact remained that a prominent poet had placed his art in the service of political and social causes.

Lowell's charm was both personal and public. "It may be that some people have turned to my poems because of the very things that are wrong with me, I mean the difficulty I have with ordinary living, the impracticability, the myopia," he remarked to Stanley Kunitz.[4] Besides these attractive shortcomings, harmless and endearing in their eccentricity, readers were drawn to Lowell's manic dramatization of his Oedipal drama, exposed through engagement with both personal and public subject matter. For Lowell, the personal became the public, regardless of how awkwardly those distinct realms coupled. His audience responded to the interplay of personal and political demons, and flocked to his readings. The audience reaction to Lowell's reading on the occasion of the 1967 march on the Pentagon was vividly chronicled by Norman Mailer: "They adored him—for his talent, his modesty, his superiority, his melancholy, his petulance, his weakness, his painful, almost stammering shyness, his noble strength."[5] Reinforcing the idea that Lowell's audience was attracted to him for his personality as much as his poetry, Mailer then quotes the opening stanza of "Waking Early

Sunday Morning," a poem that perfectly entwines the political and the personal, or perhaps demonstrates that they are one.

Beginning with early essays in the *Vindex,* a prep-school journal, Lowell addressed public and political concerns through literature.[6] And from the start these concerns emerged in self-contradicting ways. Assembled and partly written while Lowell served a prison term for refusing the draft during the Second World War, *Land of Unlikeness,* his first collection of poems, was explicitly antiwar, yet enthralled with war, as I will demonstrate. In *Lord Weary's Castle,* the political concerns are muted but detectable, particularly in poems like "After the Surprising Conversions," which lends itself to being read as a commentary on the economic, social, and spiritual difficulties of the immediate postwar period. The title poem of *The Mills of the Kavanaughs* locates a madness in the heart of stolid American achievement, while *Life Studies* in its entirety generates a bottomless vortex of psychological and public concerns and a commentary on the vapid culture of the Eisenhower years. In "For the Union Dead," Lowell wrote himself out of private obsessions to reach perhaps the highest level of political and personal unity. This much-admired poem not only merges private and public concerns but places the Civil War where it belongs, at the heart of America's darkness. Vereen Bell remarks that "the effect of the pressure of history is to narrow the gap for Lowell between art and life and therefore to foreclose any chance of redemption through mere sensibility."[7] But I would argue that Lowell attempted to develop a sensibility so open to the interaction of life and art that the gap would cease to exist, and the redemption of history itself would be within reach. Impossible though this ideal might seem, I find almost every major shift in Lowell's style pushing in this direction.

When in 1965 Lowell famously refused an invitation to a White House festival of the arts by noting that "every serious artist knows that he cannot enjoy public celebration without making public commitments," he was in fact speaking for only himself and a very few of the most perceptive writers.[8] Edmund Wilson was the only other writer to refuse to participate, though many noninvited writers endorsed the protest. Jean-Paul Sartre's refusal of the Nobel Prize is one of the few comparable instances of a writer resisting such public celebration of literature. The publicity engendered by Lowell's resistance gained him a considerable audience. His collection *For the Union Dead* had been published only the year before, and its amiable mixture of free verse and metered, rhymed and unrhymed poems on a wide variety of subjects, including Lowell's travels and past love affairs, Jonathan Edwards, Nathaniel Hawthorne, the threat of nuclear war, and the civil rights movement, reached many people who may have read little contemporary poetry. As a Book-of-the-Month Club offering, *For the Union Dead* far outsold most collections of poetry other than large collected volumes or anthologies.

Time magazine came to Lowell because of his public presence, not because of the quality of his poetry. Lowell in 1967 was news, and would stay news through Eugene McCarthy's campaign, in which Lowell was a conspicuous participant. After the publication of *Notebook 1967–1968*, though, Lowell lost some of his critical status. William Meredith's front-page review in the *New York Times Book Review* called *Notebook* "serious and imperfect, like most of the accomplishments of serious men and women today," but other reviewers found the unrhymed sonnets verbose and dull.[9] When Lowell died in 1977, *Newsweek* devoted two full pages to his obituary, but noted that "Lowell's preeminence is not universally accepted," dissenting from *Time's* assertion a decade previously that Lowell was "by rare critical consensus, the best American poet of his generation."[10]

Such critical consensus never existed. Lowell's books, even *Life Studies* and *For the Union Dead*, received mixed reviews, as most books do. His later work alienated even some of his most dedicated readers and struck many reviewers as self-indulgent, sloppy, unfinished, or dull. In 1973, *The Dolphin* explored a partly fictional version of the breakup of Lowell's second marriage and the entry into his third. Despite winning a second Pulitzer Prize for its author, *The Dolphin* seemed to many readers unkind and unethical in its use of private correspondence as source material. It elicited a serious public attack from Adrienne Rich, who had previously been a close friend but who was appalled by the careless way in which Lowell invaded the privacy of his wife and daughter. After Lowell's death, his reputation further waned. The 1981 publication of Ian Hamilton's biography, which chronicled Lowell's bipolar disorder, brutality toward his father and first wife, seeming callousness in marital affairs, and other failings and life problems, diminished respect for a man who in his lifetime most friends and students found to be charismatic, charming, kind, and politically sensitive, despite the problems caused by recurring manic episodes.

However, with the further passage of time and the renewed interest in a more contextual criticism, Lowell's work stands out as the preeminent example in recent years of a poetics rich enough to compound political and personal concerns in a distinctly literary manner. This compounding of psychological self-exploration and political critique is not wholly unique to Lowell. Much of Wordsworth's earlier poetry, especially the ninth and tenth books of the *Prelude,* on the French Revolution, constitutes another modern example of how the personal and the political entwine. In the pre-romantic era, the work of Pope, Dryden, Rochester, Herrick, Shakespeare, Marlowe, Ralegh, and many others demonstrates that dramatic, narrative poetry, and even lyric poetry, can make itself comfortable among worldly affairs. But our age is more specialized, and poetry is more marginal than ever. When Lowell's poetry was appearing in the dark days of the 1960s, it comforted and inspired its readers in a way that most poetry no longer can. It represented a partial solution to the difficulty of participation in a supposedly democratic society that had apparently gone out of control. In counterpoint to the social vision of Jürgen Habermas, Lowell's published work, widely circulated and complexly questioning, embodies one answer to the problem of public participation in a capitalist public sphere dominated by media materialism and no longer based on a liberal consensus. For this reason, although not everyone would agree that Lowell was the greatest poet of his generation, we should cherish his example, his refusal to regard his work and his status as poet as marginal, and his willingness to comment on and participate in the social and political dialectics of his time.

Lowell, like Eliot and Pound, based his poetics on the violation of received modes and standards, discarding as soon as he had mastered them the various formal modes of Anglo-American modernism. Though critics have correctly detected in this process a steady groping toward autobiographical candor, I find more interesting another complex unfolding, an aesthetic development shaped at least as much by formal considerations as by the psychological imperative that seems to have become the leitmotif of Lowell criticism. Through this development, Lowell became a public poet, one whose work embraced political and social problems as well as his private difficulties, and made these seemingly disparate concerns coincide.

The many paradoxes of Lowell's poetics include a faith in inspiration rather than craft, and a patience for revision that matches almost any other poet's; an attraction to violence and a longing for quietude; a documentary eye and a surrealist's respect for the unreality of dreams; a religious sensibility and a skeptic's grip on the world of matter. At any point in his career, such paradoxes generate tensions his poems embrace but do not necessarily resolve. A reviewer of *For the Union Dead* criticized Lowell for failing to find more resolute closures, but by then Lowell resisted tidy endings because he realized that no individual poem could terminate the lifelong obsessions that kept him writing.[11] Rather than regret his occasional lack of satisfactory closure, I see it as a clue to his poetics of process. Lowell believed that his poems were extensions of himself, autobiographical not necessarily in subject but in a more profound sense. He lived for his poems, and they helped keep him alive. They affirmed the stubborn persistence of a difficult life haunted by mental illness. Lowell's ability to rebound repeatedly from serious disorders and write his way back into the world was a measure of his courage and dedication, but this perpetual recovery also spoke of the conditions and contours of his poetics.

Lowell's romantic attempt to identify himself with his art, though another paradox he would never quite resolve, portended a dubious future for his work. Drawn to organic metaphors, he had to acknowledge their consequence. If he wielded "words meat-hooked from the living steer," the "perishable work" that resulted would not long outlive its maker.[12] But he also understood that metaphor does not necessarily determine actuality. More than twenty years after the death of the author, the poems retain their urgency, and their singular voice seems as sharply defined as when first encountered.

Regardless of where literary history finally places him, Lowell will be read because his poems are a crucial index to the temperament and emotions of the era. Elsewhere I have argued that "the story of Lowell's career is his attempt to move poetry as close as possible to experience."[13] That experience was not merely his own but that of postwar America as well. Despite his firm belief that inspiration, not craft, is the shaping force of poetry, he retained a certain healthy skepticism for the products of his own imagination. His poetry changed repeatedly because no self-created world, no finished poem or body of poetry, could satisfy his tireless perceptions. His appetite for phenomena, which was both sensuous and intellectual, required him to reject generic conventions by assimilating an obdurate, unaesthetic actuality impervious to the ideal. As Neil Corcoran has noted, Lowell's work consequently engenders "a permanent air of risk, of recklessness, and restlessness," refusing the "polished or the finished" and the "stasis of lyric perfection."[14]

The consequences of this refusal sometimes results in work that seems unnecessarily obscure or unpolished, work that withholds some of the ordinary poetic satisfactions. "Poetry," Wallace Stevens argues, "is a satisfying of the desire for resemblance."[15] But the logic, if any, of Lowell's resemblances persuades less effectively than their passion and urgency. His poetry resists metaphorical consistency in favor of emotional candor because, he wrote in 1977, his work "almost always comes out of some inner concern, temptation, or obsessive puzzle."[16] True to that "inner concern," his work typically retains the imaginative ordering of its inspiration rather than superimposing clarity. Though few poets have worked harder at revision, it is revelation, not refinement, that constitutes his poetic ideal.

In recent years, the rise of academic and even popular interest in the work of Elizabeth Bishop (notably absent in her lifetime) seems to have displaced some of the interest in Lowell. He would have been (and was) the first to promote Bishop's work to the status it deserves. That this status should be gained at his own expense, however, would bemuse and frustrate him, since he was both ambitious and admittedly sexist in his rankings of poets. He and Randall Jarrell retained the irritating habit of classifying Bishop, Marianne Moore, and others as "women poets"—a category Bishop rejected—thus placing them outside of the main arena of competition. However, he never allowed this old-fashioned attitude to conceal his enormous respect for Bishop, so perhaps he would not be entirely surprised that some serious readers now consider her the major figure of the Lowell-Bishop poetic generation. But Bishop's work falls outside of the New England tradition of politically committed writing. Despite recent attempts to recast her as a spokesperson for feminist and same-sex causes (a role she would have abhorred), her poetry does not project a powerful public voice, as Lowell's does.

Bishop's aesthetic values, as described in Lowell's 1947 review of *North and South,* markedly differed from those Lowell had practiced in *Land of Unlikeness* and *Lord Weary's Castle.* "The structure of a Bishop poem is simple and effective," he notes. "In her bare effective language she also reminds one at times of William Carlos Williams."[17] These are hardly the terms one might use to describe the baroque language, gnarled syntax, and elaborate structures of the poems Lowell wrote before the mid-1950s. But by the time he began writing the free verse of *Life Studies,* he had broken out of his old style into something closer to Bishop's, closer to Williams's, and yet wholly his own. His admiration for Bishop was one of the threads that led to this new way of writing, but only one. Lowell was also following the lead of Allen Tate, his early mentor (as I have shown in *The Years of Our Friendship*), in using openly autobiographical subject matter to redirect his aesthetic.[18]

Harold Bloom describes Lowell's early verse as "tense with impasse," clinging to an aesthetic that ignored Whitman and Wordsworth in favor of a taste inherited from T. S. Eliot and the Fugitives.[19] But Lowell himself came to judge his early work harshly, and complained that his poems "seemed like prehistoric monsters dragged down into the bog."[20] In 1957, he went on a West Coast reading tour. It was the "era and the setting of Allen Ginsberg, and all about, very modest poets were waking up prophets."[21] Lowell had written few poems since the publication of *The Mills of the Kavanaughs* in 1951, and the style of those few no longer satisfied him. Exposure to the Beats (although he did not greatly admire their work), the recent autobiographical poems of Tate, as well as Bishop's increasingly conversational voice, encouraged him to discard the metrical verse he had written in the mode of John Crowe Ransom, the earlier Tate, and Hart Crane, to free his meter, and to embrace a candor none of his early poems to any degree had achieved.[22] Although David Kalstone pointed out that some of the early poems contain autobiographical lines that could occur in *Life Studies* (because "specific and prosy enough"),[23] this is quite different than writing from an aesthetic that makes candor and the appearance of autobiographical truth primary goals. The autobiographical impulse, as with most lyric-mediative poets, appears in all of Lowell's work, but only at certain times in his career does it dominate.

As I argue in "The Corporate Fifties" (chapter 5), the new freedom that came with the writing of "Skunk Hour" also responds to the stifling social and cultural situation of the 1950s. Lowell's poetry—like Whitman's in this way if no other—responded dramatically to changes in the social and cultural climate, as well as to direct aesthetic influences. The "public poetry" of *For the Union Dead*, *Near the Ocean*, and *Notebook* not only in subject matter but in formal characteristics represents complex responses to events such as the civil-rights movement and the Vietnam War. The free verse of "For the Union Dead," a response to Allen Tate's elegiac canticle "Ode to the Confederate Dead," opposes its lanky rhythms to high modernist formalism; while conversely, the tetrameter octet borrowed from Marvell for "Waking Early

Sunday Morning" and "Fourth of July in Maine" wages battle with language perfectly formed to rebuke the shabby illiterate speeches of the
politicians.

In his prolonged engagement with unrhymed sonnets, beginning
in 1967 and lasting until 1973, Lowell adapted the most exhausted
form in Western poetry to new uses. Autobiographical, political, and
baroque in a new way, different from the early work, these sonnets jux-
tapose diverse elements as freely as the Dadaists did, but with greater
cunning and a strong sense of the dignity imposed on the sonnet by literary tradition.[24] Although *The Dolphin* has been condemned as an em-
barrassingly shameless autobiographical work,[25] the sonnets generally
resist making simple claims on truth. Their world is a relentlessly formal one, shaped by the layering of images and the generation of what
Lowell calls the "bent generalization" that resists easy correlation with
experience.[26] The sonnet volumes received some of the harshest reviews of any of Lowell's work, but although he certainly wrote—or at
least published—too many, some of these blank-verse poems have to
rank among his strongest. Scrutinized individually, they are miracles of
tight construction, startling imagery, and devious shifts of mood and
registers of diction. And perhaps most importantly for Lowell, *History*
firmly placed his own imaginative life in a larger context of culture and
social development, satisfying, at least for the time, his desire to make
a poetry that is both epic and lyric, personal and public, and freeing
him to work in the less ritualist mode that followed.

Day by Day, Lowell's final collection, escapes the confines of the
sonnet and wields free verse so limber and casual that it alienated many
of the reviewers who had not yet learned to read the sonnets. Contain-
ing his most openly autobiographical work and his most fluent associative structures, *Day by Day* presented yet another challenge to those
critics concerned with fitting the pieces of Lowell's work and life into a
reasonably coherent mass. *Day by Day* culminates his autobiographical
impulse, but several explicit poems about aesthetic concerns suggest
that he was by no means satisfied with his new accomplishment. In
"Shifting Colors," he expresses an envy of Mallarmé, "who had the

good fortune / to find a style that made writing impossible," and wishes to write "only in response to the gods."[27] This new writing, an embrace of the ineffable, if it happened would presumably satisfy Lowell's visionary-religious drive, the last of the three objects—history, self, otherness—of Lowell's aesthetic imagination. But because poetry was the vital extension of himself, and because language, not the topics it engages, was his emotional anchor in this world, he would have gone on writing, generating new concerns as he progressed. Certainly he would have become dissatisfied with the retreat from the public voice that made this last book less forceful than *For the Union Dead* and *Near the Ocean.*

As Kalstone remarks, "It is easy to portray Lowell's career as one of dramatic change."[28] Nonetheless, Kalstone, like most of Lowell's other critics, tried to attribute those changes to a single impulse—in Kalstone's view, the desire for autobiographical expression. Other critics make similar attempts to totalize Lowell's work. Alan Williamson privileges the political impulse, while Vereen Bell finds a smoldering nihilism at the root of Lowell's concerns.[29] Stephen Yenser finds an unlikely continuity by mapping a schematic formalism, somewhat Yeatsian, in which Lowell's later books generate a cone-shaped coherence thematically focused on death, the creative process, and the self.[30] Henry Hart attributes Lowell's shifts in form and style to a growing obsession with the sublime.[31] Other critics give primacy to Lowell's desire to shed the influence of Eliot's authoritative modernism, or the need to distinguish himself from his mentors Tate and Ransom, or the search for religious certainty, or the desire to understand history.

Each of these impulses—the formal, the political, the nihilistic, the religious—appears in Lowell's work at various points. But no single desire or generative force dominates the career, unless it is the desire to learn to express public and private selves as a single entity. The allegorical groping toward a religious sublime in *Land of Unlikeness* and *Lord Weary's Castle* seemed for the young Lowell a natural mode of expression, though by 1953 he had abandoned this overly compressed style. This rejection signaled his attempt to find less artificial, more demotic modes of expression that would give him greater emotional access to himself and to a more utile and less apocalyptic version of the sociopolitical world. His attitude toward the sublime, which had deeply drawn him during his student years, shifted from one of desperate seeking to a skeptical bemusement.[32] As Lowell changed—and he apparently changed as much in his personality and his manner as did his poems—his previous formal stances resisted the shape of his shifting vision of his work and his role as poet. One sign of this shift in aesthetic stance is his revision of "The Mills of the Kavanaughs" from a dramatic monologue or narrative into a lyric-meditative poem. Over the years from the early 1950s to the mid-1970s, Lowell realized that his talent, as he said, was for the shorter poem, so in reworking his most ambitious failure he made it conform to strengths with which he had only gradually come to terms.

The education of every poet is a formal one; that is, through the experience of writing, poets learn what literary structures their talents will bear. Robert Frost embraced the blank-verse eclogue partly because he couldn't write a novel, or so he joked. Wordsworth had to face, at some point, the fact that he simply could not write the philosophical poem Coleridge desired. Ezra Pound learned late that *The Cantos,* regardless of their many great beauties, did not cohere. Faulkner wisely turned from poetry to the novel, as did Hemingway. Lowell's poetic education taught him the value of rethinking himself, his poetics, and his relationship to poetry, history, and the culture. Having learned this, he simply could not repeat himself because, as he suggests in "After Enjoying Six or Seven Essays on Me," a poem is a person, and he was his poem. To repeat himself meant not only failing aesthetically but as a person, no longer able to grow or change.

By rejecting the confinements of craft, Lowell opened his work to a fuller realization of an incorporative poetic vision, one that engages both the self-created and the social-historical worlds. The resources and strategies of his personal vision (through exploitation of that vision's limitations and flaws) reconcile a historically situated inexhaustibility with the shifting limitations of various formal stances. But his poems are language-acts of complex imaginative dimensions, aloof from the particular religious or political commitments to which some readers have tried to reduce them. Lowell sacrifices received ideas of poetic and dramatic decorum for a late-twentieth-century concern with the poem as a field of action, and in doing so generates tensions and complexities that exclude the "objective validity" he said religion should have; as he further notes, "by the time [religion] gets into a poem it's so mixed up with technical and imaginative problems that the theologian, the priest, the serious religious person isn't of too much use."[33] Religion and politics were important to Lowell, and pervade his poems. But unless we fully consider how and why the possibilities of language—rather than of religion, morality, politics, history, or even the subconscious—most centrally engage him, we cannot begin to appreciate his accomplishment. This study attempts to redirect the focus from Lowell's difficulties and shortcomings to his self-renewing strengths as a poet of originality and power who used his talent to acknowledge and attempt to embrace the whole massive complexity of the modern world.

In surveying the range of Lowell's aesthetic development rather than identifying a thematic unity, I hope to demonstrate more fully his concern with the relationship between the personal and the public. I privilege formal and aesthetic considerations over psychological or social ones, although "The Corporate Fifties" locates the generative impulse of *Life Studies* in social rather than strictly aesthetic concerns, and "Vision, Landscape, and the Ineffable" (chapter 8) emphasizes the thematic unity of *History*. Thematic considerations have formal implications at every stage of Lowell's career; but I can't accept the notion that any single philosophical, religious, or social stance shaped the entirety of his work, or that his poems were wholly at the mercy of his ideas. While not wishing to isolate aesthetic considerations from textual and contextual ones, I do not want to treat Lowell as either a religious or an autobiographical poet (although he embraced both of those identities). Nor do I want to present Lowell principally as a public poet, although he was our last public poet of note. Rather, I believe that his desire to merge personal and public expression, the complex cultural forces and influences of the period, and his uncertainties about his values and beliefs, working in concert, caused him periodically to rethink his poetics and led him into further experiment with rhythm, registers of diction, and all of the other formal strategies he had mastered by the time of his second book. "Life by definition breeds on change," one of his poems notes, and Lowell extended that notion to poetry as well.[34]

This study traces some of the signs of growth and change, some of the ways in which unresolved paradox and psychological difficulties necessitate aesthetic development, some of the formal, psychological, and philosophical difficulties on which Lowell's work thrived. It is not, by any means, an attempt to read all of his work. Many of his important works, including "Near the Ocean," "Between the Porch and the Altar," "Mother Marie Therese," "Falling Asleep over the Aeneid," *The Old Glory, Imitations,* and the whole of *The Dolphin* go unexplored. I have written about *The Dolphin* and *Imitations* elsewhere, while *The Old Glory* and Lowell's other plays require consideration as drama—consideration that I simply do not feel qualified to give. Lowell's opus is a large one, and could not be exhausted in a hundred essays or twenty full-length studies, so I make no further apologies for omissions.

I have, however, tried to point to specific issues that previous critics have neglected or misunderstood. In the first few chapters, I argue that the ambiguity of Lowell's social and religious beliefs, as far as the poems express them, are functional, and that the formal restraints of the poems reveal rather than contain the difficulties Lowell found in formulating public and private values. "Crossing the Styx" examines Lowell's important uncollected poem "Caron, Non Ti Crucciare" as a complex and summarizing religious statement as well as a stylistic bridge between his first two books. Chapters 4 and 6, "Cut Down, We Flourish" and "One Gallant Rush," examine two key poems—"The Mills of the Kavanaughs" and "For the Union Dead"—and show how the first poem frustrated Lowell by working against his talent until he rethought it into a different genre, and how the second illustrates the immense flexibility of his process of composition and complicates the idea of intention. Other chapters consider the strengths and complexities of *History,* Lowell's varied ways of absorbing the Maine landscape, the role of cultural and societal stress in shaping *Life Studies,* and the generative impulse shaping some of the poems of *Day by Day.* I have tried to emphasize the importance of difference in Lowell's aesthetic, the need to avoid repeating himself in exhausted formal terms. Further, in what I take to be Lowell's own spirit, I have emphasized the process of his writing whenever possible, rather than trying to make the opus cohere.

Robert Lowell's Shifting Colors

1 | War and Redemption

I N 1943, ROBERT LOWELL, DISTURBED BY THE ALLIED
bombing of German cities and facing induction, sent a "declaration of conscience" to President Roosevelt and his local draft
board. Lowell declared himself unalterably opposed, not to war as
such but to the conduct of the war then in progress, particularly to the
bombing of civilian populations and to the intransigence of the Allied
requirement of unconditional surrender, which he felt would lead to an
untenable postwar situation, as Versailles had:

> The war has entered on an unforeseen phase: one that can
> by no possible extension of the meaning of the words be called
> defensive. By demanding unconditional surrender we reveal
> our complete confidence in the outcome, and declare that we
> are prepared to wage a war without quarter or principles, to the
> permanent destruction of Germany and Japan.[1]

The most astonishing aspect of this letter is the confidence with which
Lowell's voice assumes the authority to enter the public sphere.[2] Of
course, Lowell was partly motivated by the desire to "provoke attention
and give offense," as Anthony Hecht has noted, but immature motiva-
tions cannot account for the self-assurance of this statement.[3] Lowell's

American genealogy, though a distinguished one, does not include the prominent political voices associated, for instance, with the Adams or Roosevelt families. The Lowells and Winslows were merchants, and although mercantile success in the United States confers privilege, it was notably absent from Lowell's nuclear family. More importantly, Lowell, who frequently questioned the value of personal ancestry, descended from a distinctly literary tribe. James Russell Lowell, the first Robert T. S. Lowell (poet, novelist, pastor of the prestigious Cambridge Street Church), and Amy Lowell were ancestors. But more importantly, Thoreau, Emerson, Hawthorne, and the adopted New Englander Robert Frost were some of his many contiguous ancestors. Hawthorne had written Franklin Pierce's campaign biography and received a diplomatic appointment. James Russell Lowell had boldly spoken on the social and political issues of his day, including slavery, the unjust amassing of personal wealth, and the problems of immigrants. Margaret Fuller and Julia Ward Howe promoted women's peace and suffrage movements long before such causes became fashionable in this country. Thoreau spoke as uncompromisingly of abolition as John Brown himself. Thomas Wentworth Higginson and Robert Gould Shaw (commemorated in "For the Union Dead") led the earliest black regiments of the Civil War into battle. Frost, a social and political conservative, by the 1940s had begun to address public issues, though unfortunately with sad consequences for his poetry. The New England tradition was one of direct intervention into complex national affairs at a time when language and action often coincided. Whether that intervention came from the liberal-radical mind or the conservative-traditionalist did not matter as much as the confidence and sense of entitlement that shaped its expression.[4] Of course, that confidence often coexisted with a manic idealism, especially in the instance of self-sacrificers like Shaw; but that idealism, even when it led to virtual suicide, was at least as attractive to Lowell as the projection of social responsibility.

Drawing upon the privilege of ancestral background and cultural tradition, confusing, perhaps, his rebellion against his family with his rebellion against the state, Lowell drew heavily upon this received authority, which depends upon a willingness to accept the coincidence of language and action. The exercise of the freedom of speech in the nineteenth century could and often did lead to public consequences, including mob violence and legal prosecution. Emerson sternly rejected the tenets of even the most reformed religion of his day, gave up a comfortable ministry, and speaking at conservative Harvard defied received cultural standards and demanded a new voice for America. Excoriating supporters of slavery, William Lloyd Garrison printed what he pleased, ignoring their threats. Thoreau spoke in defense of John Brown over the shouted objections of those who believed in law and order at any moral cost. Shaw literally gave his life for abolitionist beliefs that he had publicly expressed in a milieu of bankers and merchants who depended on Southern cotton to fuel their textile mills. Emily Dickinson refused to publish rather than revise her poems to please a reading public already debased by flimsy newspaper verse. Frost defied the left-leaning political orthodoxy of 1930s intellectual America to work out his belief in individualism through his poetry, alienating much of his audience. Discourse that avoided consequences was not central to the New England tradition.

Though Lowell in "Memories of West Street and Lepke" would with hindsight refer to his letter to Roosevelt as a "manic statement," his first important public intervention retains authority because it came at considerable personal risk. Neither this protest nor his later re-fusal of President Johnson's invitation to a White House arts festival should be dismissed as motivated by "ambivalence and self-aggrandizement," as one critic has put it.[5] Draft resistance in 1943 inevitably meant familial disapproval, strong public censure, and prison. But beyond its boldness, the specific content of this letter of protest raises questions and problems. Although a conscientious objector in a limited sense, Lowell was not a pacifist: he indicated his willingness to fight in a purely defensive situation. Moreover, the poems he wrote in the early years of the war demonstrate that he was not only fascinated by modern warfare but determined to use it aesthetically. The poems of *Land of Unlikeness*

(1944), Lowell's first book, show him struggling with two opposing desires: to embrace the coldly objective but enthralling beauty of modern warfare and to subsume the imagery of war in metaphors and allegorical constructs of penance and redemption.[6]

Lowell faced two other difficulties in composing this early work. One was psychological: as just mentioned, although not a pacifist, he was intrigued by war and drawn to it, so his impulse toward atonement and redemption, insofar as they require the rejection of violence, was not consistent with some of his other feelings. The other problem was the formal difficulty of finding an adequate trope or body of figuration (in Eliot's term, an objective correlative) to express his desire for personal and national penance. His solution was to force conventional Roman Catholic iconography into contorted juxtaposition with the imagery of war; but the resulting grotesquerie embodies rather than opposes the cultural disintegration that the poems attempt to defy. The refusal of unmediated tradition and simultaneous embrace of the preconditions and privileges of tradition, which are the central strategies of Eliot's version of modernism, shape Lowell's poems, frustrating his attempt to embrace a more Thomistic and hierarchical Catholic iconography. Thus in a "land of unlikeness"[7] the powerful but unholy aesthetic of Protestant resistance appropriates the sacred imagery of Roman Catholicism, and the poems achieve a partial but unwieldy synthesis.

"On the Eve of the Feast of the Immaculate Conception: 1942," "The Bomber," "Christmas Eve in the Time of War," and "Cistercians in Germany" illustrate the tension between competing desires to acknowledge the poet's fascination with war and to censure both war and his own unruly will. Lowell desired to normalize modern warfare by imposing the language of classical and Napoleonic wars. His objections to the bombing of cities derive not only from conventional moral outrage but from his sense that the aesthetic continuity of war—which is an ethical as well as an artistic construct—has been violated. Underlying this paradoxical dilemma is Lowell's recognition that war, like poetry, is a mode of discourse, one that in this instance has been usurped by the ultrarationality of post-Enlightenment thought, to which he instinctively opposes an almost medieval sense of the mystical power of religious discourse. Long before Michel Foucault would systematically delineate the failure of rational humanism (in studies such as *Madness and Civilization* and *The Order of Things*), Lowell's early poetry embodies a Nietzschean sense of the insidiously antihuman quality of the Enlightenment faith in reason.

In "On the Eve of the Feast of the Immaculate Conception: 1942" the primary figure of absolution and redemption is the Virgin Mary, the "Mother of God, whose burly love/Turns swords to plowshares," while Eisenhower represents a Caesar-like secular heroism that has "won/Significant laurels" that perhaps more properly belong to poetry itself. As with many of Lowell's early and later poems, the modifiers betray the tension between conflicting desires.[8] That Mary's love should be "burly" indicates its worldly dimension, its bulk and brawn and utility; while Eisenhower's "significant laurels" link the present to the glorious history of warfare. Further, the wish to "make this holiday with Mars/ Your feast Day" would bring Christian and pagan, military and religious worlds together in a suitably ecumenical manner. But Lowell must resist the kind of idealism that finds religious fervor and militaristic ambition compatible, acknowledge his ancestry in violence, and empathize with the victims of the war:

> Bring me tonight no axe to grind
> On wheels of the Utopian mind:
> > Six thousand years
> Cain's blood has drummed into my ears,
> Shall I wring plums from Plato's bush
> When Burma's and Bizerte's dead
> > Must puff and push
> > Blood into bread?[9]

Grinding an axe on wheels of the Utopian mind is undesirable not only because it would blunt both his distaste for and admiration of war, but because it would distance Lowell from the blood and bread, the texture of suffering. As a poet he would find this loss of empathy intolerable; but any attempt to reconcile his conflicting desires might generate exactly the Utopian state of mind that would ease the rough and tumble of his imagery. Because the language is so aggressive and jaggedly referential (naming Mary a Nimrod, for example, after the hunter-king of Genesis 10: 8–9), the last two stanzas uncomfortably mingle holy communion, war, sexuality, and cannibalism. This unusual range of reference does not intend to conflate or equate these competing discourses but results from his fevered embrace of tactile and sanguinary images:[10]

> Oh, if soldiers mind you well
> They shall find you are their belle
>   And belly too;
> Christ's bread and beauty came by you,
> Celestial Hoyden, when our Lord
> Gave up the weary Ghost and died,
>   You shook a sword
>   From his torn side.
>
> Over the seas and far away
> They feast the fair and bloody day
>   When mankind's Mother,
> Jesus' Mother, like another
> Nimrod danced on Satan's head.
> The old Snake lopes to his shelled hole;
>   Man eats the Dead
>   From pole to pole.

The poem seems at first to abandon militaristic leanings and embrace a sentimental reconciliation in which Mary, assuming the roles of both lover and mother, would comfort and heal the soldiers, then drive "The old Snake" to a "shelled hole," thus replaying the familiar drama of sin and redemption. Here Satan, as in other poems of this period, seems a failed trickster rather than a threat, an unsuccessful usurper easily driven from the field. Perhaps depicting this undignified failure, challenging Milton's portrayal of rebellious grandeur, allows Lowell to empathize or identify with Satan in poems from "The Quaker Graveyard in Nantucket," with its complex mingling of the demonic and the reverential, to the self-deprecating stance of "Skunk Hour." The old Snake is a humorous figure that needn't be taken seriously.

The last two lines of "On the Eve of the Feast," however, shock the poem back into a mordant satire. Lowell's concluding image of cannibal passion is one that Jerome Mazzaro sees as one of hope,[11] but which I take as ironic recognition that, even with Satan banished, humankind continues to devour itself on a global scale. The difficult juxtaposition of religious and geographical metaphors indicates the poem's failure to sustain the tension between religious fervor and war fever. Lowell's attempt to reconcile the two by making Mary the "belle/And belly too" of the soldiers produces a grotesque conflation of tactile and spiritual metaphors that reveals more of his fascination with the physical immediacy of war than with the spiritual glory of the Mother of Christ.

"The Bomber" seems a more straightforward attempt to satirize war and violence, ridiculing the bomber for assuming the role of God the avenger. Without the complementary role of redeemer, the bomber, despite its destructive force, merely plays at its role:

> The Master has had enough
> Of your trial flights and your cops
> And robbers and blindman's bluff,
> And Heaven's purring stops
> *When Christ gives up the ghost.*

The bomber fails to understand that with godlike powers and easy access to the sublime go the responsibilities of a god. To pretend to power one does not possess is childish, tolerable only until the Master tires of such antics. But the satire turns uneasy when the poem notes how cruelly effective this child's play is:

> You nosed about the clouds
> And warred on the wormy sod;
> And your thunderbolts fast as light
> Blitzed a wake of shrouds.
> O godly Bomber, and most
> A god when cascading tons
> Baptized the infidel Huns
> For the Holy Ghost . . .

Though intended to satirize the bomber with the language missionaries have used for centuries to rationalize the destruction of native peoples in the name of God, this passage also betrays Lowell's fascination with the destructive power of the bombings, and it is in part his own fascination that causes his revulsion. The language—"Blitzed a wake of shrouds," and the odd conflation of ritual terms—describes a cartoon-like killing, too unreal to convince the reader that real people are dying here. And the phrase "baptized the infidel Huns" suggests that the apparent killing is actually a Catholic salvation offered to wayward Protestants. The hard Anglo-Saxon consonants of this passage may intend to approximate the harsh mechanical grind of modern warfare, but the language is so removed from gruesome actuality that it privileges the bomber, however unwillingly, as the only real function. One need only compare this to Randall Jarrell's "Eighth Air Force" poems (though they too have been criticized for their dreamlike distance from their subjects) to see how detached from reality this poem is, how like a comic book, and how ambivalent.

The Yeatsian italicized refrain "*And* [or, as in the quoted passage, *When] Christ gave up the ghost*" adds a note of seriousness that the rest of the poem doesn't quite attain, partly because the poet, despite his rage at the way the "Freedoms" have chosen to "police the world," finds the bomber with its "goggled pilots" a figure of fascination as well as of irresponsible destruction. The "unlikeness" in this poem is not only in the way in which the bomber is unlike the god that its role suggests, but in the ways the figure of destruction both repels and attracts Lowell. Again, modifiers reveal his ambivalence: "Daredevil" sky, "wormy" sod (exalting the sky-god bomber over the lowly earthlings), "thunderbolts fast as light." Caught up in admiration of the bomber's power, he only half recovers his censorious stance in the second and third stanzas, and as a result the pious refrain seems mawkish and insincere.[12]

The central motif in "Christmas Eve in the Time of War" is the further torture of Christ by capitalist greed and the threat of further, war-inflicted agonies ("Tomorrow Mars will break his bones"). By juxtaposing Christian and classical figures, the poem attempts to suggest that the war represents a conflict between opposing visions or versions of the world, a conflict that finds a psychological parallel in the psyche of the speaker of the poem. According to the subtitle, the speaker is "A Capitalist" who "Meditates by a Civil War Monument." The capitalist pleads for materialist heroes (Santa Claus and Alexander Hamilton) to "break the price-controller's strangle-hold" and by freeing capital restore the pre-apocalyptic world of his childhood. Perhaps influenced by Ezra Pound's vision of a new economy, he also hopes to "spare the Child a crust of mould," but cannot, because in his world, even in his childhood, the anti-ethic of money has replaced religious consolation:

> Twenty years ago
> I strung my stocking on the tree—if Hell's
> Inactive sting stuck in the stocking's toe,
> Money would draw it out.

The argument in this poem occurs between the trope of suffering, which belongs to Christ but the capitalist wants to claim for himself, and the trope of war-as-power, of Mars, which represents an ironic apocalypse (ironic because also embodied in the Christ of apocalypse with his drawn sword) that reflects the world's refusal of the consolations of the Redeemer:

> Brazenly gracious, Mars is open arms,
> The sabers of his statues slash the moon:
> Their pageantry understanding forms
> Anonymous machinery from raw men,
> It rides the whirlwind, it directs the drums.

Hardly any wonder that, faced with this whirlwind, the capitalist weeps "for Santa Claus and Hamilton," but he cannot conceal his awe, if not admiration, for the power of Mars. The capitalist himself has wielded such power, presumably on a smaller scale, by using his money to manufacture a different kind of "Anonymous machinery from raw men." "Christmas Eve in the Time of War" speaks in the voice of a persona; in its revised version, in *Lord Weary's Castle,* as "Christmas Eve under Hooker's Statue," the poem speaks in the voice of a poet musing to himself, a voice that however inwardly directed seems even more fiercely intent on confronting war with its fruitless history. The speakers of both versions, however, remain enthralled by the dumb power of war, the "blundering butcher."[13]

The "unlikeness" at the heart of "Christmas Eve in the Time of War" has internalized the figure of Christ, who though in danger of having his bones broken by Mars has "come with water and with fire," wielding the elements and asserting his apocalyptic role. The child-Christ, like the child-capitalist, is subsumed in the absent figure of the capitalist's "child . . . dead upon the field of honor," so the poem rightly concludes "woe unto the rich that are with child" because gold cannot compensate for the loss of a child, or even for the loss of childhood. In fact, venery is to blame for this state of loss, both the literal loss of the dead child and for the lost childhood, corrupted early by the love of money and the belief that it constituted a bulwark against sin.

The trope of war-as-power dominates the poem by excluding the trope of redemption and absorbing the trope of suffering. The despairing note of the closure, though properly Old Testament–prophetic, suggests how much more appealing are the images of punishment than those of forgiveness and redemption. The theological paradox lies in the invocation of the Christ-child rather than God the Father, necessitating an uncomfortable conflation of the gentle child Jesus with the stern warrior-Christ of the Second Coming. But this conflation is precisely the point of the poem, which centers on the capitalist's loss of his childhood to money-love and his perception of the war as retribution (a just retribution?) for this sacrifice of childhood and religion. Since rejection of one's own childhood implies rejection of the childhood of Jesus, and with it the refusal of Christ's role of savior, the capitalist has for solace only the dour Christ of the apocalypse. The later version of the poem drops this melodrama and becomes a simpler and more focused meditation on the statue of General Joseph Hooker. While possessing great personal bravery, General Hooker had trouble following orders and finally resigned his command in protest at being passed over for promotion. Invoking the statue of an eccentric and undependable Civil War figure effectively renders ironic the memorialization of war. The earlier version of the poem, however, better portrays Lowell's sense of cultural disintegration, and with dramatic effectiveness portrays the complex relationship between the social corruption that begins in childhood and its consequences for the adult.

In "Cistercians in Germany," the monks of the title are figures of renunciation, for whom "corpse and soul" *should* "go bare," but who have been functionally displaced by Hitler and his supporters. The opposing and central trope of the poem is embodied in the Third Reich's vulgar ideal of social order:

> Here corpse and soul go bare. The Leader's headpiece
> Capers to his imagination's tumblings;
> The Party barks at its unsteady fledglings
> To goose-step in red-tape, and microphones
> Sow the four winds with babble. Here the Dragon's
> Sucklings tumble on steel-scales and puff
> Billows of cannon-fodder from the beaks
> Of bee-hive camps, munition-pools and scrap-heaps,
> And here the serpent licks up Jesus' blood,

> Valhalla vapors from the punctured tank.
> Rank upon rank the cast-out Christians file
> Unter den Linden to the Wilhelmsplatz,
> Where Caesar paws the gladiator's breast;
> His martial bumblings and hypnotic yawp
> Drum out the pastors of these aimless pastures;
> And what a muster of scarred hirelings and scared sheep
> To cheapen and popularize the price of blood!

Because renunciation is not the opposite but the complement to order, the poem presents, surely inadvertently, the possibility that the Nazis, not the Cistercians, represent the only redemption available. The "cast-out Christians" seem both disfranchised and deflated. The poem describes as "sheep" both the followers of Hitler—witless pawns —and the followers of Christ, who forego the ego to save their souls. The speaker of the poem, we learn at the close, is one of the monks who "lift bloody hands to wizened Bernard, / To Bernard gathering his canticle of flowers," and assert the survival of the Christian ideal. But this vision of actual redemption arrives too late to save the poem from becoming a rather morbid dwelling upon the vicissitudes of totalitarian order that seems to suggest that for the common lot of humanity this secular cruelty is the only appropriate means of salvation:

> Here
> Puppets have heard the civil words of Darwin
> Clang Clang, while the divines of screen and air
> Twitter like Virgil's harpies eating plates,
> And lions scamper up the rumps of sheep.
> The Shepherd knows his sheep have gone to market;
> Sheep need no pastoral piping for the kill,
> Only cold mutton and a fleecing.

Lowell's infatuation with puns not only generates the "fleecing" at the end of this cruel pastoral but tempts him to confound and then fuse disparate meanings of "sheep" and so deconstruct the religious center of the poem, the orthodox argument that submission leads to salvation. Fascinated against his will by the harsh images of order generated by his poem, Lowell admits that Christian passivity and meekness might too readily submit to Fascism. It is possible to claim that this poem demonstrates how complementary Christianity and Fascism are, though this observation violates the conscious ethical stance of the author. The ambiguity of his language, however, suggests how attractive Lowell found the vocabulary of social and military power, how tenuous was his faith (his aesthetic faith, at any rate) in the figure of Christ the redeemer, and how fragile that faith seemed when under the pressures of war.

The effect of this poem, then, is to appropriate the sacred imagery of "Lycidas" and other Christian pastorals—the trope of Christ the Shepherd leading his flock to God—to fulfill the poet's need to synthesize metaphors of power and order and metaphors of redemption into an aesthetic whole. The unsatisfactory nature of the result is clear in the way Lowell rewrote the conclusion of "Cistercians in Germany" to suit the new poem "At the Indian Killer's Grave" in *Lord Weary's Castle*.[14] "Cistercians" concludes by invoking the figure of Bernard "gathering his canticle of flowers" and transforming his soul into "a bridal chamber fresh with flowers,/And all his body one extatic womb." This transcendental experience, though, inappropriately mixes sexual overtones by confusing genders, abstracting the metaphor too far from concrete actuality. It confounds a quasi-sexual moment of religious ecstasy with one of unwitting transvestitism, as if the masculine world of war, power, and imposed order had crushed the last vestiges of manliness from the saint and driven him to the embrace of his anima. Though this reading may seem forced, the poem invokes it by inadequately dramatizing the transition from scabrous social vision to transcendent metaphor. Because the earlier imagery has been so dramatic, one might expect comparable dramatization of the ecstasy of Bernard as he escapes, through the gathering of flowers (itself a sexual dramatization), the violent quotidian world. Unfortunately, such dramatization requires visualization, and this sort of religious imagery is not intended to be visual but spiritually tactile. That is, one should apprehend it with the meditative faculty rather than the perceptual one. But Lowell has already committed his poem to the imagery and language of dramatic excess. He partially mitigates this excess by the use of a capital *S* for *Shepherd,* which warns us that we are moving toward the world of religious allegory. But the conclusion occurs too abruptly and attempts to depart too radically from the tone and movement of the bulk of the poem. Lowell's purpose is to draw a violent contrast between the frenzied order of Nazi Germany and the abstract world of contemplation occupied by the monks; however, the imagery of the early part of the poem is so strong and engaging that the effect is to make Bernard's meditative ascension seem faintly ridiculous. Lowell has not yet learned how decisively the tone of a short poem, once firmly established, shapes the reading of the whole.

Only a year or so later, when he revised the closure of "Cistercians" for "At the Indian Killer's Grave," a much stronger poem, Lowell would demonstrate how apt was John Crowe Ransom's comment in 1945 that "I don't know who has grown up in verse more than you, these last few years."[15] "At the Indian Killer's Grave" shows how early Lowell began to move toward a more personal poetics of testimony. Here the voice of the poem seems coincident with the voice of the poet, so the reader may understand the concluding moment of religious vision as an expression of a psychologically verifiable presence rather than as an inchoate attempt to portray a saint's peculiar experience:

> I ponder on the railing at this park:
> Who was the man who sowed the dragon's teeth,
> That fabulous or fancied patriarch
> Who sowed so ill for his descent, beneath
> King's Chapel in this underworld and dark?
> John, Matthew, Luke and Mark,
> Gospel me to the Garden, let me come
> Where Mary twists the warlock with her flowers—
> Her soul a bridal chamber fresh with flowers
> And her whole body an ecstatic womb,
> As through the trellis peers the sudden Bridegroom.

Because the soul and womb are now Mary's, rather than the visionary's, the sexual content no longer requires unusual suspension of disbelief. It remains somewhat awkward (especially in the phrase "Gospel me to the Garden"), but placed in a less insistently violent and dramatic yet more historically situated meditation it seems a fit conclusion to a poem concerned with the religious and social hypocrisy of early New England. The Roman Catholic vision of Mary, however fraught, in this instance, with overstated sexuality, is an appropriate rebuke to the Protestantism that motivated the excesses of cruelty and the self-deluding rationalizations of Puritans and Nazis.

However, when Lowell revised his poems for *Lord Weary's Castle*, most overt references to the war disappeared, along with poems like "The Bomber," not because they had suddenly become dated but possibly because Lowell realized how difficult it was for him to control a seductive and compelling language of violence and power. Allen Tate, in his introduction to *Land of Unlikeness,* correctly observes that Lowell is "consciously a Catholic poet"; but unconsciously Lowell demonstrates a fascination with violence, imposed order, and unchecked power. The real source of unlikeness is not the land but the mind of the poet. When eventually Lowell recognized that for himself, to deal with these personal complexities, he turned to the writing of more frankly autobiographical, self-exploratory poems. Once Lowell, like Wordsworth, began to contemplate his own development, he had no difficulty portraying his early and ongoing fascination with war and his propensity for violence:

> There was rebellion, father, when the mock
> French windows slammed and you hove backward, rammed
> Into your heirlooms, screens, a glass-cased clock,
> The highboy quaking to its toes. You damned
> My arm that cast your house upon your head
> And broke the chimney flintlock on your skull.[16]
> * * *
> And I, bristling and manic,

skulked in the attic,
and got two hundred French generals by name,
from *A* to *V*—from Augereau to Vandamme.
I used to dope myself asleep
naming those unpronounceables like sheep.[17]

In much of the early work, Lowell writes in an impersonal voice and finds himself struggling with unlikenesses that impose conflicting languages of varying but unequal strength, and very often poems of religious intention veer perilously close to becoming paeans to arbitrary power. But with the fashioning of *Lord Weary's Castle*—building on strong first-person poems from *Land of Unlikeness* such as "In Memory of Arthur Winslow"—it became clear (or seems clear, in retrospect) that Lowell's proper voice—his surest and most controlled—was not that of a dramatic figure or persona but what T. S. Eliot calls "the voice of the poet" either talking to himself or "addressing an audience."[18]

This is not simply a matter of Lowell suddenly discovering himself, either as person or poet, since he would continue to evolve in sometimes radical ways as both poet and citizen for the rest of his career. Rather, it is a matter of rhetoric. Lowell's poems needed to learn to persuade themselves before they might persuade an audience, and to do this they needed the fiction of a central speaking-consciousness, not the picture of a division between consciousness and unconsciousness. In time-honored lyric tradition, Lowell found that fiction most readily embodied in the first-person speaker, especially when that speaker could be firmly placed in a landscape. If Lowell at the time of *Land of Unlikeness* was writing work that, as Stephen Yenser argues, "assumes a disjunction of the verbal symbol and the actual world," and "ignores the incorrigible referential function of words," he found this excursion into "pure poetry" unsatisfactory, and gradually moved toward a poetics more firmly rooted in experience.[19]

Consider the difference between the openings of "Cistercians in Germany" (quoted above), with its generalized if vivid social description, and the opening of the "Five Years Later" section of "In Memory of Arthur Winslow" (the version in *Land of Unlikeness*), which establishes the speaker's consciousness at the center of the poem:

> This Easter, Arthur Winslow, five years gone,
> I come to bury you and not to praise
> The craft that netted a million dollars, late
> Mining in California's golden bays
> Then lost it all in Boston real estate;
> Then from the train, at dawn,
> Leaving Columbus in Ohio, shell
> On shell of our stark culture struck the sun
> To fill my head with all our fathers won
> When Cotton Mather wrestled with the fiends from Hell.

Lowell still entwines considerable social commentary into the latter passage, but he also establishes a particularized consciousness to testify to the psychological authenticity of these perceptions.[20] Perhaps more than many other poets, Lowell would require this centering to control the tendency of his rhetoric to assume a life of its own and expose fascinations too politically or socially unkempt, and perhaps too unauthentic. The war poems of *Land of Unlikeness* reveal much about Lowell's fascination with violence, power, and authority, and reveal as well how thin a veneer was his Catholicism, which he gave up only a few years later.[21] They also reveal his first tentative movement toward the conflation of self and history, a decisive rejection of the Enlightenment belief in objectivity and the conventional limitations of genre.

Most interestingly, perhaps, these early poems reveal how powerfully the rhetoric of war grips the modern (and postmodern) mind, how firmly entrenched are the languages of sex and violence, how readily they overwhelm metaphors and other figures of religious consciousness and vision. Dredged from the ambiguous parts of the psyche, language, not reason, shapes the controlling ethos of poems like "The Bomber." To overcome the unconscious candor of his language, Lowell would have to face it "without face" in the naked first-person, the exposed romantic ego of *Life Studies* and *The Dolphin*. In the late poem "Facing Oneself," he admits how constructed that ego is—how necessarily unrepentant and honest, and even how unreligious:

> After a day indoors I sometimes see
> my face in the shaving mirror looks as old,
> frail and distinguished as my photographs—
> as established. But it doesn't make one feel
> the temptation to try to be a Christian.[22]

Lowell's struggle to face himself, which required a temporary surrender of epic and satiric ambitions in favor of lyric or meditative intimacy, was as hard-fought as any of the other struggles of modern literature.[23] In writing *Land of Unlikeness*, he hadn't yet learned that this struggle, not the attempt to satirize America and the world back to sanity, would consume most of his career; but already by 1944 his language was pushing him inward, toward the only source of fragile stability he would ever find.

2 | Crossing the Styx

"CARON, NON TI CRUCCIARE" IS ONE OF Robert Lowell's most difficult, enigmatic, and least-known poems. In style and stance it links the caustically satirical *Land of Unlikeness* to the more elegiac *Lord Weary's Castle*, so it is appropriate to examine this poem before moving on to Lowell's first major success. Though "Caron" appeared in *Portfolio* (1945, under the title "On the Right Hand of God") and in Selden Rodman's *A New Anthology of Modern American Poetry* (1946), this complex sequence (except for one sonnet) was excluded from *Lord Weary's Castle*, which was published the same year, and never reprinted by Lowell. Besides retaining some of the immature aspects of Lowell's earlier satiric style, "Caron" mimics the form and subject of Dylan Thomas's comparably difficult "Altarwise by Owl-light," so Lowell may have suppressed his poem because he thought it too openly revealed his debt to the already famous Welsh poet. Perhaps Lowell recognized in his own poem one of the faults he found in his 1947 review of Thomas's *Deaths and Entrances*: "Substitution of repeated symbols or description for logic or narrative. Because of this, the three longest poems are swamped in rhetoric and never develop."[1] Lowell's poem is more convoluted than Thomas's, however. While Thomas's poem, for all of its rhetorical complexity, rather straightforwardly dramatizes the dreams of Jesus during the days between his crucifixion and his resurrection, Lowell's poem shifts among at least three voices: the dominant one is the human voice of Jesus contained in fallen flesh, "cleft heel and horn," which resents his role as sacrificial lamb; another is that of the thieves, one or both; a third is a composite voice, also half-satanic, the expression of the collective memory of human history.

In his review of *Lord Weary's Castle*, Randall Jarrell observes that Lowell's poems "understand the world as a sort of conflict of opposites," and then locates those opposites as first "that cake of custom in which all of us lie embedded like lungfish—the stasis or inertia of the stubborn self, the obstinate persistence in evil that is damnation" and then "everything that is free or open, that grows or is willing to change."[2] Most of the evil has solidified as social institution, including Calvinism, political structures, militarism, and so on. That which is free and open is represented by the grace offered by Christ, but its relationship to traditional Christianity is dubious and problematic. In "Caron, Non Ti Crucciare" the conflict occurs between ideal spirit, muted by Jesus's sufferings, and the corruption of the body—both the human body of Jesus and the body political and institutional. Equally important is the tension between the private voice, represented by Jesus expressing his agony, and the public voice of history. Later, in Lowell's more plainly secular poetry, this tension between private and public voices becomes a problem in reconciliation as autobiography and history approach each other. In "Caron, Non Ti Crucciare," however, the voice of Jesus obliquely speaks for the poet but expresses a conflict between the satanic humanity and the divine idealism present, perhaps, in all individuals.

Critics have generally attributed Lowell's early style to the impact of Allen Tate's, Hart Crane's, and T. S. Eliot's allusive, formal, highly compressed verse. But Dylan Thomas also offered a usable model of densely figurative, rhetorically complex verse. As Lowell described Thomas in his review, "He is a dazzling obscure writer who can be enjoyed without understanding."[3] And for Lowell writing in 1945–46, when he considered himself a devout Catholic convert, Thomas's was an example of modernist religious poetry that wielded irony without compromising devotion. "Altarwise by Owl-light," like "Caron, Non Ti Crucciare," is a ten-sonnet sequence, conventional in form but written in Thomas's most difficult surreal vein, featuring lines like "The planet-ducted pelican of circles / Weans on an artery the gender's strip."[4] The first seven sonnets were published in *Life and Letters To-Day* in December 1935, and the entire sequence in *Twenty-Five Poems,* Thomas's second book, published in 1936. Although the general purpose and movement of the sequence seems clear enough to me, Daniel Jones, in the notes to his edition of Thomas's poems, observes that "Altarwise by Owl-Light," because of lines like those quoted above, defies interpretation.[5] As an example of the problem the poem offers the critic, Jones remarks that Elder Olson, in reading it on the basis of its astrological content, produces a critical paraphrase even more difficult than the poem itself, which calls into question the whole notion of critical reading. Jones believes "Altarwise" to be "'absolute poetry' . . . a pattern of images and words, held together not by ordinary logic, but by the logic of a common relationship of those images and words with certain allied subjects: sex, birth, death, Christian and pagan religion and ritual."[6] Lowell's poem answers equally well to this description. However, both of these poems have a dramatic movement or shape that prevails, though certain passages remain impenetrable. As Thomas helpfully pointed out, "this poem is a particular incident in a particular adventure."[7] That adventure is the death and resurrection of Christ.

"Altarwise" and "Caron, Non Ti Crucciare" both open by introducing a dramatic character in a particular setting. In Thomas's poem that character is a "gentleman" in a "half-way house" who lies "graveward with his furies." The late Henry Vincent Grattan, in an unpublished lecture, observed that the gentleman was Jesus, just crucified, and that the poem would trace his archetypal dreams to the point at which he prophesies his resurrection and a general dispensation of mercy ("My nest of mercies in the rude, red tree"), thus revealing a basic dramatic movement. Though not quite everything falls into place, this seems to me the key to the poem, and renders the reading of it at least possible if not entirely transparent. Most importantly, this apparently is Lowell's reading of Thomas's poem, since this is the dramatic movement he replicates in ten sonnets.

Lowell's title, from *Inferno,* Canto III, is spoken by Virgil, the master-poet and guide, who is responding to Charon's objections to taking a living being across the Styx. After exclaiming "Charon, do not rage," Virgil continues (in Charles Singleton's translation), "Thus it is willed there where that can be done which is willed; and ask no more."[8] The Italian *crucciare* suggests the English *crucify,* generating an interlingual pun; but more importantly the passage reminds us that Jesus, too, occupied for three days a state between life and death, and that this adventure was willed by a superior power. Lowell's subtitle, Mark 15:27, "And with Him they crucify two thieves, the one on His right hand, the other on His left," in its original context is followed by another passage that like Virgil's argument places the passion in a seemingly preordained historical context: "And the scripture was fulfilled, which saith, And he was numbered with the transgressors."

The poem is a journey across the Styx, back through the Old Testament and forward into medieval history and the Second World War. The first of the ten sonnets opens by invoking the ideal of beauty in the Song of Solomon (Christ in typological readings is both bride and bridegroom) as Jesus addresses the two thieves crucified beside him:

> My beauty is departed: they will square
> My hands and feet, and Omar's coarse-hair tent
> Towers above the Kedron's Torrent, Sent,
> Ben Himnon and the hide-bound outlands where
> The little fox runs shivering to its lair,
> Fearful lest the short-sighted Orient
> Mistake it for this shambles of dissent
> Where the red victims of the gallows stare
> And dazzle the trenched highways with their blood.
> My brothers, if I call you brothers, see:

The blood of Abel, crying from the dead
Sticks to my shaven skull and eyes. What good
Are *lebensraum* and bread to Israel dead
And rotten on the cross-beams of the Tree?[9]

Lebensraum, Hitler's vision of territory for a dominate Aryan nation—
a typological inversion of the Old Testament image of Israel as a land of
chosen people—is the ultimate perversion of Christ's sacrifice and the
end-product of history. Both Lebensraum and Israel are valueless concepts because they are predicated on the death of Jesus. The sonnet illustrates many of the difficulties of the sequence. The allusions are
inexact—"Himnon," for instance, probably should be "Hinnom," a valley south of Jerusalem mentioned in Joshua (Hebrew, *gê ben-hinnom*,
valley of the sons of Hinnom)—and the punctuation is confusing.
Some of the modifiers—"trenched highways," "hide-bound outlands"—
seem to require explication, and the phrase "shambles of dissent" raises
endless difficulties. One might say of this sonnet and of Lowell's work
generally in this era something similar to what Lowell himself observed
of Thomas: "If Thomas kept his eye on his object and depended less
on his rhetoric, his poems would be better organized and have more
to say."[10] In some instances, however, the complexities of Lowell's metaphor and syntax yield to the imperatives of rhetoric in ways that clarify
rather than confuse. In the closure of the second sonnet, for example,
the image of the last line, though not drawn from the immediate dramatic situation, invokes Dante's wild wood to strong effect:

O why did God climb out on this bald hill,
That Young Man, worse than prodigal, and lie
Upon the gallows of our brotherhood?
The wolves go round in circles in the wood.

The opening sonnet marks the boundaries of the entire sequence,
which proceeds by depicting the agonies of the crucifixion through the
eyes of the thieves (II), reviewing the life of Jesus (III, IV), examining

the perversion of Christianity by medieval and Protestant theology (V), shifting to a historical second-person plural to speak as the Hebrew nation (VI, VII), invoking and elegizing the classical pastoralism of Virgil (VIII), revising the Twenty-third Psalm in the voice of Jesus in his last agony—the voice of a tattered, decayed Christianity—(IX), and finally eliciting a confession by the satanic voice of history and rebellion, accepting responsibility for both earthly and heavenly suffering and sacrifice (X).

A view of spiritual evolution as a process liable to be tainted by misdirected human will frequently appears in the works of Roman Catholic theology that Lowell was reading in the 1940s. Like those works, the poems of *Land of Unlikeness,* despite their pessimism and crude satire, look toward a new Incarnation as a source of renewal. "Caron, Non Ti Crucciare," too, concludes with a suggestion that the new Incarnation is forthcoming. Though Lowell could have formulated this view from a number of sources, a passage in Christopher Dawson's *Progress and Religion* (a book Lowell owned) in discussing St. Gregory Nyssen's *Cathetical Discourse* illuminates some of the theological assumptions underlying Lowell's poetry of the early and mid-1940s:

St. Gregory of Nyssa sees in man not only "the god-like image of the archetypal beauty," but the channel through which the whole material creation acquires consciousness and becomes spiritualized and united to God. Just as in the material world itself, he says, there is an inner organic harmony of creation, so, too, there is, by the Divine Wisdom, a certain commingling of the intelligible world with the sensible creation, so that no part of creation might be rejected or deprived of Divine Fellowship. And the bond of this mixture and communion is to be found in human nature. Man was created by God "in order that the earthly element might be raised by union with the Divine, and so the Divine grace in one even course, as it were, might uniformly extend through all creation, the lower nature being mingled with that which is above the world." This created nature, however, is essentially changeable. It continually passes through a process of evolution, which so long as it acts in accordance with nature will always be progressive, but which on the other hand, may become a movement of degeneration and decline, if once the will should become perverted.[11]

The "beauty" that has "departed" in sonnet I, then, is the god-like image, the divine aspect of the self. Lacking that link to divinity, the material creation loses its spirituality. Consequently, Jesus in the agony of crucifixion not only exposes his humanity but a humanity deprived of divinity and thus in a state more degraded than the rest of the creation. This is the most sacrificial aspect of the crucifixion: not the humiliation of Christ through the punishment and corruption of his material body but the separation of flesh and spirit. In uniting itself with humanity, the "Divine Nature" intended to further human evolutionary progress, but, as Lowell's poems observe, "degeneration and decline" have displaced progress. The material suffering of Jesus in the name of an unrealized ideal is the rebuke "Caron" offers.

Everything in the poem develops out of this conviction that the passion of Christ was at least partly in vain. The version of the life of Jesus presented in sonnet III typologically confounds him with Ezekiel. While there is precedent for this, Lowell uses the opportunity to emphasize the mortal, sinning dimension rather than the self-denying spiritual self:

> I wandered footloose in the wastes of Nod
> And damned the day and age when I was born.
> I weary of this curse, Almighty God,
> Which solely falls on my cleft heel and horn;
> My shepherd brother led the lepers back
> To Jordan. Then I strayed to Babylon
> Where gold-dust sands the sidewalks, lost the track
> Of Abel through the fallow to thy Son.
> Here merchants trim the sheep and goats in mills

> Where woolen turns to gold and dollar bills:
> The merchants snare us in the golden net
> Of Mammon. O Jerusalem, I said,
> If I forget thee, may my hand forget
> Her cunning. Let the stranger eat my bread.

The "shepherd brother" of Jesus is his spiritual self. While this spiritual being goes about his ministry, the mortal Jesus becomes involved in the capitalism of the era.

This conflict between spirit and flesh is exacerbated in the following sonnet, in which Joseph counsels his son in the ways of sin. The whore of Babylon is an economic crime, not a sexual one, but honoring its material licentiousness leads to modern war. Flesh and money cohabit, and the whore of Babylon embodies the illicit relationship that engenders material misery. Appealing to the Mother of God, the mother of his spiritual self, Jesus asks to be reminded of Jonah's suffering (Jonah being another typological harbinger of Jesus) and ultimate triumph:

> "There is a woman, if you find her, Son,"
> My worldly father whispered, "Where each street
> Bubbles and bursts with houses of concrete,
> There shall you know the whore of Babylon."
> In this way Cain's instruction was begun,
> Mother of God, before I could repeat
> An *Ave* or know the fabulous clay feet
> Of Babylon are dynamite and gun;
> Mother of God, I lie here without bail.
> Instruct a lasher of the sheep and goat
> In Jonah, who three nights of midnights lay
> Buried inside the belly of the whale,
> Then, grappling Nineveh by its mule's throat,
> Hauled a great city to the Scapegoat's hay.

Unlike the voice of Jesus, which is torn between spirit and flesh but alert to the qualities of each, the plural first-person of historical consciousness in sonnet VII speaks in the mystified voice of someone as blind as the failed clergy in "Lycidas" and inert to his own cultural and religious ironies:

> But peace, in Israel bearded elders keep
> The peace as they have always kept it. No
> Wolves break into these pastures where the sheep
> Wait for the hireling hind to shear them. O
> People, let us sleep out this night in peace.
> Jehovah nods, the doors of Janus slam,
> Cocks on the weathervanes will never cease
> Crowing for our defilement of the Lamb.
> Lamb in the manger, come into our house:
> Here you may find and buy all you can eat,
> Dirt cheap. On high, till cockcrow, Lord of Hosts,
> The gallows' bird is singing to his spouse,
> And mad-cap Lamb is gambolling in the street
> And splatters blood on the polluted posts.

The reference to "mad-cap Lamb" confounds the metaphorical Jesus with Mary Lamb, who in her insanity murdered her mother. The very awkwardness of this allusion underscores the preposterous notion of keeping the peace as the bearded elders have always kept it. The history of Israel is one of bloodshed as mad as Mary Lamb's rampage. The public voice here speaks nonsense, appealing to Jesus ("Lamb in the manger") as a consumer instead of a savior.

That the classical era offered a model of pastoralism easily confounded with the biblical version is the subject of sonnet VIII, which by invoking Virgil echoes the title of the sequence, and by underscoring the consumerism of the golden age suggests the cultural bankruptcy of the pagan era. Here the pastoral is consumed and the political sublime collapses, making way for the harsher and yet more promising sublimity of the passion of Christ:

> Virgil, who heralded this golden age,
> Unctuous with olives of perpetual peace,
> Had heard the cackle of the Capitol Geese,
> And Caesar toss the sponge and patronage
> Of Empire to his prostituted page.
> The gold is tarnished and the geese are grease,
> Jason has stripped the sheep for golden fleece,
> The last brass hat has banged about the stage.
> But who will pipe a new song? In our land
> Caesar has given his scarlet coat away.
> But who will pipe a new song? In our land
> Caesar has given his crown of thorns away.
> But who will pipe the young sheep back to fold?
> Caesar has cut his throat to kill the cold.

The passion, to which the sequence returns in sonnet IX, is harshly depicted because it is a material experience, Baudelairean and yet eased by a vision of grace relieving the flesh of itself:

> God is my shepherd and looks after me.
> See how I hang. My bones eat through the skin
> And flesh they carried here upon the chin
> And lipping clutch of their cupidity;
> Now here, now there, the sparrow and the sea
> Gull splinter the groined eyeballs of my sin,
> Caesar, more beaks of birds than needles in
> The fathoms of the Bayeux Tapestry;
> Our beauty is departed. Who'll discuss
> Our scandal, for we are terror and speak:
> "Remember how the Dove came down to us,

Broke through your armor of imperial bronze
And beat with olive-branch and bleeding beak
And picked the Lord's Annointed to the bones."

Lowell would reprocess and tame the closing image for "Where the Rainbow Ends," the concluding poem of *Lord Weary's Castle*: "Stand and live, / The Dove has brought an olive branch to eat."[12] The anachronistic reference to the Bayeaux Tapestry, like the reference to Dives (Andreas Divus) in sonnet V, evokes the medieval era when Catholic and Orthodox Christianity's apparent hegemony concealed whole worlds of dissent, rebellion, and heresy. The tapestry, its fathoms of hidden depth emblematically linked to the Baudelairean vision of aggressively carnivorous birds, makes art of the material horror of the crucifixion.

In the final sonnet, the personal and public voices converge and the first-person singular speaks for the world, confessing not only to the sin of pride but to the desire to bring Satan's rebellion, a crime of the flesh, into the uppermost heaven. It confesses also that the sacrifice of Jesus is too good for it, too good for a horned creature of sin. And yet that sacrifice promises an end to suffering and ignorance, reconciling the human, the divine, and the bestial:

I made this Babel. Pushed against the wall,
With splintered hands and knees and sky-sick blood,
I pieced together scaffolding. O God,
To swing my cloven heels into the tall
Third heaven of heavens, where the Prophet Paul
Fathoms that Jacob's Ladder is the wood
Of Christ the Goat, whose hanging is too good
For my unnourished horns, gone wooden, all
Splintered. God even of the goats, that was:
The fearful night is over and the mist
Is clearing from the undemolished shore

> Of Paradise, where homing angels pass
> With the dunged sheep into the manger. Christ
> Swings from this Tower of Babel to the floor.

To say "I made this Babel" is also to say "I made this poem." Lowell confesses to a confusion of tongues, a promiscuous mingling of incongruous images, much as the historical voice confesses to history itself. This early punning convergence of historical and personal voices would not recur in this manner, but it serves as a prototype of other attempts to merge personal and public historical concerns.

Lowell sent his poem to Jarrell, his best critic, who responded in November 1945 that "'Caron, Non Ti Crucciare' is the most Lowellish poem there ever was. I'm too exhausted to judge it."[13] But he did judge it, tactfully and at first indirectly. In his next letter to Lowell, Jarrell complains, "I think your biggest limitations right now are (1) not putting enough about people in the poems—they are more about the actions of you, God, the sea, and cemeteries than they are about the 'actions of men': (2) being too harsh and severe—but this is already changing, very much for the better too, *I* think."[14] Jarrell is referring to a group of Lowell poems, including "The Quaker Graveyard in Nantucket," but "Caron," being the most Lowellish poem, may display the most characteristic Lowell limitations.

Jarrell's subsequent letter (January 1946), reviewing the whole manuscript of *Lord Weary's Castle,* confirms his earlier judgment, but suggests that he thinks the poem worth further revision: "'Caron, Non Ti Crucciare' has some of your best patches in it: it seems to me rather an extrapolation of your method, Lowell 2 rather than Lowell, but I haven't read it again and won't talk about it till I go over it some."[15] "Patches" is a telling word. The poem does seem patchy, with strong passages alternating with awkward metaphors and clumsy diction. In the second sonnet, for example, "clocks/Of Heaven bawl and falter," and in the fourth the "fabulous clay feet/Of Babylon are dynamite and gun"—a clumsy merging of Old Testament and World War concerns.

On the other hand, the opening of sonnet III, quoted above, is metrically graceful and metaphorically coherent. There Lowell displays his talent for unifying word-choice. "Footloose" and "solely" pun against the damnation of "cleft heel and horn" without being awkwardly satirical, while the rhymes are carefully modulated by the syntax to mute their stark clarity. And sonnet VI, in the collective historical voice, describes the mystic desert of Exodus, captures its naked sublimity, and dramatizes the conflict between Hebrew and Egyptian culture by invoking the latter as a soul-destroying institution:

> We saw Mount Sinai and the Holy land
> In Egypt, compound of black earth and green
> Between a powdered mountain and red sand
> Scoured by the silver air-lines: we have seen
> The sworded Seraphim, the serpent-tree,
> The apple, once more distant than light-years,
> Falling like burning brands about our ears.
> The hydra-headed delta choked with sea;
> On that sarcophagus of the Nile's mud
> And mummies, the Destroyer clamped a lid,
> Weightier than King Cheops' pyramid,—
> Coffin within a coffin. In whose blood,
> Or Jordan, will our spiked and burdened hands
> Cup water for a mummy and his lands?

Among the qualities Jarrell detected, one is surely a tendency to overstate, rhetorically or metaphorically, the conflicts that according to Jarrell empower most of Lowell's early work. In "Caron, Non Ti Crucciare" this overstatement often occurs as unhappy anachronisms, as Lowell wrenches his biblical-classical subject matter into congruence with the present. When the anachronism is unobtrusive, such as the use of "light-years" in the above sonnet, it is effective. When the anachronism is insistent, as in the application of dynamite and gun to Babylon's clay feet, it evokes the less successful satirical groans and strains of *Land of Unlikeness*. Jarrell was correct to discourage Lowell's satirical impulses, push him toward dramatic situations, and encourage his elegiac voice. "Caron, Non Ti Crucciare" amalgamates satire and elegy and therefore suffers from tonal inconsistency. Thomas's "Altarwise by Owl-Light," in comparison, regardless of its difficulty, successfully maintains a single solemn note, giving the sequence a unity critics have not induced from its surreal imagery.

In the same January letter, Jarrell remarks, "About the only thing I regret about your book is that you didn't save 'Caron, Non Ti Crucciare' for the second book (and give yourself a chance to re-write sections that don't seem good after a year or two) and use the 'France' part of it in this. But it doesn't matter, since you can always do a second version of it later, then put that in another book."[16] Lowell did include "France" (a combination of sonnet I and sonnet IX of "Caron, Non Ti Crucciare") in *Lord Weary's Castle*, but did not revise the rest of the sequence for later publication.[17] He provided a new, more secular opening for "France": "My human brothers who live after me, / See how I hang," replacing "God is my shepherd and looks after me," the opening line of sonnet IX. Dropping the last six lines of sonnet IX and adding the last five of sonnet I, adding the uncompromising exclamation "God wills it, wills it, will it: it is blood," Lowell generated a single sonnet that spans the width of his former sequence, emphasizing the role of fate and the sense of despair that began the sequence, abandoning the note of hope that concludes both sonnets IX and X. There the intervention of the Dove and the descent of Christ from the Tower of Babel to the ordinary world ("the floor") indicate that "The fearful night is over and the mist / Is clearing from the undemolished shore/Of paradise, where homing angels pass / With the dunged sheep into the manger."

By 1946, Lowell the poet was quickly evolving toward a more secular view of the universe, one that found it difficult to place much hope in an idealized Christianity, whether Catholic or Protestant. Though Lowell would always cling to a sense of the importance of a religious view of the cosmos, he would never, after the mid-1940s, place his faith in any particular theological view of the relationship between God and the human world. A few years after abandoning the bulk of "Caron, Non Ti Crucciare," Lowell wrote another sonnet sequence, one that signaled his retreat from religious salvation in favor of a secular, cultural reconstitution of the self.

"Beyond the Alps" literalizes and secularizes the crossing of the Styx as a crossing of the Alps from a religious milieu to a secular one. In leaving Rome, Lowell "left the City of God where it belongs," and in reaching Paris he enters a "black classic," a tragic, secular, pre-Christian pagan culture. Though Lowell recants his Catholicism, rejects the natural sublime of the Alps (as Henry Hart has pointed out),[18] and ridicules the religious iconography he had only a few years before taken quite seriously, "Beyond the Alps" is not a wholly renunciatory poem but a move toward a new poetics, one exemplified by pagan classical tragedy. What Lowell renounces is the religious cant of Catholicism and the secular cult of the sublime ("even the Swiss had thrown the sponge/in once again and Everest was still/unscaled");[19] what he embraces is dramatic realism ("Our mountain climbing train had come to earth") and secular and tragic (because devoid of a vision of salvation) culture. The four-sonnet version of "Beyond the Alps," by including the Ovid sonnet John Berryman admired,[20] reinforces this shift to secular drama by invoking a poet of political exile to address the unreliability of institutions and proclaim the permanence of art:

> "Imperial Tiber, Oh my yellow dog,
> black earth by the black Roman sea, I lie
> with the boy-crazy daughter of the God,
> *il Duce Augusto.* I shall never die."[21]

Subtly again, Lowell wields anachronism to link the past and present. The apostrophe *il Duce,* Mussolini's preferred title, links ancient Rome to modern Italy, and Ovid, the exiled poet of his age, to Lowell, the poet of a Guggenheim fellowship and three years' residence in Europe. In mourning the death of Roman republicanism and the ascent of imperialism, Ovid embodies the shifts in political institutions that undermine religion and culture alike. In comparison, the "killer kings on an Etruscan cup," kings in the fixed world of art rather than the uneasy world of politics, however smashed by time, embody an enviable stability.

"Beyond the Alps" places more faith in experience and individual perception than most of Lowell's previous work, and shows how far he has moved since "Caron, Non Ti Crucciare" toward committing himself to an autobiographical voice. Much simpler in diction and metaphor than "Caron," "Beyond the Alps" stands as the first poem in *Life Studies,* a collection in which Lowell momentarily resolves the tension between public and private voices by foregrounding the private voice. That this foregrounding is only a temporary solution, though a strong one, is demonstrated by Lowell's further development in *For the Union Dead*—the title poem of which, more decisively perhaps than anything else Lowell wrote, merges public and private concerns in a single fulfilled poetic gesture.

Also in the early 1960s, concurrent with the composition of *For the Union Dead,* Lowell wrote several poems (published after his death as "Three Poems for *Kaddish*") that recall the baroque rhetoric and religiosity of his poems of the 1940s. These were part of a collaboration with Leonard Bernstein for his symphony *Kaddish.* The third of them makes a particularly interesting counterpoint to "Caron":

> Winter and darkness settle on the land;
> above the river, green, avenging ice
> advances and resumes its old command,
> our north and south poles hold us in a vise.
> The sun has dropped, and there is nothing here
> but frozen fishermen whose lanterns burn
> above the ice-holes. Listen, you will hear
> the saber-tooth and mastodon return,
> dazed monarchs of this arctic wilderness,
> they rule with shaggy, crushing stubbornness.

The sun has dropped, We listen for a sign:
the manna scattered from God's hand like bread,
a pillar of fire to show our path and shine,
a hero with a rainbow on his head.
No, none of these. The sun has dropped. We must
suffer the silence of the dead machine,
whose self-repairing wheels need no unseen
mechanic, when they grind us into dust.
The system runs on its own steam. The clock-
maker has no surprises for the clock.

Yet still we stand and sing into the cold,
and trust we never can annihilate
the old, established order of the world;
we know that by creating we create.
Poor little Father, are you looking down
on us without volition to resist?
Our hands have turned creation on its head.
Oh Father, do not bite your lip and frown;
it hardly matters now if we made God
or God made us. Both suffer and exist.[22]

Here the religious emotion, however heartfelt and committed, lacks the theological confidence of "Caron." The deist, world-weary agnosticism would come only when Lowell had abandoned the overwrought voice of satire and developed the more neutral tone of historical examination found in poems like "For the Union Dead." With that wider embrace, finally, came a certain tolerance of God and humanity unavailable to the zealot, who seemed forever disappointed and enraged. The passions of Lowell's mature poems never sound like dogma.

In "Caron, Non Ti Crucciare" Lowell hadn't yet fully untangled the public voice that speaks for and to historical and political concerns from the private oedipal voice of personal suffering. He would have to separate them in *Life Studies*, then rejoin them in altered poetic stances in *For the Union Dead* and *Near the Ocean*. Crossing and recrossing the Styx, the boundary between the individual and the cosmos, "Caron, Non Ti Crucciare" hints at the complexity of his subsequent career, and in its reckless embrace of history claims a subject with which Lowell would struggle for the rest of his life.

3 | "The Sudden Bridegroom"

HEN JARRELL IN 1947 CALLED LOWELL'S poetry "essentially post- or anti-modernist," he meant that *Lord Weary's Castle,* Lowell's second book, summarized and attempted to move beyond the rhetorical and aesthetic achievement of a strain of poetics defined by T. S. Eliot, who was at that time the epitome of modernism for both Lowell and Jarrell; he further noted that Lowell had organized his poems so that their wrenched "dramatic, dialectical internal organization" strained against traditional forms.[1] Though Jarrell does not develop its social and rhetorical implications, this observation points to the larger significance of Lowell's book: it is one of the major efforts of his generation to engage the aesthetic, rhetorical, and social consequences of the internal contradictions of modernism, which it expresses by imposing traditional iconography (Christian and Roman Catholic) on a narrative of insistent skepticism. This skepticism is not merely social or cultural but linguistic, and derives from Lowell's doubts, made explicit only many years later, about the adequacy of his chosen medium.

Lowell's relentlessly intelligent poetry exposed cultural and societal tensions that prevented him from accepting the poetic inheritance of Eliot, Crane, and Tate. These tensions are readily discernible in *Land of Unlikeness;* but in revising poems from this small-press collection for his second book, Lowell modulated and carefully directed competing bodies of imagery to create a heightened aesthetic effect. The resultant exposure of the cultural and psychological anxiety underlying the Anglo-American modernist project (as Lowell discovered it in Eliot's *Four Quartets,* for instance) appears most characteristically in *Lord Weary's Castle* as a series of figural wrenchings of conventional religious iconography. This anxiety derives from Lowell's perception of the fragmentation of systems of religious, social, and cultural order, as well as from his inability to assert, as Eliot does, a faith in the possible renewal of such systems through the efficacies of language. Later, in *Life Studies,* Lowell would personalize this anxiety and devise what Harold Bloom subsequently termed the "trope of vulnerability" by replacing the archetypal voice of *Lord Weary's Castle* with a more personal lyric voice and by devising figures of self-exposure to replace the religious and societal metaphors of the early work.[2] But the poetics of *Lord Weary's Castle,* still torn between high modernism and unvoiced psychosemantic desires, precluded such direct expression of aesthetic anxiety.

Anglo-American literary modernism, as defined by Eliot's poetic practice and criticism, critiques but does not entirely reject the post-Renaissance continuum of literary, religious, or social tradition. It strains between the desire to embrace tradition and the desire to displace it, as some of Eliot's early poems do, by assuming the voice of an individual consciousness devoid of traditional religious and social convictions. Lowell's work is tempered by exposure to Crane's encomia to the machine age, Williams's nihilistic view of history, and Tate's sonorous nostalgia. In exposing the paradox of Eliot's position, Lowell's slightly revisionary stance suggests how the modernist social and aesthetic critique, despite its reactionary tendencies, barely resists cultural promiscuity and aesthetic nihilism. The strain against nihilism on the one hand and reaction on the other colors the tonalities of Lowell's poems; his speakers, whether they represent him or others, cannot deny their perceptions and experience, but feel compelled to struggle against the precipitous descent into apparent cultural anarchy represented by the elevation of metaphorical delineation of worldly experience over the symbolic language of religion and literary tradition.

Lowell's metaphors express his will as well as his perception. His figurative language consists not only of simple metaphors but of dialogically opposed rhetorical figures. On the one hand, these figures assert the continued power of the emblem, the trope of received meaning; on the other hand, they attempt to persuade both reader and speaker that contingent imagery may be equally or even more powerful and persuasive. Whether contingent or traditional, these figures may consist of isolated images, groups of images, or coherent bodies of imagery; but whether they function metaphorically (in the traditional sense), symbolically (linking the concrete and the ineffable), or contextually (deriving their meaning from immediate experience) determines whether the poem sustains, critiques, or rejects the religious, social, and literary traditions Eliot traced into this century. Because this use of figurative language represents will, desire, or pathos, it may well work against the apparent intention of the author (as a function of knowledge rather than will) and it may better represent his psychological or sexual needs than his spiritual or intellectual ones. It may also represent a clash among conflicting needs. Derived by Eliot from a strong body of urban poetry by Charles Baudelaire and Jules Laforgue, and built upon a powerful rhetorical development extending from Shakespeare through Robert Browning, the characteristic metaphors of modernism effectively translate will or desire into verbal acts and function as figures of ethos, or willed presence. The will to undo one's psychological bondage to the past without utterly rejecting its aesthetic efficacy shapes the poetics of Eliot, Pound, Williams, and Crane.

Lord Weary's Castle generates a dialogic power through opposing-yet-complementary rhetorical strategies that bear complex cultural, personal, and political implications. The willful use of metaphor inherited from high modernism attempts to persuade the reader that the relationship of the text to the past is continuous but problematic in some new way, and that the voice of the text does not merely speak for tradition but critiques it.³ The metaphors generated in *Lord Weary's Castle* overcome the modernist aesthetic, however, by confronting it with certain of its consequences, especially by exposing the irrationality and inadequacy of faith. The resultant aesthetic critique struggles with the will to reject the modern subject and reveal the failure of modernist cultural, literary, and social history to define the present by adequately distinguishing it from the past.⁴ This conflict originates with Eliot as the central paradox of Anglo-American modernism, which wants both to retain and reject the comforting structural constants of the past. The unintended irony with which Lowell in his review of *Four Quartets* describes Eliot's poetic movement in terms of a geometrical solipsism proves symptomatic of this paradoxical conflict: "Probably the contemplative's life, as distinguished from his separate acts, can only be dramatized by a circular and thematic structure. His actions, unlike the tragic hero's, have no beginning, middle, or end: their external unity is a pawn to their unity of intention. His discipline is repetitive and his moments of ecstasy disconnected. Eliot has this one theme in all of his writings and its nature in part explains the excellence of the longer poems and the relative failure of the plays."⁵

In *Lord Weary's Castle,* Lowell invents a mode of representation that reveals the self-deception in the modernist voice of the text, the sort of deception that the contemplative's discipline may unwittingly encourage. But in this early stage of invention, this body of figuration lacks adequate verbal means of translating the will and insists on distorting highly conventionalized iconography into psychologically satisfying but almost unrecognizable shapes, such as the figuration of Mary that concludes "At the Indian Killer's Grave," discussed in chapter 1. When this passage appeared as the conclusion of "Cistercians in Germany," the womb did not belong to the Virgin Mary but to the soul of Saint Bernard, to whom the Cistercian monks raise their "bloody hands" in despair as Europe and their monastery go up in flames. "At the Indian Killer's Grave" delves more deeply into history for its figuration of oppression and slaughter, and more deeply into Catholicism for its figure of redemption. Puritanism here and throughout *Lord Weary's Castle* displaces the war as a source of cultural and social tension. Its conflict with Catholicism distorts conventional religious iconography, just as, in the world of these poems, domestic and political doctrines distort the social compact.[6] In much the same way, the war distorts the social compact and warps the religious imagery in *Land of Unlikeness*—at the behest of the poet—to emphasize the judgmental rather than the redemptive function of Catholic theology.

Judgment remains a motivating force in *Lord Weary's Castle,* but even when socially directed it also indicates aesthetic failures and, paradoxically, the inadequacy of religion itself. The grotesque iconography at the end of "At the Indian Killer's Grave" points in three directions: toward the aesthetic inadequacy and stubborn persistence of faith, toward the psychological inadequacy of the modernist aesthetic inherited from Eliot and Tate that issues in this compressed imagery, and toward the post-Freudian recognition of sexuality as the open secret of the unrepentant id.[7] The will cannot quite overcome the modernist voice, but it can critique it by forcing it to speak in terms it cannot adequately represent. Adequate representation would require a different cultural context, however—one that would finally reject the tradition rather than attempt to revise it. Lowell's own poetics verge upon this rejection, and this Freudian critique of Mary as a culmination of the pagan tradition of vegetation goddesses reveals the sexual anxiety that would dominate much of Lowell's later work, especially *The Dolphin.* In "At the Indian Killer's Grave," however, the imagery of faith resists being subsumed entirely into sexual domesticity. The tension between Puritan and Catholic imagery, between the Roman Catholic embrace of Mary's virginity and her florally enfigured fecundity, keeps the poem focused on the social hypocrisy of the puritanical spiritual legacy rather than allowing it to drift into the personal. Mary's presence represents a richness and generosity of spirit that the Puritans rejected in favor of a stark, death-oriented culture where her warlock-destroying powers would be honored rather than her innocence and purity.

At this stage in the development of Lowell's poetics, his will, lacking adequate means of representation, seizes upon its own inadequacy of voice and generates from religious iconography a series of uneasy figurations of pathos. But however troubled and incomplete, this development represents Lowell's revisionary reading of T. S. Eliot as a poet who contrived a modernist poetics only to spend a lifetime repudiating the modern ethos he helped create. That ethos was surely problematic to Eliot and Tate, both of whom made explicit their repugnance for certain aspects of modern culture.[8] Regardless of how he saw himself in relation to the tradition represented by Eliot, Lowell had ample precedent for seeing the modernist project as one of escaping from the state of being modern. Because this is a paradoxical project, Lowell's reformulation of it would also have to be paradoxical.

Lord Weary's Castle, its aesthetic shaped by modernism, its psychological desires producing conflicted forces that undermine the modernist view of tradition, attempts to superimpose the pathos of self-awareness onto the ethos of modernism. The means are a rhetoric dominated by a clash of competing languages: one determinedly secular, urban, and sexual, another committed to literary tradition, and another psychologically drawn but not theologically committed to Catholicism. The net result is that concealments of the will, its figures of pathos, shape some of the most powerful moments of poems like "Christmas in Black Rock" and "Where the Rainbow Ends." In aiming to transcend modernist poetics and critique the modern state, *Lord Weary's Castle* undertakes to persuade the reader that Mary, the eternal virgin at the heart of a dying European culture, can function as the muse of the violence that would topple the modern state. Despite her virgin innocence, Mary can wield force when necessary, and in poems like "On the Eve of the Feast of the Immaculate Conception: 1942" in *Land of Unlikeness,* the poet quite openly requests that she, like Athena, intervene in an unjust war. In *Lord Weary's Castle,* Mary and Jesus (who explicitly threatens to return with a sword) occupy less insistent roles, but their presence remains associated with violence, most obviously in poems like "The Dead in Europe."

While in *Land of Unlikeness* such poems as "The Wood of Life" and "Satan's Confession" use parable as a structural device, Lowell in *Lord*

Weary's Castle abandons this structural use of religious motifs without voiding their emotional imperative and anchors his work more firmly in the present-day urbanized world. He attempts to will Boston into a place of symbolic desire, but since the poems trust no body of figuration (and even Catholic symbols become distorted self-parodies) the embrace of modernism serves mostly to reveal the poet's own fear of the modern and his will to escape it. In revising "Christmas Eve in the Time of War" into "Christmas Eve under Hooker's Statue," Lowell secularized the poem by removing much of the religious imagery of the original version.[9] In the new version, the central trope, taken over the modernist revision of the English poetic tradition, is the statue—the representative public work of art—that links art, society, and history. Here, however, General Joseph Hooker, the unsuccessful commander of Union forces at Chancellorsville, figures a loss of innocence that bridges the gap between history and the individual. As a descendant of the New England puritan tradition, Hooker embodies the moral and social hypocrisy that has "blackened" the "statehouse," since his god is Mars, not Christ the redeemer. As twenty years ago the child "hung [his] stocking on the tree, and hell's/Serpent entwined the apple in the toe/To sting the child with knowledge," so Hooker's statue exudes the hellish knowledge that transforms boys ("'All wars are boyish,' Herman Melville said"[10]) into ironic, self-aware, and guilty men. Christmas Eve should foster commemoration of the origin of true religion; but Lowell's poem confounds the birth of Christ with the American republic's loss of innocence as represented by a rusting and ineffectual "cannon and a cairn of cannon balls," and Lowell's own twenty years of aging out of childhood into the chill of knowledge.

The modernist impulse of "Christmas Eve under Hooker's Statue" is to critique the history of the matured republic in terms of the high idealism of Christianity (primarily Roman Catholicism); but the sense of personal loss that makes Lowell ironic and skeptical overcomes the childlike requirements of faith and necessitates further revision of the Christian outlook. "We are old," he observes, and will remain so "Till Christ again turn wanderer and child." Imitation of Christ requires a return to a childhood that Lowell finds personally improbable, so he looks to the Second Coming as a source of renewal, since it would bring into focus a new manifestation of Christ. The whole thrust of the poem, however, collapses the imagery of faith into naive innocence. A winter-dominated poem of age, collective guilt, and frustrated faith ("I ask for bread, my father gives me mould"), "Christmas Eve under Hooker's Statue" inscribes in its very title one aspect of the modernist dilemma —the relationships among competing bodies of iconography, none of which mean any longer what they were once thought to mean, and that now signify only in terms of an immediate context.

The personal element of this poem, the memory of a bland and secularized Protestant Christmas with its childhood innocence poisoned by adult understanding, refutes the public element. The latter would extend this compromise of innocence by confronting Christian idealism with the politics of expediency that led to the Civil War and perhaps to the Second World War. In place of the conventional narrative of salvation through the sacrifice of Christ, the poem substitutes a personal narrative of knowledge, untouched by redemption except in its postulation of an improbable version of Christian idealism, one in which Christ reverts to his own childhood, a more human state of unrealized possibility.

In the characteristically modernist dynamic of this poem, a personal narrative confronts the iconographies of war and religion. But iconography no longer functions as a body of symbols; instead, it serves as a source of contingent but contextually empowered emblems. The "blackout" of this Christmas Eve is both an event of modern warfare and a blotting out of inherited meanings. Whereas in *The Waste Land* Eliot transplants traditional symbols with inherited meanings into a dissociative context that preserves strong traces of the narrative that originally empowered them, Lowell places the symbols of this poem in a personal narrative that simply if regretfully negates them by illustrating how inadequately they function outside of their original narratives. In the second stanza, the voice of the poet, only half-disguised in biblical paraphrase, neatly undercuts the accumulated power of faith, myth, and history by invoking the psychological anxiety of a speaker, his alter ego, for whom the dialogue among symbols no longer provides intellectual sustenance:

> Now storm-clouds shelter Christmas, once again
> Mars meets his fruitless star with open arms,
> His heavy saber flashes with the rime,
> The war-god's bronzed and empty forehead forms
> Anonymous machinery from raw men;
> The cannon on the Common cannot stun
> The blundering butcher as he rides on Time—
> The barrel clinks with holly. I am cold:
> I ask for bread, my father gives me mould . . .

Not only the speaking voice but almost every modifier in the poem weakens the traditional efficacy of the symbolism. "Fruitless," "empty," "anonymous," and "blundering" attest to the failure of meaning and the collapse, not merely the modification or reassessment, of traditions. By undermining the poem's entire symbolic structure, the skepticism of the speaking voice, though rooted in biblical struggles between faith and doubt, rejects the use of language as a transcendent medium.

The tones of this insinuated private voice, colored by distrust of the tradition it invokes, distinguished Lowell's work from that of many of his contemporaries long before he fully accepted the voice and began to write openly autobiographical poems. By contrast, the characteristic voice of high modernism in American, British, and a great deal of French poetry is discrete, distant: archetypal and ceremonial rather than personal, "a kind of incantation," as Mallarmé describes it.[11] It purports to be a voice of objectivity and impersonality, though recent critical thinking has cast doubt upon its actual distance from personal concerns. Certainly it places great faith in the incantatory power of language, sometimes even confounding representation with presence—a heresy in the postmodern linguistic world. Eliot, Pound, Stevens, and Yeats generate almost infinite possibilities with this formal voice. Overawed by the achievement of the major modernists, yet unable to quite duplicate their successes, the subsequent generation would gradually return to the more personal lyric voice categorically rejected by Pound and Eliot. They associated that voice with the nineteenth century, particularly with Wordsworth, for whom their admiration was decidedly qualified, and with Tennyson, whom Eliot in the 1936 essay on "In Memoriam" had just begun to rehabilitate after years of refusing him a suitable place in the tradition.[12]

After the publication of *Life Studies* in 1959, the gradual return to a lyric voice would become a rush. Though by then many poets, notably Weldon Kees, W. D. Snodgrass, Frank O'Hara, and Allen Ginsberg, had adopted radically personal poetics, in 1946, those of Lowell's contemporaries who challenged the inherited modernist positions had not confronted the doctrines and voice of objectivity and impersonality with aesthetic and psychological imperatives that could serve as convincing alternatives. During the 1940s, perhaps only Delmore Schwartz (*Genesis,* 1943), Muriel Rukeyser (*Beast in View,* 1944), Elizabeth Bishop (*North & South,* 1946), and Theodore Roethke (*The Lost Son,* 1948) challenged the characteristic modernist voice as productively as Lowell did.[13] Some of the most progressive and interesting poets of the era, including George Oppen, Charles Reznikoff, Louis Zukofsky, and Carl Rakosi, chose instead to emphasize or even exaggerate the objective voice, building upon the precisely descriptive aspect of William Carlos Williams's work while rejecting (for the moment) his example of a frankly personal voice.[14] Eventually, however, Williams, almost alone in his generation, would provide a strong model for the rediscovery or reinvention of the lyric "I-you" voice of intimacy and personal discovery.[15] Lowell himself rediscovered Williams in the early 1950s (his undergraduate notebooks show him experimenting with Williams-like free verse).[16] Although Williams would inspire him with a new sense of the possibilities of a more casually intimate voice—one less strained and self-conscious than that of "Christmas Eve under Hooker's Statue" —some of Lowell's poems of the war years were already clearly drifting in that direction.

"The Drunken Fisherman," virtually unrevised (except for one line) from its appearance in *Land of Unlikeness,* goes a step further than "Christmas Eve under Hooker's Statue" in reinventing this personal lyric voice. Lowell here is an adult Huckleberry Finn—which means an Ahab—who toys with the allegorical imagery of his avocation, rejecting the idea that one might fish for the symbols of redemption ("Truly Jehovah's bow suspends/No pots of gold to weight its ends") and arguing that only real fish—"the blood-mouthed rainbow trout"—are his prey. His initial rhymes establish his hungover bloodshot state ("Wallowing in this bloody sty/I cast for fish that pleased my eye"). The pun on "sty" (both a bloodshot eye and a pigpen) and the many purposes of "bloody" (invoking the river of the damned, invoking the war, and referring to his drink-muddled vision) trigger an allegorical unfolding that repeatedly evokes and then veers from conventional religious allegory and returns to the quotidian. After establishing his credentials as an actual fisherman, complete with "A whiskey bottle full of worms," Lowell toys with the allegorical dimensions of his occupation—the savior and the blasphemer, Christ and Melville's Ahab—and acknowledges that there is no way "to cast [his] hook/Out of this dynamited brook," no way entirely to resist the pressure of significance.

To distance himself from allegorical roles that require transcendent faith, Lowell distorts them almost beyond recognition, relegating the Ahab-role to the "pot-hole of old age" and asserting that he "will catch Christ with a greased worm" to enact his role as the ironic figure of the "Man-Fisher": not only Christ as fisher of men, but Lowell as fisher of Christ. This recognition of the role-reversal implicit in metaphor suggests how deeply compromised is the conventional imagery of the fisherman. The symbol no longer retains its shape. The fisherman is both the savior and the destroyer, the hunter and the prey. Here the "Prince of Darkness" embodies the uncertainty of such archetypal imagery in a contemporary world. By stalking Lowell's "bloodstream," he is deconstructing the relationship between tenor and vehicle, undoing the knots of metaphor to expose the arbitrary character of referent. Lowell's casual blasphemy (as opposed to Ahab's calculated blasphemy) and the

mock-drunken jauntiness of his voice make available this casual attitude toward metaphor.

Whereas in "Christmas Eve under Hooker's Statue" the poet's first-
person voice carries a note of regret and nostalgia for the compromised
iconography of religion and history, the voice of "The Drunken Fisher-
men" revels in acknowledging of the arbitrary nature of language and
metaphor:

> Once fishing was a rabbit's foot—
> O wind blow cold, O wind blow hot,
> Let suns stay in or suns step out:
> Life danced a jig on the sperm-whale's spout—
> The fisher's fluent and obscene
> Catches kept his conscience clean.
> Children, the raging memory drools
> Over the glory of past pools.

That these "past pools" are now fished out does not bother the drunken
fisherman—he accepts the absurdity of his enterprise and embraces the
chaotic declension of metaphor that he has precipitated. The poem
moves dialogically between his acknowledgment of the traditional
fisher-metaphors (savior, destroyer of nature, the fisher-king) and his
drink-loosened sensibility, which playfully exploits the failure of these
metaphors to retain their precipitous grip on traditional significance.
When Eliot in *The Waste Land* invokes the fisher-king as a metaphor
of the individual's dilemma in a decaying, corrupt culture, he leans
on the figure's long history, updating rather than refusing its literary
and historical resonance. But Lowell in "The Drunken Fisherman" undermines traditional metaphors by manipulating the early Christian
symbol of the fish, baiting his hook with a "greased worm" to catch the
fisher of men as if Christ were himself an ordinary fish like the "blood-
mouthed trout" in his creel.

That the roles of fisher and fish should be so easily reversed illustrates how arbitrary metaphor is—how inadequately language engages
such mysteries as salvation and blasphemy. This sense of the inadequa-

cies of language, while hardly unique to the twentieth century, characterizes much contemporary poetry not only as attitude but as topic. Occurring in Lowell's work as a flash of awareness, this sense usually results from self-consciousness, a moment when not only the absurdity of language but the awkwardness of the poet-speaker becomes palpable—and it is usually rather quickly glossed over by a shift to a more public voice. This dialectic of private and public voices characterizes some of Lowell's finished later poems, such as "For the Union Dead" and "Waking Early Sunday Morning." "After the Surprising Conversions," a dramatic monologue cast in the voice of Jonathan Edwards, seems safely to historicize this dialectic, but nonetheless exposes the tension between Lowell's modernist and nihilist sensibilities.[17] As Lowell himself points out, this poem reworks a passage from Edwards's *A Faithful Narrative of the Surprising Work of God in the Conversion of Many Hundred Souls in Northampton, and the Neighboring Towns and Villages* (1737).[18] The poem opens in epistolary mode by imitating Edwards's characteristically formal diction:

> *September twenty-second*, Sir: today
> I answer. In the latter part of May,
> Hard on our Lord's Ascension, it began
> To be more sensible.

It concludes with a cluster of images whose more naturalistic tenor (including a nonitalicized repetition of the date) offsets and to some degree neutralizes and secularizes the rehearsal of spiritual woe that constitutes the bulk of the poem:

> September twenty-second, Sir, the bough
> Cracks with the unpicked apples, and at dawn
> The small-mouth bass breaks water, gorged with spawn.

Edwards's original letter (from which the finished *Narrative*, with some additions, derives) addresses Benjamin Coleman, minister of the Brattle Street Church in Boston, who had written for information about the religious revival. The letter, dated 30 May 1735, has a postscript describing the suicide of Josiah Hawley, Edwards's uncle and one of the most prominent citizens of Northampton. In writing his poem, Lowell re-dates the original account and sets it in the fall (though accurately placing Hawley's suicide in May) presumably so that he can conclude with autumnal imagery of ripeness and mature fecundity.[19] As though waking from a bad dream, Edwards acknowledges that in stark contrast with the suicide of Hawley—a "gentleman / Of more than common understanding"—the natural world of apples and small-mouth bass seems a place of unfallen innocence, or, better still, perhaps a place in which the terms of sin and redemption no longer apply.[20] By contrast, Hawley, whose name the poem withholds (as does the relevant passage in the published *Narrative*), worried over his bible late at night in his attic, and the poem suggests that he shut himself into a world of language where phenomenal existence seemed a religious or epistemological construction rather than material reality. In his spiritual malaise, if not in his drastic response, he represents his misguided brethren. The spirit of God seems to have turned against Northampton and negated the communal sense of purpose:

> Content was gone.
> All the good work was quashed. We were undone.
> The breath of God had carried out a planned
> And sensible withdrawal from this land . . .

Unlike Edwards's original narrative, which orders the cold solace of a day of fasting after Hawley's suicide, the poem offers a secular and material palliative. To resist the impulse to "Cut your own throat. Now! Now!" one must turn from the world of metaphor to the phenomenal world of apples and bass, from the world of tradition to the world of immediate observation and experience. This is the very direction that Lowell's poems would take in the following decades. Like the voice of Lowell's Edwards doubting the efficacy of his former theological views and considering how the contemporary situation modifies his position, the modernist aesthetic requires a skepticism in mediating tradition.

This voice, drifting toward atheism, acknowledges that the breath of God might well withdraw and leave the chosen people at a loss.

Metaphors of self-awareness require unmediated imagery, refusing irony and skepticism because they have already rejected whatever there was to be ironic or skeptical about. Thus the voice of Lowell's Edwards must turn for its images to the cultural or natural world at hand, rather than to the heavily mediated world of biblical mythology. By closing his letter as he does, Edwards regains in peace of mind whatever he loses in resonance. The self-aware, self-conscious contemporary world, finally, proceeds to final refusal of medieval, Elizabethan, and Victorian worldviews. The new language of self-representation acknowledges that the old constructs of the gods no longer function, no longer even resonate. Resonance still occurs, however, when the personal voice insists that experience, and not history or tradition, bears authority. The initial voice of "Where the Rainbow Ends" is that of the Christian visionary who witnesses the imminence of apocalypse in Boston. Jerome Mazzaro notes that this "vision parallels St. John's in Apocalypse 21:2 'And I saw the holy city, New Jerusalem, coming down out of heaven from God, made ready as a bride adorned for her husband.'" He then aptly remarks that "as the reader soon learns, Boston exists outside of the rainbow of God's will."[21] Though Hugh Staples has characterized it as "metaphysical,"[22] Lowell's poem offers a thoroughly modernist application of this apocalyptic imagery—modernist in Eliot's manner because traditional to the core. Yet the immediacy of witness determines the pivotal image of the poem, the "Pepperpot, ironic rainbow, [that] spans / Charles River and its scales of scorched-earth miles." The authenticity of Lowell's vision does not inhere in the authority with which he deploys the trope of biblical revelation, with its archetypal images of serpents, doves, and "scythers, Time and Death," but rather in the trope of geographical presence generated by invoking—in the middle of a poem full of visionary images—the Longfellow Bridge, an utterly ordinary sight to all Bostonians.[23] This graceless bridge, braced with green steel girders readily visible beneath its arches, carries a rapid-transit line as well as four lanes of automotive traffic. How else could we be sure that the referent of this apocalyptic vision is Boston except by Lowell's invocation of a utilitarian if whimsically ornamented land-mark?

The distrust of visionary imagery, the unwillingness to allow it to bear the full weight of the poem, derives from those passages in *The Waste Land* that suggest the domesticated gray London of Eliot's bank-clerk career and hint at buried autobiographical impulses. Lowell's poem, also haunted by unspoken self-revelatory desires, relies more heavily than he may have intended on the actual Longfellow Bridge. By comparison, the other images of the poem seem somewhat distant and unauthentic, as if Lowell were dissatisfied with allegorical figures like Time and Death wielded with little modernist irony, and halfway through his poem realized how unsatisfactory a basis for a poem is a re-ligious vision unmediated by actuality.[24] This half-articulated note of anxiety exposes the psychological inadequacy of religious imagery in modernist poetry, an inadequacy that to a great extent shapes Eliot's *Four Quartets*. When Lowell called Eliot's masterpiece "a quasi-autobio-graphical testimony of the experience of *union with God*, or rather, its imperfect approximation in this life" he revealed his theoretical view of the role of religious poetry at the time he was writing of *Lord Weary's Castle*.[25] The imperfection noted by Lowell is not only aesthetic but also thematic; it reflects the structural imperfections that secular cul-ture and personal neurosis impose on the subjective literary ideals of romanticism and modernism. As Lowell would acknowledge in later years, language is public and belongs to culture and society rather than to the isolated romantic imagination:

> Those blesséd structures, plot and rhyme—
> why are they no help to me now
> I want to make
> something imagined, not recalled?[26]

By 1977, when this poem was published, Lowell's formal skills could no longer effectively mediate between the social world of experi-ence and the private, lost world of the subject.[27] But the poems of the

1940s have not yet fully surrendered to the loss of romantic and religious solipsism. If for Lowell, as for Eliot, in "wrestling with language, artistic craft is analogous to contemplative discipline," then in "Where the Rainbow Ends" the contemplative act consists of reconciling the aesthetic attraction of the immediate phenomenal world with the visionary world of religious symbols.[28] This appropriately suggests the tension between the desire to surrender and the desire to fully realize the self, which is resolved when the contemplative realizes they are the same desire. In the larger context of *Lord Weary's Castle* and Lowell's later development, this tension between aesthetic and visionary desires emerges as a struggle between high modernist rhetoric, derived from conventional religious discourse, and metaphors of unmediated experience.

The summation of Lowell's struggle to mediate between personal reflexivity (both self-deceptive and self-aware) and the complications of Catholic and Protestant religious expression that shaped his New England inheritance is "The Quaker Graveyard in Nantucket." Torn between a Miltonic Protestant-elegiac poetics and a richly symbolic mode derived from Melville and Thoreau, Lowell's attempt to impose a Catholic serenity in the midst of this stormy, fog-shrouded, richly rhetorical miniature epic strains his language into an eloquence unmatched in his own work or that of any subsequent poet working in English. The Catholic iconography appears most explicitly in the "Our Lady of Walsingham" section (which echoes Eliot's "Little Gidding" in subject and tone), while the arrogance of New England Protestantism, its inability fully to engage the implications of Christianity, and its eagerness to exploit the natural wealth of the New World constitute the driving force of the poem.

The poem opens with a conventionally iconographic scene: a warship finds a drowned sailor, whose corpse resembles the one described by Thoreau in the shipwreck scene in *Cape Cod:*

A brackish reach of shoal off Madaket,—
The sea was still breaking violently and night

Had steamed into our North Atlantic Fleet,
When the drowned sailor clutched the drag-net. Light
Flashed from his matted head and marble feet,
He grappled at the net
With the coiled, hurdling muscles of his thighs:
The corpse was bloodless, a botch of reds and whites,
Its open, staring eyes
Were lustreless dead-lights
Or cabin-windows on a stranded hulk
heavy with sand.[29]

Here the poem strikes the essential note of contrast between experience and intellect. A real corpse and a literary corpse become one. Like the "corpse-cold" Unitarianism that repelled yet inspired Emerson, this drowned sailor motivates a reconsideration of everything Lowell has thought, experienced, and read, and in the course of the poem it will become identified with every figure from the harpooned whale to Our Lady of Walsingham with her corpse-like undynamic calm.

Any elegy for the drowned is likely to suggest Milton's "Lycidas." In this instance, the parallels are inescapable, as Hugh Staples has pointed out: "For example, the nine sections of the poem (as originally printed in the *Partisan Review*) contain 194 lines, divided like the 193 lines of 'Lycidas,' into a loose stanzaic structure of pentameter lines, varied by an occasional trimeter."[30] Staples goes on to cite other similarities, then finds a number of ways in which Lowell has "made his own unique contribution" to "the great tradition of the English elegy."[31] However, Lowell's poem represents, I believe, a questioning of the very roots of that tradition. For one thing, Lowell rejects all the possible consolations that tradition offers, including the consolations of religion and literature. His commitment to a self-conscious modernist rhetoric leads him to wrench every rhetorical figure in the poem into configurations modeled upon Hart Crane's and Dylan Thomas's extreme compression of metaphor:

The winds' wings beat upon the stones,
Cousin, and scream for you and the claws rush
At the sea's throat and wring it in the slush
Of this old Quaker graveyard where the bones
Cry out in the long night for the hurt beast
Bobbing by Ahab's whaleboats in the East.

Though as critical of some religious conventions as "Lycidas," which excoriates a smug and ineffectual clergy, "Quaker Graveyard" bears little of the conviction that empowers Milton's elegantly organized poem. It does, however, develop the aura of vengefulness embodied in Milton's "two-handed engine at the door, / [that] Stands ready to smite once, and smite no more." This vengeance, embodied in "Quaker Graveyard" in the sea itself, the emblem of a chaotic creation, has overtaken Lowell's cousin, whose evolution from origin has come to naught: "All you recovered from Poseidon died/With you, my cousin, and the harrowed brine/Is fruitless on the blue beard of the god." Similarly, "The end of the whaleroad" for Ahab is death at sea with no one to mourn, no one to "dance/The mast-lashed master of Leviathans / Up from this field of Quakers in their unstoned graves." The only mourning that Ahab, lashed to the great bulk of Moby-Dick, may expect is the cry of gulls and wind.

The poem imagines God as the vengeful, jealous creature of the Old Testament, ironically opposing him to the pacifism professed by the same Quakers who produced Ahab, an irreverent figure who claimed he'd strike the sun itself if it insulted him. In the tension between the principles of Christianity and the material corruption of the world, embodied in the whale ("When the whale's viscera go and the roll / Of its corruption overruns this world . . .") the poem finds its rhetorical imperative. To combine the language of material corruption, most vividly presented in part V with the deception of the actual slaughter of the whale, and the language of salvation, which finds little sure footing in the poem except in part VI in the figure of Mary, "too small for her canopy," is the project of the poem. The struggle to combine antithetical metaphors, given Lowell's modernist self-consciousness, generates language of agonizing, muddled, and compelling materiality. The most moving passages of the poem are those that most vividly invoke the atmosphere of the sea:

> Sailor, can you hear
> The Pequod's sea wings, beating landward, fall
> Headlong and break on our Atlantic wall
> Off 'Sconset, where the yawing S-boats splash
> The bellbuoy, with ballooning spinnakers,
> As the entangled, screeching mainsheet clears
> The blocks: off Madaket, where lubbers lash
> The heavy surf and throw their long lead squids
> For blue-fish? Sea-gulls blink their heavy lids
> Seaward.[32]

But the moments of rhetorical crisis, where modernist conventions compete with the conventions of the elegiac tradition, invariably negate received literary motifs and posit the industrial world of the nineteenth-century whalers or the Second World War as the dominant reality of the poem:

> ask for no Orphean lute
> To pluck life back. The guns of the steeled fleet
> Recoil and then repeat
> The hoarse salute.[33]

Consequently, the consolations offered in part VI seem antiquated. "There once the penitents took off their shoes/And then walked barefoot the remaining mile," but in the modernist world no one walks barefoot; no one has the patience or self-abnegation to humble one's self before the icon. This is an aesthetic as well as a religious actuality. No icon, no emblem, no symbol compels such a humble demeanor. Instead, the arrogant Quakers cry,

"If God himself had not been on our side,
If God himself had not been on our side,
When the Atlantic rose against us, why,
Then it had swallowed us up quick."[34]

The sea in this poem belongs to Poseidon, the vengeful part of God. The land belongs to Mary, who if she lacks "comeliness" and "charm" is "expressionless" enough to express God in a benign manner. But the sea, too, expresses God, indeed is the "rainbow of His will," which He and only He survives. The Atlantic, "fouled with the blue sailors," too much embodies the origin of the world, "When the Lord God formed man from the sea's slime." To return to the point of origin means not only death but obliteration, as cousin Warren Winslow has found. Origin is an undesirable, impossible state, an abstraction untenable in the material world of the modernist aesthetic, in which the self has to mediate among competing ideologies, aesthetics, and faiths. The only surety in this poem is that God survives His own creation. Walsingham does not end the poem, and the world has not come to it. The storm-tossed Atlantic remains the center of the poem's consciousness. Everything else, especially the relationship between God and his creation, remains in doubt. The poem that embodies this doubt, that finds itself torn by Melville's vision of elemental arrogance and Thoreau's documentary perceptions, Milton's puritanical certainties and the Catholic vision of a benevolent mother-figure, rhetorically benefits from its stresses and strains. Lowell is forced by the logic of competing aesthetic forces to settle for a worldview hardly "that of the traditional Christian mystic," as Staples argues.[35] In this worldview, no metaphor finds God generous enough to sustain the modernist conviction of material self-presence.

Lowell's poetics, informed by skeptical modernism but compromised by social and aesthetic disillusionment, could not sustain unmediated religious experience, largely because the language of such experience no longer corresponded to his experiential and aesthetic world. This is one reason he drifted away from Catholicism and religious poetry in general. The new mode of linguistic self-awareness, still more radical, displaces skepticism with a weary knowledge: God is not dead, he simply never existed except as a language-construct, and the visionary is the prisoner of his own experience. The trope of vulnerability, identified by Bloom as Lowell's primary contribution to poetry, derives from the knowledge that inhabitants of a world deprived of religion are more vulnerable to personal and societal experience than had been realized, and this deprivation appears to Lowell primarily as a failure of language. Its themes underlie "Mother Marie Therese" and "Falling Asleep over the Aeneid," and they also undermine much of the religious iconography of *Lord Weary's Castle* to expose the psychosexual or egoistical longings beneath the religious impulse, as in the conclusion of "At the Indian Killer's Grave." This passage, as sexual as Yeats's "Leda and the Swan," is decidedly heretical in Lowell's desire to "come / Where Mary twists the warlock with her flowers," especially since her "whole body" is an "ecstatic womb," attuned to pleasures that are simultaneously religious and libidinous.[36]

Surely Lowell knew what he was writing here, and why. Far from being committed to a conventional religiosity, he was determined to expose the awkward writhings and even the failings of language in portraying ecstatic or visionary states. But in doing so he also exposed what would become the central issue of a contemporary dilemma: the recognition that the arbitrariness of language exposes the arbitrariness of culture itself. The trope of Mary's sexuality is also the trope of the failure of language to mediate between itself and whatever is outside of or beyond language. Jarrell thought that Lowell's mind was exclusively "traditional, theocentric, and anthropomorphic," failing to see that the wrenching of imagery that characterizes these poems is caused by tension between a modernist language of skepticism and a weary dismissal of the traditional worldview represented both by Roman Catholicism and the high modernism of Eliot.[37] But Jarrell saw modernism and tradition as opposites or incompatibles. From the vantage of our era, this no longer seems entirely true—in fact, it did not seem true for Eliot, who never repudiated his positioning of the modern poet in a line of succession in "Tradition and the Individual Talent." Jarrell was deeply indebted to the categorically American worldview of Whitman, however, and was already leaning toward a poetics of self-consciousness both in his own verse and in his expectations as a reviewer; consequently, he correctly identifies the world of *Lord Weary's Castle* as one of struggle between the "Old Law" and a new "accessibility to experience."[38] From a perspective of fifty additional years, we can better understand how deeply implicated are larger issues of language and culture in this struggle, and how decisively the language of personal experience would come to displace, in both poetry and the larger culture, the received symbolic language of religion and literary tradition—including, perhaps especially, its high modernist revisionary modes.

4 | "Cut Down, We Flourish"

LOWELL'S EFFORT TO ESCAPE CLOTTED SYM-
bolism and a debased religious sublime finds expression in
his years of struggle with the most ambitious of his early
poems. *The Mills of the Kavanaughs*, Lowell's third book, and
first after the public and critical success of *Lord Weary's Castle*, appeared in 1951 to sometimes laudatory but more often mixed or negative reviews. Reviewers generally admired "Mother Marie Therese" and
"Falling Asleep over the Aeneid" but found the other poems clotted,
confusing, forced, or uncertain.[1] Most disturbing was the ambitious
title poem, which daunted readers with its length, rigid structure, hallucinatory quality, and, some felt, unreal atmosphere. In a February
1952 letter to Randall Jarrell, responding to Jarrell's friendly but heavily qualified notice, Lowell defends his title poem in ambiguous and
suggestive terms:"The poem is meant to be grandiose, melodramatic,
carried on by a mixture of drama and shifting tones, rather like Maud.
I agree with most of what you say, except the heroine is very real to *me*
and that in a freakish way the poem has more in it than any of the others. Anyway I am delighted with your review and have read it many
times out of vanity. Perhaps I agree with it all, but since I've finished
nothing new I go on overrating the Kavanaughs."[2] The version Jarrell
reviewed as part of the book was Lowell's second; the first one, sub-

stantially different, had appeared in a journal. Lowell wasn't satisfied with his revisions for the book appearance, though. As late as the mid-1970s, he would continue to worry over this difficult poem, using parts of it in *History* and producing an attenuated version for the American edition of his *Selected Poems* (1976). The poem obsessed him for a variety of reasons, both aesthetic and biographical. Begun immediately after the breakup of his marriage with Jean Stafford, set in Damariscotta Mills, Maine, where he and Stafford lived in the mid 1940s, "The Mills of the Kavanaughs" embodies many of the aesthetic and personal complexities that challenged Lowell during his entire writing life, and that still interest his readers, including the psychological impact of history and the personal past, and the ways in which the formal qualities of art both bond with and distance it from life—a problem Lowell never quite resolves in this or any of his poems.

The heroine of the poem was real to Lowell, if not to many of his readers, because she is partly based on Stafford, and some of the key incidents in the poem come directly out of their troubled marriage. Linked to an unpublished draft of Stafford's "A Country Love Story," Lowell's poem recalls an incident in which, according to Frank Parker, Lowell woke Stafford from a dream of a former lover. As they then made love, Stafford, still half-asleep, mentioned the lover's name. According to Stafford, as told to Parker, Lowell had then tried to strangle her, but by digging her nails into his wrists she freed herself.[3] This incident corresponds to the central moment of "The Mills of the Kavanaughs," when Anne Kavanaugh recalls her husband Harry's similar attempt to kill her. Like the traumatic incident in which the novice poet struck his father for interfering in his relationship with Anne Dick, this assault on Stafford, regardless of whether he had actually attempted to murder her, would haunt Lowell for the rest of his life. The story of the writing and revision of "The Mills of the Kavanaughs" is in part the story of Lowell's attempt to first bring into focus, then later exorcize, a self-imposed nightmare. Jarrell's complaint that the poem "is too much a succession of nightmares and daydreams that are half-nightmare" was truer than he may have realized.[4] Lowell's comment that he had written

something like Tennyson's *Maud* is true insofar as both poems attempt to dramatize madness, melancholy, suicide, and the failure of a proud family. But the language of *Maud* attains a melodramatic urgency that Lowell's cannot match, so its succession of "nightmares and day-dreams," though perhaps equally morbid, does not tax but tantalizes the reader. Further, despite its length, *Maud* varies its formal design and avoids the metrical doldrums that quickly fall over "The Mills of the Kavanaughs."

The actual Kavanaghs (who spelled their name the way Longfellow spelled it) were a distinguished Roman Catholic family whose large nineteenth-century house (built in 1803), like the Stafford-Lowell house, overlooks Damariscotta Lake.[5] The first Kavanagh in the area was James, from County Wexford, who provided the lands and two-thirds of the cost of building St. Patrick's Church across the road. The last Kavanagh in residence was actually a Mrs. Cabot, whom Stafford reported as once saying "Imagine, a bogus Cabot talking to a bogus Lowell."[6] The Kavanaghs, like many coastal Maine families, had made their fortune in the lumber trade. Their money continued to support St. Patrick's, the oldest Roman Catholic church still standing in New England. Lowell, still a Catholic in 1946 when he and Stafford lived in Damariscotta Mills, was interested in the brick church structure, dating from 1808, designed by Nicholas Codd, with its handsome, Federalist interior. He was equally interested in the Kavanagh family, which had a history of public service comparable to the Lowells and Winslows. Edward Kavanagh (1795–1844), for instance, buried beside the church with his father and many of his descendants, served as ambassador to Portugal and governor of Maine. A prominent Catholic family would naturally appeal to Lowell, but the poem he wrote using their house and a version of the family name bears no relationship to authentic Kavanagh history. Even the purported Kavanaugh motto, "Cut down, we flourish," is actually that of Lowell's maternal family, the Winslows.

Both of the long versions of the poem bear prefatory notes that describe Anne Kavanaugh in her garden in 1943 playing solitaire, her opponent a bible, in the poem named "Sol." Her husband Harry, who retired after Pearl Harbor (and killed himself, according to the *Kenyon Review* version of the prefatory note), lies buried at the end of the garden, a flag flying above the grave of this man who could not lie in consecrated ground. A marble statue of Persephone—"who became a queen by becoming queen of the dead," as Anne has claimed the Kavanaugh estate on Harry's death—stands by a millpond. Anne was adopted by the Kavanaughs long before she married Harry. "Most of the poem," the note concludes, "is a revery of her childhood and marriage, and is addressed to her dead husband."[7]

The first version of "The Mills of the Kavanaughs" was accepted for publication sometime in 1950 and appeared in the *Kenyon Review* in the winter 1951 issue. While living in Rome, faced with the galley proofs of the book version late in 1950, Lowell thoroughly revised the poem—and others in the new collection—along lines that suggest he may have anticipated criticism like Jarrell's. In a letter to Elizabeth Bishop he described himself as working over "the fuzzy places," and adding new lines, "filled with Miltonic mythology, hard for a rhetorician to resist."[8] Both of the long versions are haunted by Anne Kavanaugh's sense of herself as Persephone, who goes "underground/into herself." As Hugh Staples first pointed out, Lowell derived much of the material for this poem from Ovid's tale of Persephone and Pluto, and for good measure merged into it the stories of Cyrane and Arethusa.[9] This mythopoeic stance shapes the poem, and along with the insistent meter and rhyme scheme is partly responsible for an oppressive air of artifice against which the banal domestic violence and emotions ring falsely. In revising it from first the *Kenyon Review* version to the book version to the much briefer *Selected Poems* version, Lowell first dilutes the mixture of classical and Christian myth, then in the full maturity of his aesthetic development altogether eliminates the machinery of mythology and the domestic jealousy and violence.

The *Kenyon Review* version consists of thirty-seven sixteen-line stanzas rhymed in couplets, one fewer stanzas than the book version. However, the differences between the two versions are greater than this suggests. Nearly every stanza undergoes extensive revision for book publication: one disappears entirely, two are added, two are reversed in order, and the final stanza is wholly revised, half of it pushed back into the penultimate stanza. Though Staples argues that Christian references (St. Patrick, the Virgin Mary) disappear so that the classical ones may dominate, the net effect is to trim some of the more artificial mythological parallels, slightly diminish the violence, clarify the action, and ease the sometimes rather stilted couplets.

For instance, to make the poem more domestic and less insistently archetypal, in revising the sixth stanza of the *Kenyon Review* version (seventh of the book version), Lowell replaces St. Patrick, presumably the family's patron saint, with a dog:

> He is Saint Patrick; that is why the brush
> And boulders wriggle, when the children rush
> Hurrahing . . .
> (*Kenyon Review* version)

> The setter worries through the coils of brush
> And steaming bramble, and the children rush
> Hurrahing . . .
> (book version)

And in the fourteenth stanza of the book version, Lowell changes Demeter—"'The Harvest's Daughter'" (Demeter, the corn goddess, is the mother of Persephone and sister of Pluto)—to a woodsman. This is a crucial change, since in the original version Anne actually seems to imagine Demeter to be her mother:

> "The Harvest's Daughter's wind-prints left a track
> Straight as an arrow to the blacksmith's shack
> Where I was born . . . "
> (stanza 13, *Kenyon Review* version)

Further, in this first version Harry seems a kind of Pan, "dressed/in Lincoln green," while in the revision they have both dressed in holly, anticipating their wedding, and take an oath to honor the memory of the Abenaki Indians, the pagans who preceded them in this landscape. The pagan quality of their wedding, in both instances, unlikely as the odd act of John Adams giving a Roman Catholic church a bell (see below), suggests how awkwardly Ann and Harry find themselves placed in twentieth-century America, how unsuited to dealing with the stresses that apparently drove Harry to suicide and Anne to a widowhood of hallucinatory loneliness.

The most obvious revision to the book version, besides the new final stanza, is the deletion of this stanza bristling with violence and associated with the bombing of Pearl Harbor, a crucial event in Harry's navy career:

> "The radio was saying ' . . . undeclared
> War seems to . . . ' static, ' . . . the United States
> And Honolulu . . . no! we mean . . .' THE WAR.
> Your ship was burning; and I thought you cared
> Little and that was why you turned to creak
> The rusty hinges of the oven door;
> And while you whistled, Harry, all your plates
> Of seabirds seemed to smash through glass, and shriek . . .
> Your whistling stopped. We ran. I tried to tell
> You marriage salvaged. . . . but we ran until
> Our brick church staggered on us from the hill—
> A bloody bandage! Then we must have passed
> The granite quarry, but I could not hear
> The workers; I was in a diving bell,
> Until the distant dynamiter's blast
> Broke, and the bell-boom broke from my ear.[10]

Lowell may have deleted this stanza for dramatic reasons, since it introduces a false climax that both anticipates and defuses the actual climax a few stanzas later. Or he may have simply found it too grotesque to convey the necessary tension between public and private worlds, as he apparently did when he revised several other passages to tone down the violence of their language if not their action. When Lowell re-thought Harry's death and decided to omit his suicide in the prefatory note (the poem still implies it), this stanza must have seemed awkward with its melodramatic depiction of Harry's frenzy.

Lowell made few changes to the three climactic stanzas in which Anne dreams aloud of making love with "a boy" in Harry's absence. The boy is all sensuous textures; his "chin/is bristling," he has "gored" her "black and blue," and made her "all prickle-tickle like the stars." He has made her "hide / Split snakey," apparently revealing an Anne her husband has never known. Harry in a rage at this adulterous dream strikes his wife, shakes the bed, and mocks her. In the first version, Harry chokes on his mockery and Anne runs, while in the book version she gags and runs while the maid knocks at the door. In both versions she is glad Harry tried to kill her, exposing his madness: "Hus-band kills / His wife for dreaming," she taunts. This entire stanza owes a great deal to Robert Frost's "Home Burial," but the mutual cruelty of the situation, if it does reflect an actual occurrence in the Lowell-Stafford marriage, suggests one reason for their divorce.

After this harsh drama, the poem slowly closes through a musing upon the emblematic landscape spread before Anne: "And now the mussed blue bottles bead her float:/Bringers of luck," one stanza ironi-cally begins. Another opens with a glimpse of a heron fishing. These stanzas, occurring in this order in the first version, are reversed for the book version. The heron stanza, though coming late in the poem, pro-vides a good deal of historical background, which seems introduced at this point to ease the tone and demonstrate how far Anne's thoughts have drifted from the moment when her life seemed forfeit, how muted her emotions:

> The heron warps its neck, a broken pick,
> To study its reflection on the scales,
> Or knife-bright shards of water lilies, quick
> In the dead autumn water with their snails
> And water lice. Her ballet glasses hold

> Him twisted by a fist of spruce, as dry
> As flint and steel. She thinks: "The bird is old,
> A cousin to all scholars; that is why
> He will abet my thoughts of Kavanaugh,
> Who gave the Mills its lumberyard and weir
> In eighteen hundred, when our farmers saw
> John Adams bring their Romish church a bell,
> Cast—so the records claim—by Paul Revere.
> The sticks of *Kavanaugh* are buried here—
> Many of them, too many, Love, to tell—
> Faithful to where their virgin forest fell.[11]

This glimpse of natural process and calm historical musing, the most easeful conjunction of nature and culture in the poem, may suggest why this stanza became the opening one of the *Selected Poems* version, and why, beginning with so placid a meditative moment (though with a hint of suppressed violence in the "broken pick") that brief version seems so comfortably stalled in circular, lyric time. A much-revised fourteen-line version of this stanza appears as "In the Forties 2," in *History,* Lowell's first attempt at salvaging "Kavanaugh" material by recasting it in lyric form.

Lowell revised the final stanza of the *Kenyon Review* version by removing the picture of Harry swinging a string of yellow perch and placing those lines in the preceding stanza to make room for this closing meditation on death and the Persephone theme:

> "God knows!" she marvels, "Harry, *Kavanaugh*
> Was lightly given. Soon enough we saw
> Death like the Bourbon after Waterloo,
> Who learning and forgetting nothing, knew
> Nothing but ruin. Why must we mistrust
> Ourselves with Death who takes the world on trust?
> Although God's brother, and himself a god,
> Death whipped his horses through the startled sod;

> For neither conscience nor omniscience warned
> Him from his folly, when the virgin scorned
> His courtship, and the quaking earth revealed
> Death's desperation to the Thracian field.
> And yet we think the virgin took no harm:
> She gave herself because her blood was warm—
> And for no other reason, Love, I gave
> Whatever brought me gladness to the grave."

The net effect is to make the closure less hallucinatory, though less concrete, and to suggest that Anne's vision of herself as Persephone has so deeply penetrated as to explain her very presence in the garden at this meditative moment.

Hugh Staples argues that the poem "operates in an atmosphere of Greek tragedy," and that its "final meaning" lies in Anne's acceptance of the dualisms with which she has contended throughout her life, most especially her own dual nature as Anne Kavanaugh and as Persephone, queen of the dead.[12] But in this dualistic scheme and courting of dramatic expectations lie the problems of the poem. It is too static in form and diction, too torn between the meditation mode of the dramatic monologue and the chronological unfolding of the narrative poem to satisfactorily function in either genre. Although it has the air of tragedy, it lacks action and interplay of characters. Anne is a figure in repose, and her memories are psychologically horrifying but lack the statuesque grandeur of the events of Greek tragedy. Harry's suicide is so offstage it seems almost irrelevant, and her recollection of the central episode seems as much imagined as authentic. The poem opens and closes on a static garden landscape of patrician New England ease that lacks the hard surfaces of the stony Greek world or the harshness of the lonely farm settings of Robert Frost's harrowing dialogues. The poem is too violent for its setting and mood, and yet not violent enough for the tragic air it attempts to capture. It misses the "melodrama" Lowell wished to catch, achieving instead a nervous hallucinatory quality in which even the "mood of stoic resignation" detected by Staples seems uncertain and temporary. The poem generates many powerful effects, numerous memorable images, and a psychologically convincing voice. But it seems ill at ease with the very formalism that makes so much of its language memorable, and fails to fulfill its own dramatic necessity. Anne Kavanaugh convinces in her tone and mood; but unlike the women in Frost's "Home Burial" or "Death of the Hired Hand," poems much admired by Lowell, she lacks full dramatic characterization. She seems rather an interesting aspect of the poet's own voice.

Most commentators over the years have judged "The Mills of the Kavanaughs" a failure to one degree or another. Jerome Mazzaro wrote that "it offers little besides its gothic machinery to entice a reader,"[13] Richard Fein called it "a poem we read because it is by an author who interests us,"[14] and Stephen Yenser noted that much in the poem "depend[s] upon an understanding of some odd joints and strangely twisted members in a fascinating and awkward Goldbergian infrastructure."[15] Lowell must have thought a great deal about his poem over the years, trying to determine what, if anything, he could salvage from all this gnarled and imperfect grandeur. His solution was a drastic one: to discard all of the narrative machinery, almost all of the classical mythology, everything except the final five stanzas, jettisoning everything linked to the public effort to purge himself of a shameful domestic episode, every attempt to aggrandize domestic sadness by linking it to Greek tragedy.

In paring the poem down to the last five stanzas, Lowell salvages it by changing its genre from narrative to lyric-meditative. The poem succeeds in this genre because the rhymed couplets, which are too harsh and willed to generate the flexibility that would further a narration, successfully mime the turnings of the mind, catching Anne Kvanaugh's shifts in mood and perception far better than they caught the unfolding of her lengthy story. Further, Lowell chose stanzas that in this isolated grouping—the dramatic trappings discarded—expose some of the topics that by 1976 had become primary for him: the relationships among perception, history, art, and nature; and the difficulty of formulating a living relationship with death. These topics always resided in the poem, as they do in many of Lowell's earlier poems, but now, freed of the violent narrative and clarified by distillation from a poem that simply went on too long, this brief version illuminates them.

The opening stanza of the *Selected Poems* version, the heron stanza quoted above, presents the vexed relationship between history and nature as a difficulty in assessing the present in terms of the past when that past clearly has shaped the immediate instance. That is, the heron is "Old,/A cousin to all scholars" because it embodies a species perfectly represented by each individual (unlike the human species), and thus is as old as its evolution. The history of Kavanaugh is present in the scene immediately before Anne Kavanaugh (unnamed in *Selected Poems*), yet is lost because in the human mind only the individual exists, and the events of the past have to be re-created in the mind or through narration. Such re-creation lacks exactness, so the Paul Revere bell, for instance, may be unauthentic.

The second stanza ("the mussed blue bottles") touches upon the problematic relationship between nature and art, the place of the sublime, and the link between human and natural history. The picture of Kavanaugh may resemble one by Fragonard in its contrasts of light and dark: "her park,/Whose planted poplars scatter penny-leaves,/White underneath, like mussels to the dark/Chop of the shadows." In this scene, her metal boat, both the actual one on the millpond and the vehicle of her meditation, encounters whitecaps, becomes difficult to row. As long as she keeps her mind on the actual scene she moves freely among its elements, but the interpolation of a human past—"Where Harry's mother bathed in navy-blue/Stockings and skirts"—makes the afternoon sullen, the surface of the millpond choppy. The old antagonism between culture and nature looms: "The floorboards bruise the lilies that she pulled."

The third and fourth stanzas contemplate temporality—"'The day is sharp/And short, Love, and its sun is like this carp'"—as the past and present merge in a vision of Harry's mother looking from her window as the couple rows on the pond. However, when the mother asks, "'is it well?'" Anne replies, "'Yes, very well. He died outside the church/Like Harry Tudor,'" and clarifies for herself the difference between what she remembers and what she perceives. She still sees Harry, swinging "'a string of yellow perch/About your head to fan off gnats,'" but in the same sentences reminds him that his body lies in "'The buried bedstead,'" in a grave that is not only his but the marriage's.

Prepared to consider death by acknowledging Harry's status (as "'disheartened shadow'"), Anne in the final stanza asks, "'Why must we mistrust/Ourselves with Death who takes the world on trust?'" The answer, such as it is, personifies death as lacking both perception and knowledge. Yet Pluto (Hades, in Greek mythology), who fell in love with his niece Persephone and abducted her, and who has perhaps fallen in love with Anne Kavanaugh and seduced her into a death wish, has apparently done no damage: "'And yet we think the virgin took no harm,'" Anne muses, "'She gave herself because her blood was warm,'" because of her emotional need to give of herself. For similar emotional reasons (and no other) Anne sacrificed herself to Harry, whom, we would not fully realize from this short version, she detested.

That we may willingly or half-willingly give ourselves to death, sacrifice ourselves through emotion and yet do ourselves no harm, though of thematic interest, is hardly the point of this version. Rather, the unfolding of the mind in itself, the process of association, the casual rather than logical interplay of memory, knowledge, and perception, becomes the subject of the poem. Myth still plays a role, but only as one of several aspects of knowledge. History is another. The naming of natural objects is yet another. And the mental process of juxtaposing these elements to understand how they play off against each other is yet another, and a more important one. Thus simplified, its narrative and empowering dramatic incident discarded, the poem stands as a model of the mind at work, a lyric-meditative musing detached from any specific circumstance, tracing through the requisite imagery an arc from nature through history and temporality to death, completing the circle by reconciling the speaker with herself.

5 | The Corporate Fifties

IN 1961, LOWELL, IN A LETTER TO HIS ELDERLY cousin Harriet Winslow, reflecting on the cold war crises of the period, most recently the erection of the Berlin Wall, wrote, "The world's really strange isn't it? I mean the world of the news and the nations and the bomb testings. I feel it this fall and wonder, if it's just being forty three. Under a certain calm, there seems to be a question that must be answered. If one could think of the question."[1] Though this passage illustrates Lowell's tendency to read the world in autobiographical terms, it also displays his sensitivity to the power of language in crisis situations. The rhetorical, public, and communal effort of voicing the required question may be the key to "the world of the news," yet asking that question is not only beyond Lowell but everyone else, as the uncharacteristically impersonal "one" suggests.

By the end of the 1950s, voicing the need to ask such a question, which for Lowell meant making poetry where public and private concerns met, had become an intrinsic part of his poetics. He most vividly formulates this need in "For the Union Dead," a poem completed in 1960, in which public and personal dimensions powerfully cohere. However, his work of the previous decade, collected in *Life Studies*, had already plumbed the clichés, aporia, rhetorical corruption, and general verbal difficulties of the early television era, a period defined by the infusion of the corporate structure, outlook, and language into business, social, and private life.[2] The resultant cultural ethos, characterized by the misuse and corruption of the common language, made thinking of and voicing the question all but impossible.

Generally perceived as the product of Lowell's attempt to resolve a personal aesthetic dilemma, *Life Studies* also responds to the situation of public discourse in Eisenhower's America. It participates in the larger text of the age, in which Beat and popular-magazine writing, political speech, advertising, television, journalism, comics, and popular psychology compete for an audience. That competition tended to exclude or marginalize poets, especially those who weren't satisfied to write the tame verse promoted by the *New Yorker* and the *Saturday Review*. Further, language itself seemed debased by its appropriation for governmental and corporate purposes. Esme, a wispy poet in William Gaddis's 1955 novel *The Recognitions,* attempts to reinvest language with a primal innocence because "the words which the tradition of her art offered her were by now in chaos, coerced through the contexts of a million inanities, the printed page everywhere opiate, row upon row of compelling idiocies disposed to induce stupor, coma, necrotic convulsion."[3] Another poet despairing for a media-deafened America, Allen Ginsberg in *Howl* points to the "angelheaded hipsters," who "joined the elemental verbs" in protest against the failure of public discourse, attempting "to recreate the syntax and measure of poor human prose and stand before / you speechless and intelligent and shaking with shame,/rejected yet/confessing out the soul to conform to the rhythm of thought in his naked and endless head."[4]

To "conform to the rhythm of thought" in the "naked and endless head" of God has never been easy even for the rare visionary, but such poetic evangelism seemed utterly irrelevant to the material needs of the postwar world. The social and cultural atmosphere following the Korean War was fractious, nervously energetic, semiliterate, threatening, and threatened. It was the era of "duck-and-cover" drills in elementary schools, backyard bomb shelters, nuclear tests, and massive suburban housing developments. Television almost overnight had become the characteristic means of cultural expression. Bolstered by cold-war defense spending, the working and middle classes felt prosperous, but with memories of the Great Depression and the Second World War still fresh, feared losing their unprecedented material well-being. This situation made much of the citizenry easy prey for the fear-mongering tactics of politicians who either believed Communism a genuine threat or were determined to oversell defense and maintain a high level of unscrutinized government spending for the benefit of rich investors. The social and psychological consequences of this political situation shaped much of the art and literature of the period, as noted by writers alert to the debasing power of the dominant national-corporate discourse. The fiction writer R. V. Cassill, in a statement for an anthology published in 1959, comments that "the obviously special problem for a writer of the Fifties . . . is that the Cold War and the McCarthy Era have so compromised the common vision and vocabulary that honesty, even at simple levels of communication, is harder to achieve than in any other time I have heard about."[5] And Kenneth Rexroth, in an essay on the Beat Generation, argues that "it is impossible for an artist to remain true to himself as a man, let alone an artist, and work within the context of this society."[6]

Writers of many eras have complained about neglect and cultural decline, but the 1950s raised the level of discontent by embracing electronic mass media as a means of promoting the corporate ethos. The consequent debasement of language is central to our historical and literary awareness of the period, especially since it has continued, even deepened, in our own time. Distrust of the adequacy of language and the integrity of literature characterizes contemporary literary and linguistic theory, while a corresponding social cynicism has crept into ordinary discourse. Such distrust has deep historical roots, perhaps from the romantic sensitivity to the insufficiencies of literary language, but in the postwar United States, at the beginning of the "information age," even business leaders and government agencies called into question previous assumptions about discourse. One acknowledgment of a growing difficulty in the routine use of language appears in a 1954

Fortune article by Perrin Stryker ironically entitled "A Slight Case of Over-communication": "It is a problem that seems to have been completely ignored in the literature on communications. Even Wisler [John Wisler, president of United Sound & Signal Company] is not yet sure quite how to describe it. His jawbreaking definition of 'the frustration of knowing too much' is 'an awareness of some—but not all—factors of a situation resulting in the individual's inability to rationalize the particular action indicated, with consequent confusion of ideas.' In other words, a little knowledge is a confusing thing."[7]

The impossibility of apprehending the totality of information required for ideal action troubles discourse by challenging its basis in reason; further, it exacerbates the uneasy distinction between the individual and the corporation. The corporate construct, whether expressed as big business, the university, military organization, or the family, separates itself from the more general concept of communal enterprise and becomes a distinct entity, alien and yet disquietingly familiar. Discourse between individual and corporation does not occur between equals: the corporation, like the atomic bomb, embodies a powerful compressive force sufficient to annihilate most opposition. The insistent corporate commodification of American life, while routinely glorifying the individualism of the past, reinterprets the American tradition in terms of its profit motive and need to suppress the individual by assigning him or her the role of employee, consumer, or merely compliant citizen. With the cooperation or coercion of U.S. citizens, this unequal discourse defined the cold war era. The situation defies Habermas's characterization of the transformed bourgeois public sphere as one of high inclusiveness governed by a media-linked system of conflict and consensus.[8] It became apparent early in the 1950s that public discourse would soon belong entirely to the mass media, particularly electronic media, and would include only the voices of those who could penetrate or manipulate a genre of discourse that thrives on overcommunication. Despite Habermas's confidence in the flexibility and resources of democracy, the Eisenhower presidency saw a return to an elitist public sphere, this time dominated by corporate interests rather than a small group of individuals. This corporate hegemony has steadily increased its power to the present. Political attempts to nullify it, because necessarily framed in mass-media terms, only further distort communication. This political process resulted in "an era of slogans, symbols, and smooth talk which may well go down in history as the Genuine Simulated Golden Age," as Herbert Block argues in his 1955 protest against fatuous thinking in political affairs.[9]

The implications of Stryker's characterization of "the individual's inability to rationalize the particular action indicated, with consequent confusion of ideas" extend from the corporate and public spheres to the more personal but comparably frustrated discourse situations developed in *Life Studies*. Lowell's most poignant depiction of the limitations of a characteristic 1950s social and communicative stance occurs in "Memories of West Street and Lepke." Here Lowell as the speaker of the poem occupies a vantage point of leisure, a privileged position that in its casual air of comfort defines the social confidence of the era:

> Only teaching on Tuesdays, book-worming
> in pajamas fresh from the washer each morning,
> I hog a whole house on Boston's
> "hardly passionate Marlborough Street,"
> where even the man
> scavenging filth in the back alley trash cans,
> has two children, a beach wagon, a helpmate,
> and is a "young Republican."
> I have a nine months' daughter,
> young enough to be my granddaughter.
> Like the sun she rises in her flame-flamingo infants' wear.
>
> These are the tranquillized *Fifties*,
> and I am forty.[10]

In terms of locating Lowell in place and time, this is the central passage of the "Life Studies" sequence. The poem opens as a kind of postwar *L'Allegro*; Lowell's mornings spent in clean pajamas, lounging over books, his occupation of a whole Back Bay townhouse, his erudite reference to Henry James (himself the product of a privileged background), and his status as a new father all speak to his role as representative American. Middle-aged in midcentury, affluent, literate, and surrounded by unchallenged serenity (even the scavenger represents no social challenge), he seems as tranquillized as his era.

But the expression of individual sufficiency, perhaps always problematic, in the postwar era raises doubts about one's social purpose, personal fitness, or even sanity. Here the rhetorical question "Ought I to regret my seedtime?" casts Lowell's social and personal construct into doubt. Why might one regret fathering a child, even somewhat later in life than usual? One problem, the poem notes, is that Lowell has a history of manic social challenge, lack of respect for authority, and criminal disobedience. Because this social malfeasance occurred in the past, and because the present offers such ease and security, the rhetorical question and the consequent leap into the past seem oddly irrational. However, the rest of the poem, which retrospectively describes the inhabitants of the West Street jail, suggests, as does the mise en scène at McLean Hospital in "Waking in the Blue," that an allegory of an enclosed world may more incisively define the United States than does the apparently seamless, present-tense landscape of Marlborough Street. This is, after all, the America that Lowell in the winter of 1959 described as dominated by two great facts: "The decline of the west and our probable nuclear extinction."[11] While neither of these facts need be regarded as factual—the decline of the West is a debatable matter and nuclear extinction more than fifty years after Hiroshima has yet to occur—this pessimistic view, shared by many other intellectuals of the period, underlies much of Lowell's work in the 1950s and 1960s. "Memories of West Street and Lepke" closes with a portrait of an individual literally on the brink of extinction: Czar Lepke, "Flabby, bald, lobotomized," embodies a murky state of being akin to that of the more innocent inhabitants (including Lowell) of McLean Hospital in "Waking in the Blue." Lepke's "portable radio, dresser, two toy American/ flags" stake his claim to being a representative American—that is, a creature of mixed or confused motives, condemned by social and political forces he no longer quite understands. Lepke, the characteristic corporate self, tranquilized by surgery, accepts his role and plays it as the social structure requires.

What happens to the serenity of the present? Lowell's depicted ignorance ("I was so out of things I'd never heard/of the Jehovah's Witnesses") casts doubt on his earlier testimony by suggesting that the calm of the era is merely a tranquilized version of the uncertain decades preceding. Perhaps the man with the beach wagon isn't entirely prosperous, his supposed Republicanism merely a fatal lethargy. Perhaps "Ought I to regret my seedtime?" is not rhetorical but is "a question that must be answered"; perhaps Lowell is too old to have fathered a child; perhaps he is wrong to bring new life into a desperate world. But certainly he should not—and indeed, the general drift of the poem suggests he does not—unquestioningly accept the prosperity and leisure of his present life. And if his forties aren't all they appear to be, neither are America's "tranquillized *Fifties*." One of the few critical comments linking the "Life Studies" group of poems to the social and political morass of the 1950s occurs in Richard Fein's study of Lowell. Fein notes of the ending of "Memories of West Street and Lepke" that "we come across the mentally tough slogan 'agonizing reappraisal,' a phrase that during the tenure of Secretary of State John Foster Dulles in the Eisenhower years of mental vapidity was used to describe a supposedly painful rethinking of American foreign policy. In employing the phrase himself, Lowell not only indicates how *Life Studies* grew out of the atmosphere of the 1950s, but uses his own plight to rescue the words from their role as political adage. At the same time, he ambiguously connects himself to the deceptive language of the time."[12] Further, although the gulf between expression and significance is exacerbated by the duplicitous ideology of the present era, Lowell finds the roots of deceptive language in his own past, rendering his own discourse symptomatic rather than exceptional, like Ginsberg's eloquent protest.

The communal problems of discourse haunt all of *Life Studies*, but the opening poem of the sequence, "My Last Afternoon with Uncle Devereux Winslow," suggests that even in childhood the protagonist suffered the effects of unequal or incoherent discourse and the accumulation of incomplete, useless, or unusable information. Already the self in formation is partly a corporate one, too comprehensive, structured, and complex to apprehend itself fully. The opening of the poem delineates the inequalities of discourse that will shape it:

> "I won't go with you. I want to stay with Grandpa!"
> That's how I threw cold water
> on my Mother and Father's
> watery martini pipe dreams at Sunday dinner.
> . . . Fountainebleau, Mattapoisett, Puget Sound. . . .
> Nowhere was anywhere after a summer
> at my Grandfather's farm.[13]

Though it may seem the characteristic exclamation of a petulant child, this impertinent and pointless fragment of discourse fairly represents the social situation at Char-de-sa, his grandfather's farm, characterized by unsocial behavior on the part of the child's Great Aunt Sarah. Further, what we have here is a portrait of a 1920s childhood seen from the perspective of 1957, which imposes on the earlier part of the century the irrationality of postwar fear and uncertainty. The topics of incomplete, problematic discourse and the frustrations of partial or inappropriate information overlay this and the other *Life Studies* poems because they are part of the common text of 1950s America. Lowell has reinvented his childhood along the lines of rhetorical concern current at the time of writing, and this generates a highly fictional account that emphasizes a point of view alien not only to the historical child but to the aesthetic and social concerns of the earlier twentieth century. The *Life Studies* poems are genuinely autobiographical, but I would contend that their real concern is not only with childhood Oedipal conflicts but with the crisis in discourse, information, and representation Lowell and the rest of the United States faced in the postwar climate. This crisis is in itself Oedipal, insofar as it is a struggle between Lowell the poet and the politically patriarchal "military industrial complex." As Hart notes, "the conflict at the heart of Lowell's 'one story,' as Jarrell knew, was Oedipal."[14] As with all such conflicts since Sophocles, this struggle occurs offstage in heavy whispers, which the audience can plainly hear. Autobiography, as I remarked earlier, teases the reader with half-heard incomplete information, suggesting what could, under certain circumstances, be exposed; but *Life Studies* channels its conflicts into the portrayal of failed, fractured, unequal, or incomplete discourse to establish that a condition of language, not the unfolding of subject matter per se, represents the life story, insofar as the book tells one. The very incompleteness of information becomes both a mode of narration and the subject.

Following the child's outburst, "Last Afternoon" describes the grandfather's house as a kitschy collection of dated artifacts, "manly, comfortable/overbearing, disproportioned." Even these adjectives suggest how much information remains concealed. The grandfather's stern temperament, as implied by these words, remains unrevealed until he chastises Uncle Devereux and his wife for "behaving like children," leaving their three infants and voyaging to Europe in the face of a fatal illness. Yet even this incident remains tantalizingly incomplete, telegraphic in its emotional starkness. The very name of the farm signals this incompletion, since it consists of fragments of the grandfather's children's names—Charlotte, Devereux, and Sarah. The only death here has been a dog's, which indicates that despite the old-fashioned decor, this farm, though "in the Social Register," has not long been in the family, so its value as a socially redemptive possession is limited.

The child stands woefully incomplete, provisional, and tentative in his "formal pearl gray shorts/. . . worn for three minutes." His age—"five and a half"—contrasts in its breezy temporality with his timeless sculptural "perfection . . . the Olympian/poise of [his] models in the imperishable autumn/display windows/of Rogers Peet's boys' store below the State House/in Boston." This dialogue between timelessness and temporality permeates the poem, as indicated by the title. Elegies characteristically invoke this dialogue of contrast, but Lowell places even timelessness in time by specifying a particular shop, one that while still in business when he wrote the poem closed in the late 1970s, around the time of Lowell's own death. The other metaphor of the child bears an even more ironic relationship to this dialogue. The "stuffed toucan" (perhaps suggested by Elizabeth Bishop's two pet toucans) represents perfection in death, nature embalmed as pseudo-art. Its "bibulous, multicolored beak" projects the hard-drinking future, the slightly alcoholic present-tense era of the adult poet. The dialogue between temporality and timelessness is also one between past and present, a dialogue that tends to conflate its terms.

Discourse in this section of the poem signals failure by refusing adequate terms for temporality and timelessness, allowing past and present to commingle in metaphors that negate childhood without fully embracing or endorsing the adult point of view. Lowell represents his persona as a figure like his father's, out of time yet subject to its vicissitudes. That a reviewer could dismiss *Life Studies* as a collection of "snobbish memoirs" suggests how readily the slippery surface of Lowell's language could shed readers in this class-shy decade, but it also serves to remind us that Lowell's commitment to his ancestral past, even as represented by his weak father and aggressive mother, was deeper and perhaps less ironic than many critics have assumed.[15] In "My Last Afternoon with Uncle Devereux Winslow," the child persona represents, from a mixed perspective, a self as much at odds with his time and place as his father, Commander Lowell, who is usually the butt of Lowell's irony.

In the third section of the poem, the child's great-aunt, Aunt Sarah, sets a high standard for the failure of aesthetic and social discourse. She practices *Samson and Delilah* (a piece about the failure of domestic communication) on "the keyboard of a dummy piano," apparently forbidden to share her music because of her mother's nerves, though the older woman is "tone-deaf, quick as a cricket." Real crickets sing, but Grandmother with her tone-deafness rejects music, a primal and primary mode of temporal communication, in favor of playing cards. Aunt Sarah, an unequal locutor, accedes to her mother's wishes, abandoning "her bed of troublesome snacks and Tauchnitz classics" (which with their improvised illustrations, including often rather tawdry tipped-in photographs, are pathetic attempts to render dated literary works more attractive). Aunt Sarah had her opportunities for a larger, more public life, but she "jilted an Astor," and despite hours of practice "on the grand piano at Symphony Hall," a place of suitably modest aesthetic demands, its "naked Greek statues draped with purple," she simply did not show up on recital day.

Having rehearsed the inadequacies of his family and himself, having dramatized in the first line of the poem his complicity in the family efforts to sabotage communication, the child in part IV notes his lack of psychological involvement in the slow process of Uncle Devereux's dying, looking elsewhere for a clue to his mental processes as they might have been at the time:

> What in the world was I wishing?
> . . . A sail-colored horse browsing in the bullrushes . . .
> A fluff of the west wind puffing
> my blouse, kiting me over our seven chimneys,
> troubling the waters. . . .

The adult cannot find the focus of the child's vision so returns to the adult world of contingent metaphor in which "Double-barrelled shotguns" resemble (or even function as) "bundles of baby crowbars." The un-expectedness of "baby" points to the resistance with which this poem approaches its ostensible subject. Death, the core topic of the elegy, resists naming until nearly the end of this last section of the poem. Here the shotguns oddly domesticate themselves. Ordinary crowbars perhaps would seem too utile to adequately resist the threat of death borne by the guns, but "baby" crowbars suitably divert the image into a parodic domesticity that somehow mirrors the paradoxes of the poem as a whole. The very awkwardness of the metaphor points to the difficulty the adult autobiographer has in reconstructing a family life that from his present vantage seems never to have fully constructed itself to begin with. The problem is partly the massive gap between the child and the adult poet, which is not entirely explained by temporality.

The child lacks emotional focus and sees himself paradoxically as a contingent being and imperishable mannequin. This complex self-image voices itself through the adult poet's view of his childhood as product and embodiment of the failure of familial discourse. The resultant air of claustrophobia is one that speech between two equal locutors, if such were imaginable at Char-de-sa, would instantly shatter. In the last section of the poem, however, speech is limited to the grandfather's sole declaration that "You are behaving like children," which, although directed at Uncle Devereux and his wife, could apply to every one in the family. Silenced like everyone else in the poem by the grandfather's strident and socially constructed masculinity, Uncle Devereux mutely appears in uniform, "As if posed for 'the engagement photograph,'" while student posters, "almost life-size," mock lost opportunities for a larger life. The only actual child in this world "wasn't a child at all—/. . . was Agrippina/ in the Golden House of Nero." That the child may have seen himself as the mother of Nero, reversing his role in his ruling-class family, is ironic enough; that the elder Agrippina (not the one in the "Golden House of Nero") was the mother of Caligula—Lowell himself—renders the figure absurd. This complex metaphor may indeed point to the adult's "frustration of knowing too much," his awareness of "some—but not all—factors of [the child's] situation," his inability to make sense of his family, his difficulty in emotionally grasping Uncle Devereux's death, and the gap between the child's mentality and the adult's. In a situation like this, the ability to draw a comparison between the child and a figure from Roman history serves mainly to express the frustration of failed or inadequate communication, the impossibility of constructing an adequate self either inside or outside the incorporated family.

The mute Uncle Devereux, like the tone-deaf grandmother and socially irresponsible Aunt Sarah, personifies that failure. The series of metaphors inscribed on the dying uncle by an adult perspective (while the child sits on the floor and picks at the blue anchor—a family naval emblem—on his shirt) point to the impossibility of reconstructing a living presence while at the same time insisting on the materiality of ancestral presence:

> He was as brushed as Bayard, our riding horse.
> His face was putty.
> His blue coat and white trousers
> grew sharper and straighter.
> His coat was a blue jay's tail,
> his trousers were solid cream from the top of the bottle.
> He was animated, hierarchical,
> like a ginger snap man in a clothes-press.

The convoluted last metaphor summarizes the ironies and irrationalities of the poem. Both "animated" (brought to life by artificial means) and "hierarchical" (fixed in social and personal status), Uncle Devereux lacks dimension, being a creation of the child's somewhat limited and oblique imagination, or rather of the adult poet's dimensionless memory, skewed by the dimensionless present.

The child, on the other hand, returns to elemental gestures of nature and culture, the cool and warmth of earth and lime, and finally accepts the incipient absorption of Uncle Devereux into "the one color," the color of absence.[16] The impulse to elegize has come to nothing, as Uncle Devereux has, leaving the child incommunicado with the unmixed *prima materia* of the imagination heaped before him. "My Last Afternoon with Uncle Devereux Winslow," then, enacts a drama of incomplete (an elegy that does not elegize), improbable ("baby crowbars"), socially and aesthetically inadequate (Aunt Sarah) instances of communication. Yet the poem satisfies because of, not despite, its delayed, unpredictable, and thoroughly resisted progression. Its "resisted motion" satisfies Robert Penn Warren's notion that "a poem, to be good, must earn itself,"[17] a notion surely familiar to Lowell, a former Warren student. This is an important point: that in the sphere of poetics, frustrations similar to those of the corporate sphere of communication, while remaining frustrations, may signal aesthetic success. Though the age may have tranquilized itself, Lowell's poetry refuses that stupor and refines partial awareness and frustrated complexity into irrational yet compelling drama in which the poet of the present reinvents his life history to reflect and interrogate a contemporary crisis in representation.

The poems set in Lowell's adult years further explore the crisis in information and representation by refining the claustrophobia in "My Last Afternoon with Uncle Devereux Winslow" as symptomatic of American social, political, and moral decline, as well as a corporate, structural throttling of communication. "Waking in the Blue" institutionalizes familial claustrophobia in depicting a stay at McLean Hospital, a "house for the 'mentally ill.'" Here the social breakdown of communication, catalogued as a series of ironic gestures, renders class, social, and educational distinctions with clarity but deprived of their original significance. Lowell, confined because of a severe manic episode,[18] finds himself in the company of "'Bobbie,'/Porcellian '29,/a replica of Louis XVI/without the wig" and "Stanley . . ./once a Harvard all-American fullback." Because "These victorious figures of bravado ossified young" they cannot speak for themselves (Stanley is "more cut off from words than a seal"). The primary symptom of mental illness, in this context, is a communications disorder. The night attendant has fallen asleep over *The Meaning of Meaning,* a study of applied semantics by C. K. Ogden and I. A. Richards, and consequently has awakened in a slightly addled state. Lowell's humor here has not been sufficiently appreciated, nor has the importance to this poem of Ogden's and Richards's book. The night attendant's mussed hair is one kind of "mare's-nest," while *The Meaning of Meaning* is another. The humor lies in the literalizing of the ancient metaphor. The book, although not directed at the problematic state of postwar discourse (it originally appeared in 1923, though several expanded editions appeared over the years), does address a social and cultural problem in language, as the preface makes clear:

The view that language works well enough as it is, can only be held by those who use it merely in such affairs as could be conducted without it—the business of the paper-boy or the butcher, for instance, where all that needs to be referred to can equally well be pointed at. None but those who shut their eyes to the hasty re-adaption to totally new circumstances which the human race has during the last century been blindly endeavoring to achieve, can pretend that there is no need to examine critically the most important of all the instruments of civilization. New millions of participants in the control of general affairs must now attempt to form personal opinions upon matters which were once left to a few. At the same time the complexity of these matters has immensely increased.[19]

The particular aspect of meaning explicated by Lowell's poem—and that is also explored in Ogden and Richards—is the fragile, oblique relationship between locutors, between Lowell and Stanley, between attendants and inmates. And the dim halls of McLean Hospital faintly illuminate a problem in affect as well, the mock clarity of language that fails to accommodate the mock clarity of madness.[20] Language surely does not work "well enough" when the normal circuits of communication have failed because of mental illness, or because, more broadly, the old social and cultural hierarchies (represented by the Porcellian Club) have disintegrated. What use is reading so utterly rational a book in a place and era of nakedness and absence? Intellectual argument has no function in this ward, and even more basic interactions fail. With great poignancy, Lowell reasonably asks "What use is my sense of humor?" —casting into relief his skewed relationship with the humorless "Roman Catholic attendants." Lowell himself was once a Catholic, though by birth, and later in life, a Beacon Hill Episcopalian. "There are no Mayflower/screwballs in the Catholic Church," Lowell wryly notes, suggesting why his own Catholicism, incompatible with his mania, faded. With only a modest strain on one's critical sensibilities, one might argue that in these lines Lowell critiques the entire Protestant

Reformation and the later Enlightenment and rise of the bourgeoisie as producing the societal aporia represented in "Waking in the Blue" as the division between the sane attendants, who are students or working people, and the insane patients, whose actions parody their former upper-class status. The postwar boom decade, the age of the greatest working-class and middle-class prosperity in American history, an age in which going to college became normative, may represent the triumph of Enlightenment reason over Catholic mysticism at a stiff political, social, and aesthetic cost.

For Lowell and his fellow inmates, the cost is deeply personal: the stresses of the era drive them into themselves, away from the casual sociability of language. Testing his humor by grinning at Stanley elicits no response because the former All-American fullback and the other patients, including Lowell, concentrate primarily on their own seal-like bodies ("After a hearty New England breakfast,/I weigh two hundred pounds/this morning") to compensate, perhaps, for their compromised mental acuity and communicative dysfunction. The body, however, especially when self-incorporated (made corpulent) under the pressure of social stigma, is a private place, not only seal-like but sealed against intrusions; focusing on it excludes the routine interpersonal exchange that makes life bearable. This willed incorporation of the body with the overstructured psyche extends to the body politic and the obsession of midcentury America with the disease of Communism. This sort of allegorical link between the structure of madness and the structure of society haunts the literary depiction of mental institutions and has historically determined their actual incorporation and courses of treatment, as Michel Foucault has demonstrated in *Madness and Civilization*. The allegorical motif is reinforced by the poem's closure, "We are all old-timers,/each of us holds a locked razor," which not only includes the reader in its weary royal "we" but the entire corporate society that conceives and constructs such elaborate institutional structures and the appropriate psyches to inhabit them.

Another allegorical-corporate parallel occurs between government and marriage. In the first section of *Life Studies*, a poem entitled "Inauguration Day: January 1953" commemorates the opening of the Eisenhower era by describing the wintry violence of New York City's artificial landscape and invoking Peter Stuyvesant and Ulysses S. Grant as historically relevant figures of irony and pathos. Grant, in his success as a general and failure as a president, seems prophetically comparable to Eisenhower.[21] Stuyvesant, seventeenth-century governor of New Amsterdam, was forced to surrender the colony, and died in bitterness in the renamed English colony of New York. Having invoked these figures of prominence and disgrace, the brief poem concludes with a picture of mechanical, cosmological stasis:

> Ice, ice. Our wheels no longer move.
> Look, the fixed stars, all just alike
> as lack-land atoms, split apart,
> and the Republic summons Ike,
> the mausoleum in her heart.[22]

Yet in fulfilling this apparent prophecy, the close of the era presents a picture of greater complexity, as "Man and Wife" illustrates. Eisenhower, with his relatively liberal domestic policy, muddled anti-Communism, and generous budgets, by 1958, when Lowell revised this poem,[23] seemed historically a more ambiguous figure than he appeared to be in 1953, just as Lowell's second marriage would develop patterns of complexity he could not have predicted in 1949.[24] "Man and Wife" suggests something about both the public and private price of tranquility, the *Pax Americana* of the cold war. Miltown, a powerful chemical tranquilizer, has "Tamed" the marriage bed, "Mother's bed," recently inherited. It is a scene not of tranquility, however, but of violent hues and energetic dissipation: "the rising sun in warpaint dyes [husband and wife] red," and the "gilded bed-posts shine, / abandoned, almost Dionysian." The contrast in this scene between the drugged but warpainted occupants of the ancestral bed and the vividly depicted details of the world outside, including the "murderous five days' white" of the magnolias on Marlborough Street, embodies the tension in their present lives and in the history of their marriage.

Disconnection, failed communication, and aporia, which plague the lobotomized Czar Lepke, the Winslow family, the obsessive inhabitants of McLean Hospital, and the American democratic process, in "Man and Wife" have come to characterize a marriage.[25] When they met, Lowell was "too boiled and shy/and poker-faced to make a pass,/ while the shrill verse of [his future wife's] invective scorched the traditional South." The fictionalized Elizabeth Hardwick's apparent disloyalty to her home region bears an ambiguous relationship to her patience ("as if you had/a fourth time faced the kingdom of the mad") and ongoing "old-fashioned tirade—/loving, rapid merciless—" that "breaks like the Atlantic Ocean" on Lowell's head, doing, apparently, no great harm. This ambiguous marriage portrait mixes violence, mutual survival, and the failure of communication ("Now twelve years later, you turn your back") in equal doses. As a portrait of the "tranquillized *Fifties*" it suggests how precariously balanced is the ethos of the era.

Tranquilizers, the characteristic drugs of a neurotic age, do not cure but mask symptoms. "Each drug that numbs alerts another nerve to pain," Lowell later notes in "Soft Wood" in *For the Union Dead*. In "Man and Wife," not even Miltown, a powerful tranquilizer, can obliterate Lowell's sense of the past—indeed, the drug seems to sharpen his sense of the connection between past and present—can stop the "old-fashioned tirade," can erase the "hackneyed speech, . . . homicidal eye" that Elizabeth has to face whenever his mania recurs (an annual event in this pre-lithium period). Surely this poem is fraught with "the frustration of knowing too much": too much knowledge of the past, too much foresight. And surely the need for a powerful drug to tame the present indicates with what difficulty the participants rationalize a relationship so verbally inept.

Finally, "Skunk Hour," the first poem composed for the "Life Studies" group, depicts a community in corporate failure, which results in blocked, frustrated, or incomplete discourse. Lowell consequently experiences a disparity between the possibility of individual action and the appropriateness or utility of the available information, all of which symptomizes communal and personal decay.

In the early stanzas, the failure of communal structure generates clearly defined irrationalities, while the later stanzas depict the consequent failure of discourse to occur in a normal fashion. Assuming the public burden, Lowell's persona (a self-ironizing construct) finds himself unable to communicate his mental anguish in an appropriate context. Though Lowell's erudition is a source of pride, and although he places himself among those few upper-class Americans capable of reading history in the light of a classical education, he is alone in a disintegrated community indifferent to the subtleties that (for example) made his nickname "Cal" (for Caligula) so ironically amusing to his prep-school comrades. To escape this dilemma, which characterizes the plight of intellectual and aesthetic self-consciousness in this decade, he generates a Wordsworthian trope of natural efficacy that displaces the possibility of conventional discourse with an irrefutable epiphany.

"Skunk Hour," though partly derived from an unpublished poem entitled "For Elizabeth Bishop," and developed through confrontation with poems by Bishop ("The Armadillo"), Friedrich Hölderlin ("Brod und Wein"), and Annette von Droste-Hülshoff ("Amletzten Tage des Jahres"), is not primarily a poem of literary but of social allusion. This poem, more clearly than any other in *Life Studies*, depicts the psychic consequences of failing to live within the corporate ideology of the age. In a community misshapen by the breakdown of public roles and disabled by incomplete or inadequate forms of discourse, the poem attempts to gather sufficient information for Lowell to define himself before he goes mad for lack of response. Frustrating his desire for coherent discourse, the information gathered in the first four stanzas constitutes a series of metaphors of irrationality and incompletion: a "hermit heiress" (itself vaguely oxymoronic) who buys houses only to allow them to collapse into ruin; a summer millionaire whose yacht, after his death, becomes a commercial fishing craft; an unprosperous gay shopkeeper who imagines marriage to be his salvation. Wealth leads to loneliness and death, homosexuality leads to thoughts of marriage. The irregularly rhymed six-line stanzas tease the eye and ear with faint echoes of a more rigid order than they actually embody. Their appearance of order and their refusal to adhere to their own strictures suggest the tension between individualism and corporate order, but they also suggest how deceptive the idea of order is, how readily the arrangement of verse implies rationality of trope and statement, and how arbitrary is this anticipation of continuity in form and content.

The stanzas depicting Lowell's failure to contrive an effective discourse of the self contrast sharply with the village images; however, the depicted social failings imply both public and private irrationality, demonstrating that Lowell's personal failure is also a public one. Because so many examples of structural breakdown—unbalanced by examples of resolution, wholeness, or sanity—trouble the poem, Lowell can discover no appropriate model of presence, discourse, or representation. Corporate structure, the specialized organization of society, has so utterly failed that the economic pillars of the community have gone mad or died. Even sexual roles—especially Lowell's—have blurred and distorted. Perceiving this structural failure leads to "the frustration of knowing too much" that determines Lowell's venture into the irrational community of disconnected locutors. In an irrational community, only irrational behavior makes sense, so Lowell drives to the summit of a local Golgotha to spy on lovers in parked cars. Love, because apart from rationality (as opposed to being irrational), would seem an appropriate means of salvation, but as the "fairy decorator" presumably will discover, love doesn't necessarily conquer all. The familiar old blues tune "Love, O Careless Love" depicts the failure of love to generate rational discourse and warns Lowell that carelessness begets carelessness: in one version of the song, a young woman has carelessly gotten pregnant, but her mother reassures her by confiding that "She did the same when she was young." Voyeurism, one of the bases of art, is the mode of discourse engaged here, but it is one in which the interlocutors are always distinctly unequal. In art, the shaping voice engages the auditor or reader from a privileged position. In life, the voyeur partakes of the actions of others without the obligation of responding in any comparable way. Lowell, perhaps appalled by his voyeurism and discouraged by the impossibility of significant human contact, notes that his "mind's not right."

When the breakdown of the informational community results in "the individual's ability to rationalize the particular action indicated," such a conclusion may not be wholly warranted. Critics have taken his most desperate line at face value for so long that it is difficult to see how tentative it is. The realization that "I myself am hell;/nobody's here—" acknowledges through identification with Satan (the very figure of the isolated romantic poet) the alienating force of irrationality and redirects the poem from the consequences of a derationalized discourse community to an alternative model in nature, a need-driven primitivism that challenges both the dated conventions of Christianity and his sense of terminal solitude. Unlike Milton's Satan, whose alienation is permanent and unalterable, the protagonist finds himself back in the domestic world ("on top/of our back steps") at the boundary between culture and nature:

> I stand on top
> of our back steps and breathe the rich air—
> a mother skunk with her column of kittens swills the
>   garbage pail.
> She jabs her wedge-head in a cup
> of sour cream, drops her ostrich tail,
> and will not scare.[26]

The skunk's exploitation of the human community by way of a cup of sour cream (a ghastly parody of communion) underscores the animal's utilitarian natural state. It, too, is a Satanic figure, a type of the poet ("I'm a skunk in the poem," Lowell wrote to Bishop[27]). The sour cream, despite the claims of some critics, is not and was not in the Eisenhower era "snob food" but was found on every baked potato on every working-class dinner table—a symbol, as it were, of national prosperity.[28] It therefore represents a Luciferian delving into the ordinary domestic world. The attempt of the mother skunk to invade and parodically endorse national prosperity both illustrates and reinforces the arbitrary distinction between human and natural needs. This encounter suggests the paradigm that Friedrich von Schiller describes as a private encounter between nature and culture: "Man in his physical state merely suffers the dominion of nature; he emancipates himself from this dominion in the aesthetic state, and he acquires mastery over it in the moral."[29]

"Skunk Hour" generates no such feeling of emancipation, though, because Lowell cannot resolve his private situation without emancipating the entire society from its structural or corporate malaise. The poem ends with the skunks dominant and Lowell suspended in his information void. He cannot assert the moral priority of the aesthetic, which in its more conventional forms he has abandoned—cannot rationalize his presence in a debilitated culture. His actions remain shapeless, ambiguous, his attempts to embrace his community in the continuity of discourse have failed, and the village, even by moonlight, looks arid and sinister, dominated by the "chalk-dry and spar spire/of the Trinitarian Church."

"Skunk Hour," the final poem in *Life Studies,* mutually implicates the failures of public and private expression and most clearly depicts the plight of the self that attempts definition outside of a sufficiently incorporated (that is, highly structured and normalized) setting. But the inability to rationalize postwar America and reintegrate the individual into society haunts all of these poems. This difficulty functions both thematically and as a formal problem requiring withdrawal from the traditional poetics Lowell had previously practiced. When almost twenty years later in "Death of a Critic" in *Day by Day* Lowell comments that "The age burns in me"[30] he speaks as a veteran of an era in which, thanks to the pervasiveness of corporate ideology, the difficulties of finding a personal language and of explicating public history became inextricable. The *Life Studies* poems, some of the more personal writings of their decade, seem from this modest historical distance both singularly candid and yet dramatically responsive to a decade of corrupt and mystified discourse.

6 | "One Gallant Rush"

I N 1969 LOWELL DRAFTED A STATEMENT ON HIS
poem "For the Union Dead" to be included in an anthology edited
by Whit Burnett and entitled *This Is My Best*. Each poet was to se-
lect the most outstanding poem from his or her own work and
then explain that choice. Though Lowell hedged on declaring "For the
Union Dead" his best poem, in choosing it for the collection he confirmed what many of his readers had felt, that if not his "best," this was
certainly one of his most attractive, compelling, and characteristic
poems.

Lowell's statement touches on the composition and the thematic
center of the poem. Those who have not read Lowell's account of its
origins may find his assessment surprising. As originally drafted, Lowell's remarks read as follows:

> If I knew my best poem, I think I would be too elated to reveal
> the secret; like some powerful chemical formula, this knowl-
> edge should be guarded and sipped by stealth. Anyway, I have
> no idea. Each poem was meant to be alive and new, and many
> were once ambitious. I chose For the Union Dead partly be-
> cause of its length, neither overmodest nor hoggishly long for

this collection. All one winter, I cut, added and tinkered. Some of my better lines came to me a few days before I read the poem at the Boston Public Garden Festival.

> He rejoices in man's lovely,
> peculiar power to choose life and die.

I have written nothing else for an occasion, and feel no desire to try again. The demands helped and even encouraged me to try to pull three incoherent sketches together. One was about an aquarium, one about a parking lot, one about a Boston club. I do not regard ambitious interpretations of his own poems as one of the poet's most useful chores. I wished to give my own structure to the free verse I had learned from my friend, William Carlos Williams. My poem may be about a child maturing into courage and terror. My lines are on the dry and angry side, but the fish and steamshovels are Tahitian. In 1959 I had a message. Since then the blacks have perhaps found their "break," but the landscape remains.

This statement contains instructions on how to read "For the Union Dead" and important clues to its genesis. Although discussions of Lowell's work have generally emphasized its psychological and personal aspects, the public dimensions of this poem have always attracted more attention than the personal ones, such as Lowell's humorous diminution to child-level of the whale/fish imagery that empowers and even mystifies his earlier work. By remarking upon the "child maturing into courage and terror," rather than Shaw's courageous and principled self-sacrifice (which, however, involved the sacrifice of others), Lowell modestly refuses to conflate himself and the Civil War hero, but the poem's melding of personal and public concerns does exactly that. It also exposes, as Steven Axelrod has pointed out, the Ahab-like obsession of Shaw, whose idealism (like that of the Lowell of *Land of Unlikeness*) is equalled only by his appetite for violence.[1]

Tracing the process through which Lowell pulled his "incoherent sketches together" and combined them with the ur-poem called "One Gallant Rush" to create "Colonel Shaw and the Massachusetts 54th," now entitled "For the Union Dead," will demonstrate how powerfully he welds personal and public subject matter to create a single aesthetic entity. It will also expose the implications of Lowell's ingenuous suggestion that his poem "may be about a child maturing into courage and terror." Lowell wanted to suggest that the finished poem "For the Union Dead"—by then already praised by critics as a public utterance—centers not solely in its public language of history and heroism but equally in its critique of memory and psychological alienation.[2] Lowell wrote (or, perhaps more accurately, completed) the poem for the Boston Arts Festival of 1960.[3] This annual event, for many years held every June in the Public Garden, featured work by New England painters, sculptures displayed among the plantings, and a reading by a prominent poet. The year that Lowell read his poem, the Common, directly across Charles Street, had been torn up for construction of a massive, underground parking garage. Because of the scale of the excavations, the state house and the Shaw memorial, two hundred yards up the slope of Beacon Hill, required heavy planking to stabilize them against vibrations, as Lowell notes in his completed poem. Yellow power shovels and other heavy equipment, idled for the evening, stood in full view of the reading site.

Lowell recognized the dangers of writing occasional poetry, and in consciously resisting conventional pitfalls he cast his autobiographical-psychological study of historical self-presence (that is, a poem that places the self at the center of history) within the framework of a Horatian ode.[4] He thereby makes room for his own revisionary approach to modernism, which abandons Eliot's doctrine of impersonality and restores a Wordsworthian faith in the signature of individual experience. The poem presented special problems because Lowell knew he was not only taking on a famous subject but one that had already inspired an astonishing number of poems, all of them more or less occasional and commemorative, by well-known poets. Axelrod, in a note to his chapter on "For the Union Dead," lists fourteen examples, including poems by Emerson, James Russell Lowell, Paul Lawrence Dunbar, Thomas Bailey Aldrich, and John Berryman, as well as Charles Ives's program notes to "Three New England Places."[5] Lowell probably knew all of them, and characteristically would have been anxious to avoid following their examples.

The "incoherent sketches" are drafts of two separate poems, one about the old South Boston Aquarium and the other about Colonel Shaw.[6] The parking-lot sketch and the Boston club sketch in the surviving drafts have already been incorporated into "The Old Aquarium," the five draft pages of which illustrate Lowell's attempt to combine the strongest elements of one half-finished sketch with another. "The Old Aquarium" opens, "Remember how your nose crawled like a snail on the glass, / your hand, a child's, tingled / with careless confidence." A penciled "my" over the first "your," indicates that even at this early stage Lowell was making the decision to filter experience through a first-person speaker. The fourth stanza of this draft contains the remainder of the otherwise lost sketch about the Boston club:

> The curator, once the city's foremost citizen,
> the pillar and sustainer of its symphony,
> stands, a judge and beggar, in the doorway. His white scar,
> a trophy of the Civil War, is like a jawbone.

The subject of the portrait is Henry Lee Higginson, Civil War veteran and founder of the Boston Symphony Orchestra, who had died when Lowell was two years old. Perhaps in the original Boston club sketch Higginson had been portrayed with more historical verisimilitude, but identifying him as the "curator" of the aquarium is an act of fancy, irony, and satire. While Lowell's purpose in conflating the imaginary and the real is unclear, Higginson's historical presence will serve to facilitate Lowell's imaginative leap when, some drafts hence, he brings together the aquarium and the Shaw memorial as civic monuments of dissimilar public status but comparable personal significance.

Certainly Higginson was the archetypal old Boston club member, a partner in Lee, Higginson, and Co., investment bankers, and a wealthy benefactor of schools and cultural institutions. The "club" to which Higginson belonged is no particular institution but rather that class of powerful and well-educated men who once ran the city of Boston but who, by the time he died, were losing control to Irish and Italian politicians. Lowell seems to imagine Higginson in reduced circumstances as "curator" of a broken-down, snow-shrouded aquarium, ironic emblem of cultural and education institutions now bereft of their purpose and dignity. But Higginson retains his sense of self:

> Blunt humor and blunt severity
> alternately puff from his chewed cigar;   /bitten
> his exquisite, taut face,
> a grayhound's, trembles with robustness.

In spite of his longing for the antebellum world, he seems to understand that its utopian qualities have flourished only in his own mind:

> "No one I've ever met,"
> he sighs /
> ["]even remembers the code duello,
> man's peculiar and lovely power
> to deny what is and die."

Here Higginson, the Civil War survivor, offers a romantic view of combat that Lowell would later apply to Colonel Shaw. Higginson, a friend of Shaw's, was a member of the Massachusetts Second Regiment, Shaw's second military unit and the first in which he served as an officer.[7] Although Lowell proceeded no further with "The Old Aquarium" (subsequent drafts comprise his efforts to merge it with "One Gallant Rush"), he already had hit upon one of the essential strategies of his finished poem—to bridge the gap between the historically distant, heroic self-sacrifice of Colonel Shaw and the human degradation of an unheroic present through the medium of individual perception and memory. Higginson, who survived into the new century, embodies the Civil War experience and draws it closer to our own time. As such, he serves as a transition between the long-lost personal experience of Shaw and that of the contemporary first-person speaker, who views Shaw only as a historical figure.

In rhetorical terms, Lowell in "One Gallant Rush" overlays a meditative lyric stance on the structure of a historical narrative. The earliest draft, so called, derives many phrases and scenes from Luis F. Emilio's *A Brave Black Regiment, History of the Fifty-Fourth Regiment of Massachusetts Volunteer Infantry* (1891). Lowell's title, used a few years later for a book on Shaw by Peter Burchard, is almost certainly drawn from Frederick Douglass's famous words, "The iron gate of our prison stands half open, one gallant rush . . . will fling it wide."[8] The draft begins as a critique of modern war: "Fort Wagner uselessly cannonaded all day/like the French English and German trenches." As in *Henry V*, the pageantry of the battlefield almost conceals the futility of armed conflict:

> and you on the far right of your negros,
> sword out, now ankle deep, now knee deep,
> as the waves slapped the sand,
> the white flag of Massachusetts in front,
> the national flag to the rear.

But pageantry isn't combat, and once the gunfire breaks out, Shaw's sense of predestination, as Lowell imagines it, prepares him for his fate, perhaps even causes it. The syntax propelling the colonel to his death relies on infinitives, which suggest a continuing expectancy. The event itself concludes so abruptly that the poem, failing to catch the moment, simply notes that it is "all over."

> The . . . cannon and muskets,
> your men holding their fire,
> everywhere dropping,
> then the moment it was all about,
> the moment you'd been expecting,
> three days, perhaps all winter since

> you took the command,
> at last the instant, powder-lit,
> sword in hand, crouched like a cat—
> all over.

The poem's argument, insofar as it makes one, is, of course, the rather well-worn observation that war is hell, modern war even more hellish than those of earlier days. The black soldiers have no role in this poem other than to hold their fire and die. On a separate page, however, probably written as an afterthought to the first draft, Lowell begins to complicate his poem. He had adhered too closely to his single source. He needed to multiply the dimensions of this poem so that it would spring to life, and he would do so by extending his concerns into his own century. The first lines of the fragment undercut the futility the first draft projects by presenting Shaw's death as a tragic moment that somehow transcends momentariness:

> Because that fine moment ended abruptly,
> it never ended.
> It shines on distinct like a target.
> Or is it a loaded and leveled gun?

The question links the historical figure with contemporary black civil-rights leaders; nonetheless, Lowell argues, Shaw is "to[o] perfect for the moment" to be of use in the present struggle. His willingness to sacrifice, his embrace of the heroic imperative, involved not only himself but the black soldiers he led. Shaw is thus a pivotal figure, his military-heroic values rooted in the past, his democratic sympathies, though grounded in the New England aristocrat's natural sense of leadership, expanding to encompass a grander ideal of human equality.[9]

Finding the proper symbolic framework to embody the complexities of Shaw's relationship with the contemporary world would eventually require Lowell to choose a meditative, first-person speaker and to unfold the plot through personal associations. It is central to Lowell's aesthetic that the most profound links with history are revealed by means of an associative process so personal that it can only be justified by acknowledging the peculiarities of individual perception.

But before making that important leap in the composition process, Lowell again reworked his straightforward historical sketch in yet another draft of "One Gallant Rush." Focusing on Shaw's experience, it suggests that blacks and whites have been so divided since the Civil War that Shaw's personal qualities are irrelevant to the contemporary civil rights struggle. Too much a product of the war and of heroic idealism, Shaw in a sense exists only because he chose not to. If he had lived, he would have gone "on like a Strul[d]bug," in a state of death-in-life.[10]

Finding a bronze immortality ill suited to his purposes, Lowell marshals some historic anecdotes to soften the effect. The martyr is addressed: "you shaved your beard/and mustache and passed for a girl at the ball . . ." (the incident is apparently true); and: "at your mother's nagging you packed/the colonels uniform you wouldn't wear at your wedding."[11] Drawing upon such domestic details helps humanize Shaw, and permits Lowell to begin imagining a larger but more personal context in which the figure of Shaw is subsumed, but not lost, in a more contemporary meditation.

The rest of this draft concentrates on the heroic act itself. Calling the Civil War "the first modern war" (a historical truism, although some historians give the Crimean War precedent) Lowell resorts to desultory melodramatics of a sort he would never have allowed himself to publish:

> your general, soon mortally wounded,
> on his great bay charger, saying:
> "I am a Massachusetts man myself,"
> then turning and asking,
> "if the flag-bearer fall,
> who will carry the fla[g]?"
> And you tense and watchful,

> affable, easy in your movements,
> parsimonious in speech, saying:
> "I will."

Clearly this melodramatic language (taken word for word from Emilio's book) wouldn't do. Lowell realized he had to find a way to link the past to the present, to follow the line of development suggested in his opening stanza. He would look no further than his last work to find his strategy.

In *Life Studies*, published shortly before he began working on "One Gallant Rush," Lowell had committed himself to a personal, autobiographical aesthetic. While such an aesthetic functions naturally in poems about one's family life and childhood—and even about one's stay in a mental hospital—"For the Union Dead" would significantly extend the range of the approach beyond the personal, even beyond perceivable space and time, into shared history.

In the next, fragmentary draft of "One Gallant Rush," Lowell introduced poignant domestic lines about his daughter's guinea pigs. Although incorporated in a full-length draft of "For the Union Dead," the passage was later dropped—only to find its way, three or four years later, into "Fourth of July in Maine." The lines were probably intended to provide a meditative setting and therefore fulfill the same function as the childhood and present-tense landscapes of aquarium and Boston Common in the finished poem:

> Always this itch for the far away,
> the excessive, the decadent!
> Even on this dead June afternoon,
> when the air has stopped still,
> and my daughter has just brought home
> a baby guinea pig and its mother from school
> to board with us till fall,
> I dream of some flash of powder or whiff of grapeshot
> to destroy the chaff of day.

Lowell would have quickly detected the awkwardness of personifying two guinea pigs to trigger a meditation on war, but the draft justifies the connection by means of an analogy between Shaw's childhood and Lowell's, Harriet being the intermediary. As a boy, Shaw had altogether too much in common with the inhabitants of the twentieth century to excite our envy or admiration, Lowell argues, so we can be "grateful" that in his subsequent martyrdom he "managed to supersede / those fond, early out of key anecdotes."

The anecdote, cited by Lowell and recounted in detail by Burchard, refers to Shaw's ballroom cross-dressing. Though probably a typical jest of the period, it is hardly the sort of story we expect to hear about a Civil War hero, since it calls into question the rigidly conventional, nineteenth-century ideal of manhood. In war, whatever its social or political justifications, men distinguish themselves by demonstrating courage and military prowess. How could a boy amused by an activity that implicitly rejects the phallic power and privilege of manhood have become, only six or seven years later, a martyr to the cause of abolition and the republic? And Shaw was, it seems, still young enough to be "nagged" by his "abolitionist mother / into packing the colonel's uniform [he] wouldn't wear to [his] wedding."

The problem with "One Gallant Rush" was that it failed, despite Lowell's tinkering, to bridge the historical gap between the narrator and his subject. For Lowell, naked historicism was unacceptable; only through its personal dimensions could the intellectual experience of history be authenticated and only through the language of the sense could it be adequately conveyed. The attempt autobiographically to place "One Gallant Rush" on a "dead June afternoon" didn't work. But combining it with the aquarium sketch would locate it within a landscape of loss and destruction, one more richly endowed with personal memory-images and public sociopolitical dimensions.

Reworking passages from the aquarium sketch and combining them with passages from "One Gallant Rush," Lowell began to fashion the poem into the four-line free verse stanzas of the finished version. Almost immediately, the opening lines take shape (I reproduce these drafts as Lowell typed them, with numerous spelling and capitalization errors):

> The old South Boston aquarium stands
> in a sahara of snow now. The broken windows are boarded,
> the bronze weathervane carp has lost half its scales,
> the seedy tanks are dry.

> Once my nose crawled like a snail on the glass,
> my hand, a child's, tingled
> with careless confidence to burst
> the bubbles drifting from the noses of the cowed, compliant
> fish.

Establishing the essential rhythm in these two stanzas was Lowell's most important single step toward completing the poem. "One Gallant Rush" was dogged and flatfooted in its cadence; the new stanzas provided a far more effective rhythmic template which subsequent stanzas could follow or play upon.

Another central concern was to position the speaker in relation to his material, and here Lowell still has some problems. The two subsequent stanzas, which deal with Shaw (and mention for the first time the "bell-cheeked Negro infantry"), both begin with "Later," as Lowell hesitates to bring his childhood self and his contemporary persona into conjunction. "Once" places the child comfortably in the past, but only in the next draft would Lowell devise the stanza that relinquishes his childhood and valorizes the role of the Shaw memorial in linking historical past, memory, and the present:

> The Aquarium is gone. Here in the heart of Boston
> the Shaw Civil War Memorial
> still immortalizes the immortal moment,
> and stick[s] like a fishbone in the City's throat.

Extending this draft generated new problems, but also gave birth to vivid images that would survive in the finished poem, like the "bell-cheeked negro infantry," and the memorial as a hook, later a fishhook, finally a fishbone, stuck in the throat of the city like the Massachusetts codfish displayed in the Bulfinch state house. Thus the poem extends the fish-metaphor of the opening stanzas, a calculated diminishment of the whale of "Quaker Graveyard" related to the minnow-self of "Fall 1961," and parodies contemporary America as a distorted species of aquatic life. A version of lines that would eventually conclude the poem—"giant finned cars nose on like fish,/a savage servility slides by on grease"—appears at this stage, but in subsequent drafts Lowell would bury them in the middle of the poem.

Lowell now embarks on five successive complete drafts, the first two entitled "Robert Shaw and his Men" and "Colonel Shaw and his Negro Regiment," the rest "Colonel Shaw and the Massachusetts 54th," the title under which the poem would appear in the first paperback edition of *Life Studies*. These drafts all contain the essential tensions of the finished poem, the historical conversation between past and present, the violence of modern life and the dignity of Shaw's enterprise—the ironic awareness that Shaw's battle remains unconcluded.

Not until the fifth complete draft, however, would Lowell finally end his poem. Driving the giant-finned cars to the rear of the poem, Lowell refuses any hint of resolution and leaves the reader with an image of sharks schooling as if they had grown from the modest little fish the child once observed in the South Boston Aquarium. It is because of this ending that Lowell could successfully argue that his poem is about that child's maturation; the poem is about the maturation of a point of view, a widening of observation from a child's wonderment at the contained natural world to a critically informed understanding of the relationship between history and the present. Moving to giant-finned cars from cowed, compliant fish completes the trope of observation and maturation that opens the poem.

Before he settled on an adequate conclusion to what had become a

slightly unwieldy poem, Lowell made several attempts to close with his
historical material rather than with the present:

> Unable to bend his back, he leads
> his men to death, and seems to wince
> at pleasure, suffocate to be alone.
> They all died for the Republic. [complete draft #1]

. . . .

> A gay, droll gentleman—he) had no leisure (to
> distrust
> (nature at ease,) the resolute disorder
> of his bronze, bell-cheeked negro infantry,
> their eternal lubberly slogging past the Statehouse
> steps. [complete draft #3][12]

Besides generating (or rediscovering) the eventual ending, Lowell's
five drafts produce another essential image—that of the Mosler safe
and the atomic explosion at Hiroshima. This key image of modern warfare provides the historical balance against which to weigh the individual heroism of Shaw and his troops, and with which to return to the
present. With the other key image, also found in these drafts, of the
speaker's hand drawing back not from cowed fish but from "negro
school children" seen on television (who, too, are cowed like the fish),
the poem is largely complete, though many penciled notations on the
final draft indicate further polishing. This last of the Houghton drafts
still differs enough from the published version of the poem to warrant
reproduction here, with the kind permission of the Lowell estate and of
Houghton Library. I make no attempt to correct the numerous spelling
and typing errors nor to reproduce the marginal notations, some of
which include words or phrases that would be incorporated in the finished poem:

COLONEL SHAW AND THE
MASSACHUSSETTS' 54TH

Relinquunt omnia servare rem publicam

The old South Boston Aquarium stands
in a Sahara of snow now. Its broken windows are
        boarded.
The black weathervane cod has lost half its scales.
The airy tanks are dry.

Once my nose crawled like a snail on the glass;
my hand tingled
to burst the bubbles
drifting from the noses of the cowed, compliant fish.

My hand draws back now. I often sigh
for the dark, downward and vegetative kingdom
of the fish and reptile. One morning last March,
I pressed against the new, barbed and galvanized

fence on the Boston Common. Behind their cage,
yellow dyosaur steamshovels were grunting
as they cropped up tons of mush and grass
to build the mammoth parking lot.

Everywhere, the purr of commercial optimism
rises to the clang of desecration. Orange,
Thanksgiving-colored pumpkin-colored girders
brace the tingling Statehouse.

A steel frame reinforced
Colonel Shaw

and his bell-cheeked negro infantry
on St. Gaudens' Civil War relief . . .

The monument sticks like a fishbone
in the City's throat;
its Colonel is as lean
as a compass-needle.

he has an angry wrenlike vigilence,
a greyhound's gentle tautness;
he seems to wince at pleasure,
and suffocate for privacy.

When he leads his negro volunteers to death,
he cannot bend his back—
he is rejoicing in man's lovely,
peculiar power to deny what is and die.

Outside Boston,
the old white churches hold their air
of sparse, sincere rebellion; transparant flags quilt
the graveyards of the Grand Army of the Republic;

it[s] ramrod-witted stone Union Soldiers
grow slimmer and younger each year—
wasp-waisted, they doze over muskets,
and muse through their sideburns.

Here in this city, a girdle of girder;
the terminus of turnpikes,
there are no bronze monuments for the last war.
A felt, authentic commercial photograph

of Hiroshima rising like a cloud
above an American safe that survived the blast

says no thief
will break into our treasure.

The aquarium is gone. My hand draws back.
When I crouch to my television set,
the terrorized faces of negro schoolchildren
flash like bubbles on the screen.

Colonel Shaw is riding on his bubble,
he waits for the blessed break.

Everywhere,
giant finned cars nose forward like fish;
a savage servility
slides by on grease.

Before publishing the poem, Lowell added two lines to the penulti-mate stanza, revised the stanza about the stone Union soldiers to give them a little more dignity, eliminated "terminus of turnpikes," changed the "mammoth parking lot" to an "underworld garage," replaced "com-mercial optimism" with "parking spaces" that "luxuriate like civic/sand piles," eliminated the awkward lines "says no thief/will break into our treasure," and generally rendered the poem more euphonious and rhythmically satisfying.

At the Boston Arts Festival, Lowell would say (reading a prepared statement), "My poem, *The Union Dead*, is about childhood memories, the evisceration of our modern cities, civil rights, nuclear warfare and more particularly, Colonel Robert Shaw and his negro regiment, the Massachusetts 54th. I brought in early personal memories because I wanted to avoid the fixed, brazen tone of the set-piece and official ode."[13] Later, in drafting his statement for the Burnett anthology, Low-ell would recognize how deeply personal he had made his poem, how very different it is from the "official ode." In examining these drafts we can see how consistently the poem moves from wooden impersonal-ity toward a more vivid, more openly autobiographical moment, a progress consistent with Lowell's strengths as a lyric and meditative poet. History and autobiography deeply and subtly mingle in Lowell's creative process, and perhaps we can now more fully appreciate that his public voice developed not out of megalomania but as the authentic speech of an artist whose aesthetic personality merged with the vagaries of history and the contemporary American social scene.

7 | Lowell in Maine

I N CONVERSATION WITH IAN HAMILTON IN 1971, Lowell, reconsidering almost thirty years of his own work, mused over his limited sense of place and indicated the active role of the imagination in creating as well as empowering these familiar landscapes: "I found I wrote about only four places: Harvard and Boston, New York and Maine. These were the places I lived in and also symbols, conscious and unavoidable. New York is our cultural city and furthest from nature; Maine is nature, and Harvard may be somewhere between."[1] In the course of most of Lowell's poems, however, landscapes rarely embody either nature or culture alone. They become intensely complex arenas in which competing symbolic notions clash. These notions, which I have already variously described as the personal and the public, art and life, experience and imagination, assume different shadings in the neopastoral setting of Maine. Lowell, deeply attached to Maine, commented that in summer all the poets go there, spent the last difficult years of his first marriage in Damariscotta Mills, and toyed with the notion of living there permanently, though admitting the winters would probably be too difficult for him. Most importantly, he wrote a great deal in the few months of summer leisure, and the natural setting encouraged him to clarify the ruling dichotomies of his art by delineating parallels with the ancient division between nature and culture.

Perhaps because Lowell associated a high susceptivity to landscape with a romantic art of landscape that he found uncongenial, he limited himself, until his late years in England, to writing about a very few places, each realized in ways too complex to summarize in this brief chapter. If we understand his distinctions among New York, Harvard, and Maine to mean simply that Maine is the symbolic home of nature, we would underestimate the implications of his approach to landscape and society, and in particular we would miss the paradoxical resonances of his poems set in Maine. Many of his most important poems occur in Maine, including "The Mills of the Kavanaughs," "Skunk Hour," and "Waking Early Sunday Morning." In these, Maine provides a social as well as natural foreground. It embodies neither nature alone (despite Lowell's statement) nor an idealized pastoral society but the tension between nature and the artifice of being human, and the failure to devise a human society adequate to the challenge presented by the natural order. Lowell in these poems stands at the locus of a process, and does not merely function as a figure in a landscape. Though he often begins a poem in the passive role of witness, he usually becomes engaged in what he perceives to the extent of transforming, through a shift in rhetorical emphasis, his naturalistic imagery into intense and sometimes even private psychological symbolism.

Lowell most poignantly expresses the primal comforts and elemental qualities of Maine's bleak, powerful landscape in his brief elegy, "For Theodore Roethke," in which the late poet and the landscape blend in a recasting of the original act of creation, and in which the shift from dreaming to wakefulness introduces a cold realism that demands a language of natural occurrence yet is plainly inadequate to Lowell's elegiac mood:

> All night you wallowed through my sleep,
> then in the morning you were lost

in the Maine sky—close, cold and gray,
smoke and smoke-colored cloud.

Sheeplike, unsociable reptilian, two
hell-divers splattered squawking on the water,
loons devolving to a monochrome.
You honored nature,

helpless, elemental creature.
The black stump of your hand
just touched the waters under the earth,
and left them quickened with your name. . . .

Now, you honor the mother.
Omnipresent,
she made you nonexistent,
the ocean's anchor, our high tide.[2]

To honor nature is to invite a coldly empirical judgment on one's self. Lowell's affection for Maine is ample, but he is aware that the cold sea, windblown evergreens, and mysterious animal population are inimical to human consciousness. Considered as aspects of internal landscape, Maine's features reflect facets of the mind that are even more difficult to assimilate into the constructed self than those represented by the brisk, urban imagery of his Boston and New York poems. Equally, the human population of Maine reflects Lowell's conviction that American civilization has declined from the high point of New England culture, partly, he suggests, because of the dour and warped theology and narrow conception of society seeded by the founding settlers. The nineteenth-century myth of a sadistic and self-destructive puritanism finds in Lowell an ardent believer. Maine, settled early, in Lowell's view suffers like Boston (and the rest of the United States) from that poisoned legacy.

This legacy finds its apotheosis in "Waking Early Sunday Morning," Lowell's complex elegy for America, in which the pastoral simplicity of Maine reductively corrupts into a series of poignant but barely relevant details, and the whole of American greed, ambition, and psychosexual dysfunction assumes a murderous dimension in the poet's consciousness. The poem opens with an exclamation of impossible longing and transcendent passion for the natural sublime, foreshadowing the wistful closure in which the natural sublime has been displaced by the predatory sublime of political and military power. The initial encounter with the sublime, though requiring an unlikely extrahuman effort, seems in Lowell's dream a potential source of joy and purpose:

> O to break loose, like the chinook
> salmon jumping and falling back,
> nosing up to the impossible
> stone and bone-crushing waterfall—
> raw-jawed, weak-fleshed there, stopped by ten
> steps of the roaring ladder, and then
> to clear the top on the last try,
> alive enough to spawn and die.[3]

Then waking, sobering into the ordinary range of human desires, Lowell asserts a momentary solipsistic joy at being himself, free to spend his time as he pleases:

> Stop, back off. The salmon breaks
> water, and now my body wakes
> to feel the unpolluted joy
> and criminal leisure of a boy—
> no rainbow smashing a dry fly
> in the white run is free as I,
> here squatting like a dragon on
> time's hoard before the day's begun!

The poet's "fierce, fireless mind" runs downhill in more than one sense. By noticing the minutiae of the natural world—the field mouse rolling a marble, the vermin running for their holes, the termite in the wood-work—he has irreparably lowered his register of perception from the natural sublime to the material world in which church means merely "new electric bells" and hymns "shovelled out four-square." Even in Maine, the natural sublime occurs only in the imagination. Actual perception reveals another world, one of "dregs and dreck: tools with no handle,/ten candle-ends not worth a candle." Faith, like nature, has withdrawn its bounty from this landscape, as in "After the Surprising Conversions," and left only "vanishing emblems, His white spire and flag-/pole sticking out above the fog," so pointless now they resemble "old white china doorknobs, sad,/slight, useless things to calm the mad."[4]

Yet this elegiac state of mind, in which nature and religion seem unavailable, alerts Lowell to social and political imperatives that otherwise might have passed uncommemorated. Meditating upon the withdrawal of God reminds Lowell of Goliath crashing to the earth, and this in turn suggests a modest lowering of the voice, a "new diminuendo," suitable to a world devoid of epic significance. But this risks resuscitating the cycle of power, ambition, and greed, and returns Lowell to his primal desire to "break loose" and recover the grandeur of life, "something with a girl in summer," an innocence so primal it may be the very source of art. The least innocent man in America, President Johnson, comes into focus here—"girdled by his establishment" much as Lowell is "girdled" by his rural summer life, but with greater consequences. The president, like Lowell, has tired of his lust for power, and is "sick/ of his ghost-written rhetoric" (in Lowell's case, the ghost is imagination rather than another person), but the alternative to listening to one's own voice, on this quiet Sunday morning, is to hear the sound of "man thinning out his kind" as wars and assassinations proceed, assisted by fate itself, "the blind/swipe of the pruner and his knife/busy about the tree of life."

The elegy, then, mourns the planet as a whole, not merely the lost or dilapidated agrarianism of Jeffersonian America, and sublimity returns to mock Lowell with a vision of pointless sacrifice and loss:

> Pity the planet, all joy gone
> from this sweet volcanic cone;
> peace to our children when they fall
> in small war on the heels of small
> war—until the end of time
> to police the earth, a ghost
> orbiting forever lost
> in our monotonous sublime.

But the sublimity of culture, even presented ironically, is a poor substitute—indeed a disastrous one—for the sublimity of nature. Maine, unnamed though deeply inscribed in this poem, provides a setting of suitable cultural deterioration, one in which lost ideals "stick . . . out above the fog." The exclamatory "O," the lone vowel of regret and loss that begins four stanzas of the poem, speaks for the demise of the epic grandeur of poetry itself, as do the Marvellian eight-line stanzas rhymed in couplets. Elegizing not only America and the planet, this poem finds in the trivia of an ordinary Sunday summer morning the wreckage of thousands of years of culture, and mourns not only the unavailable sublime but the very monotony of expressing its absence.

However, "Waking Early Sunday Morning," with Lowell the retired Virgilian poet sifting through the detritus of a post-rural United States, only hints at another difficulty precluding the embrace of the natural sublime as an alternate to postmodern nuclear frenzy: Lowell in Maine, like Thoreau at the conclusion of *The Maine Woods*, finds himself uneasy with the wild—almost afraid of it. And for Lowell, unlike Thoreau, the pastoral always seems uneasily close to the wild. In even the mildest glimpses of wilderness he finds an uncomfortable correlative with unsettled states of mind, perhaps even with its own mania.[5] Confronting the "dregs and dreck" of agrarian life inflames his sense of the brutal failure of modern civilization, and it reminds him that, as he demonstrated in *Lord Weary's Castle*, the city, not the country, is the site in which significant moral confrontation must occur. Washington, D.C., not Castine, Maine, is where serious moral concerns focus. A dim guilt threads through "Waking Early Sunday Morning"—a sense that rural Maine has already diminished below the threshold of significance, and this generates a tension between the poet and the semipastoral setting to which he has cheerfully awakened. This tension illuminates Lowell's concurrent struggle to subsume his narcissism in the otherness of art, which is an attempt to overcome what Fein calls his "fear of being unable to cope with life."[6] Alternately, on the verge of surrender to the otherness of a hostile world and the aesthetic alienation of surrealism, Lowell considers the possibility of subsuming himself in nature, but this would be a violent, not a pastoral, surrender of the self, a clumsy attempt to equal in human terms the feat and vision of the spawning salmon.

The late poem "Turtle" illustrates how cruel a pattern this relinquishment of ego and the poetic could make:

> They lie like luggage—
> my old friend the turtle . . . Too many pictures
> have screamed from the reel . . . in the rerun,
> the snapper holds on till sunset—
> in the awful instantness of retrospect,
> its beak
> works me underwater drowning by my neck,
> as it claws away pieces of my flesh
> to make me small enough to swallow.[7]

But such melodramatic self-relinquishment is less characteristic of Lowell than a wistful longing for the simple competence and the easy joys seemingly just beyond his reach. Two other turtle poems, "Bringing Turtle Home" and "Returning Turtle," explicitly set in Maine, embrace a more documentary aesthetic, as if in Maine a turtle, however suggestive in ancestry and associations, remains a turtle even under the pressure of poetry. The first of these begins with plain, almost documentary narration, then juxtaposes a social argument about the materialism to demonstrate the difference between species survival and the individualism of the contemporary human world. Though the poem can hardly be said to anthropomorphize the turtle, it does manage to suggest that the breezy laughter on Mount Olympus lacks the solidity of the turtle-world:

> On the road to Bangor, we spotted a domed stone,
> a painted turtle petrified by fear.
> I picked it up. The turtle had come a long walk,
> 200 millennia understudy to dinosaurs,
> then their survivor. A god for the out-of-power. . . .
> Faster gods come to Castine, flush yachtsmen who see
> hell as a city very much like New York,
> these gods give a bad past and worse future to men
> who never bother to set a spinnaker;
> culture without cash isn't worth their spit.
> The laughter on Mt. Olympus was always breezy. . . .
> *Goodnight, little Boy, little Soldier, live,*
> *a toy to your friend, a stone of stumbling to God—*
> *sandpaper turtle, scratching your pail for water.*[8]

The concluding apostrophe to the turtle, italicized like the closure of Elizabeth Bishop's "The Armadillo," reads like a prayer, and suggests that Lowell finds something sacred in the turtle's stubborn persistence. The second turtle sonnet confirms that by contrasting culture (the bathtub) and nature (the Orland River) to demonstrate that the turtle, by survival and birthright, like the Native American, is entitled to access to the natural sublime, is even part of it:

> Weeks hitting the road, one fasting in the bathtub,
> raw hamburger mossing in the watery stoppage,
> the room drenched with musk like kerosene—
> no one shaved, and only the turtle washed.
> He was so beautiful when we flipped him over:
> greens, reds, yellows, fringe of the faded savage,

the last Sioux, old and worn, saying with weariness,
"Why doesn't the Great White Father put his red
children on wheels, and move us as he will?"
We drove to the Orland River, and watched the turtle
rush for water like rushing into marriage,
swimming in uncontaminated joy,
lovely the flies that fed that sleazy surface,
a turtle looking back at us, and blinking.

This turtle retains its footing in the natural sublime, even when in captivity, and eventually recovers the wholeness of it; while the turtles of urban dreams, alienated from their proper landscape and fused with the poet's childhood memory of imprisonment and torture of turtles, can function only as metaphor, and offer the poet no access to sublimity, only to the material cruelty that, as much as beauty, characterizes the natural world.

Four poems—"Soft Wood," "Fourth of July in Maine," "Water," and "Long Summer"—embody this wistfulness and sense of helplessness in the face of a natural world too easily and too deceptively appropriated by consciousness, a world in which "peace and cold" uneasily coexist as memory and actuality. Here I want to consider how Maine offered aesthetic correlatives for aspects of that "fierce, fireless mind" otherwise inaccessible to Lowell, and how pastoral rhetoric gives way to a more solipsistic voice and a view of the tattered boundaries of culture rather than of the easeful landscape halfway between the wild and the overcivilized.

A brief note Lowell composed for an anthology punningly entitled *Maine Lines* points to both the autobiographical and symbolic importance of Maine: "I can't define the role of Maine in my life and work. I spent some three summers there as a boy, and about thirteen more in my middle age. It stands for nature against the city, peace and cold."[9] The opposition of city and nature is stock pastoral, but the conjunction of peace and cold is unexpected and ominous. Lowell commonly pairs oxymoronic terms to indicate the appositions that shape his rhetoric and poetic. Life and art, nature and city, naturalism and symbolism, the objective viewer and the Emersonian visionary through their essential incompatibility generate the strained modes of rhetoric that character- ize his poetry and that some reviewers of the later books would claim had deteriorated into mannerism.

Autobiography and "peace and cold" shape "Water," the first poem in *For the Union Dead* and the first in the selection of Lowell's poems in *Maine Lines.* "Water" derives from Lowell's visit to Elizabeth Bishop in Stonington in 1948. The poem's landscape is specific and geographi- cally correct; Stonington's island granite quarries remain visible (still worked in the 1940s, some worked even in recent years) and his de- scription of

> dozens of bleak
> white frame houses stuck
> like oyster shells
> on a hill of rock[10]

depicts the village almost as starkly as John Marin's famous watercolors or Marsden Hartley's oils do. In a 1962 letter to Lowell, responding to an early version of "Water" in the preliminary manuscript of *For the Union Dead,* Bishop commented that "the houses struck me as looking like clam shells, because of the clapboarding. . . . Oyster shells is right because of the way they stick in beds in the rocks, exactly—if not for their color."[11] Lowell, who in 1948 had only recently met Bishop, brought his then-fiancée Carley Dawson to Stonington to visit Bishop, who had just rented a house there. Lowell apparently treated Dawson so distantly that she correctly decided their relationship was over, and took the train to Boston, leaving him there with Bishop. Although Low- ell apparently did not get up the courage to ask Bishop to marry him, he left feeling he had made his intentions clear—though their relation- ship remained a friendly rather than a romantic one.[12] In the fiction of the poem, Bishop (though unnamed) and Lowell apparently agreed that because "the water was too cold" for them they had renounced

marriage or romance in favor of friendship, rather than risk an exhilarating but perhaps ultimately numbing experience.

This biographical understanding of the poem is not so important as
the stony but sensuous feeling of the language, the consequence not of
autobiographical fact or geographical precision but of Lowell's tactile
choice of words, which appeals to the senses of touch and texture as
well as sight, as in the lines

> Remember? We sat on a slab of rock.
> From this distance in time,
> it seems the color
> of iris, rotting and turning purpler,
>
> but it was only
> the usual gray rock
> turning the usual green
> when drenched by the sea.

Marin and Hartley portrayed these same colors—gray, green, purple—
in expressing stone and barnacle and weed. But the query "Remember?" shifts the poem from one of landscape to one of dramatic
engagement, and the choice of "seems" indicates how memory empowers landscape by making it more than itself, infusing it with the
drama the poem alludes to but does not develop. Lowell perceives the
difference between the internal landscape of purple and the external
landscape of usual gray and usual green. By voicing that distinction, he
points to the role of landscape in human intercourse, its pliable recep-
tivity to mood and remembrance.

The modest free verse, with its occasional rhymes (usually ABCA),
allows the rhetorical shift from description to memory and the linked
sea-images of islands, oyster shells, weir, rock, mermaid, wharf-pile,
and barnacles to give the poem its structure, so that the last line—"the
water was too cold for us," a perfect negative image of chastity—becomes a renunciation of everything physical and sensuous in the world

of the poem, whether objective and empirical or transformed by memory and experience. The paradox that sensuous—or sensual—indulgence should seem potentially "too cold" (usually it is too warm) is a consequence of the poem's chilly Maine atmosphere, which embodies the mutual self-doubts of Lowell and Bishop.

"Water" deals with the immutability of events, and the dream in which the woman sees herself as "a mermaid clinging to a wharf-pile/ and trying to pull/off the barnacles with her hands" is a vision of futile opposition to nature, which in this poem is what remains after one becomes conscious of the illusory constructions of memory. To marry, then, would require the characters in the poem to oppose themselves to the natural currents of their lives. The obscurities of the poem revolve around images of departure and permanence—the departing boatloads of quarry workers versus the immovable barnacles and the fixed white houses. The divided mind of the speaker also engenders imagery of entrapment ("where the fish for bait were trapped"), decay, and death. The poem leaves no room for the pastoral vision, since everything in it either assumes an unfeeling objectivity or the tone and coloration of the participants' feelings. The cold Atlantic only reflects the frigidity of quelled emotions, and the flux of "Water" is that of will and emotion subdued by the inevitability of consciousness.

But a longing for the lost pastoral of literary convention lingers in "Soft Wood," in which the seal pack that barks past the Lowells' window "summer after summer" suggests not only the immortality of the lower animals, which live through their species rather than through the self-awareness of individuals, but the eternal summer of the young, the lotus-like forgetfulness or childlike unawareness of mortality that makes the pastoral vision possible.[13] Three lines after noting the seal pack, however, Lowell speculates that "Surely the lives of the old/are briefer than the young," indicating that this elegy is not only for Harriet Winslow, to whose memory the poem is dedicated, but for Lowell and his family and friends, who "may and will die daily," victims like Lowell and Bishop in "Water" of their own consciousness. Yet consciousness in this poem indicates perception. Though time surely has a different significance for the old, its significance for Lowell is modified by the setting of coastal Maine, where "things last," where the salt air preserves the "soft wood" and "even the hot water in the bathtub/is more than water." The salt is the difference—its preservative power, though ineffective against human mortality, here affects the larger world of landscape.

In "Soft Wood," which utilizes many of the elements of Bishop's "At the Fishhouses," the natural world includes the buildings, the seals, everything but Lowell and Harriet Winslow and his unnamed friends. Contrary to Marjorie Perloff's claim, the poem does not suggest that "along the Maine coast, one has the illusion of being able to live forever."[14] In fact, the gap between the human world of aging and death and the "healing" and "illimitable" natural world is greater, or at least more visible, here. The seals "in their barred pond at the zoo" retain their otherness, and live "as long as the Scholar Gypsy"—a figure of reputed immortality. That seals remain happy even in the zoo (though Lowell's assertion is difficult to believe) suggests how distant their lives and expectations are from ours. That otherness, that apparent immortality, in Maine expresses itself in landscape: "Here too in Maine things bend to the wind forever." In Maine, as in the zoo, "things"—that is, whatever is not human—perpetually imbibe the freshness and healing power of the salt breeze. The landscape absorbs human artifacts and makes them its own. The healing power of nature even pours into the bathtub; but even though "things last," this landscape offers "no utility or inspiration," the two qualities that the human world expects to derive from the natural. If "only children seem fit to handle children," then perhaps this is a world only for children, whose view of their own lives is one of eternal summer. Children characteristically view themselves as immortal and cannot imagine the world without them in it. In this "illimitable" landscape of self-renewal, only a child could feel at home: the old are too conscious of the gap between themselves and what they behold.

Lowell has inherited his Castine house from Harriet Winslow, but whatever pleasure he takes in it is tempered by his awareness that "it's no consolation to know/the possessors seldom outlast the possessions." The house itself reminds him of his late cousin, and he recalls her dying days, "breathing in the heat wave / and air conditioning, knowing/each drug that numbs alerts another nerve to pain." To be an adult, to be aware of growing old, is to understand that consolations only turn us toward other griefs. If the zoo-bound seals are happy, it is because they sense no disjunction between themselves and their landscape, because they aren't conscious of the "futureless future" in which they, as individuals, will have no place, while for Lowell even his house, his most treasured possession, reminds him of his mortality.

Maine in this poem, then, represents nature at its most remote and yet most attractive. The healing power of the salt, the happiness of the seals, the "wind smashing without direction" remind Lowell how brief are "the lives of the old," yet there's something cheering about perceiving one's own impermanence in the context of "painted soft wood staying bright and clean" and "the green juniper berry" that spills "crystal-clear gin." Perhaps the very cleanliness of the landscape, constantly scoured by the salt air, clarifies Lowell's vision and enables him, momentarily, to experience, while observing that "shed skin will never fit another wearer," an awareness that in contrast with the seals' indifference toward fate clarifies his relationship to his ancestors.

"Fourth of July in Maine," which immediately follows "Waking Early Sunday Morning" in *Near the Ocean,* also elegizes Harriet Winslow, but in this poem Maine is more a society than a landscape. The loss of "Independence" and "innocence," the rhymed end words of the poem's first two lines, as Steven Yenser has pointed out, is the subject of this poem.[15] What is elegiac is Lowell's awareness that the house "willed downward" from Winslow to himself represents a dead tradition and a dying line:

> Your house, still outwardly in form
> lasts, though no emissary come
> to watch the garden running down,
> or photograph the propped-up barn.[16]

The sequence ("Near the Ocean") of which this poem is a part is an elegy for American civilization, though, not merely for one aged relative, and the house here is a complex symbol of both decay and permanence. The permanence is aesthetic and formal, the house a specimen of "the Americas'/best artifact produced en masse." The decay derives from puritan obsessions with mortality and control, obsessions that "gave this land/a ministry that would have made/short work of Christ, the Son of God," and have devoured the very traditions that built the house: faith in God and in political self-sufficiency. In Maine, specifically, Lowell notes that the Independence Day celebration is now for children, who in this poem are innocent both of their mortality and of the decay of tradition. The adults, "poor and Republicans," in attempting to "uphold the American dream" have perverted "Emersonian self reliance" into the "lethargy of Russian peasantry." Is this what American independence and self-reliance have come down to? Maine resists "the communist and socialist," but to what end? The lesser consciousness of the uneducated peasantry serves them ill, but the greater consciousness of Lowell troubles him with a sense of impermanence.

For consolation, Lowell turns to the "white Colonial frame house" willed to him by cousin Harriet, but it, too, represents the crumbling tradition. This tradition of sturdy utilitarian architecture ("modest, functional . . . without bragging about it," he later wrote),[17] uncompromising theology, and fiery independence carried the seeds of its own decay—indeed, willed itself into decay. The "dark design/spun by God and Cotton Mather" enmeshed the culture. Each generation, like the Hawthornes, has declined from the one before, so that the house "willed downward" has passed into less capable hands than Cousin Harriet's. The decline since the Founders has been precipitous, and Harriet is not exempt. Though the poet's tone is affectionate, he is ironic about her talents and interests:

> If memory is genius, you
> had Homer's, enough gossip to
> repeople Trollope's Barchester,

> nurses, Negro, diplomat, down-easter,
> cousins kept up with, nipped, corrected,
> kindly, majorfully directed,
> though family furniture, decor,
> and rooms redone meant almost more.

Surely authentic genius wouldn't so obsess itself with trivia. This description of Harriet makes her resemble the field mouse in "Waking Early Sunday Morning" that "rolls /a marble, hours on end, then stops," or the other "creatures of the night /obsessive, sure of foot" that "go on grinding, while the sun's/daily remorseful blackout dawns." In her illness, Harriet comes to represent the general decay of New England culture, "not trusting in the afterlife,/ teasing us for a carving knife." The failure of faith is one of the dominant motifs in this poem, as in "Waking Early Sunday Morning." Religious faith is only one of the many kinds of faith one might lose. The decline of self-reliance into lethargy represents one sort of loss of faith; and the belief that contemporary New England seems doomed by the "dark design" woven in the first hundred years of settlement represents another sort, one of which Lowell may not have been entirely conscious.

Yet, even in decline, this culture offers certain compensations that can be passed from generation to generation:

> High New England summer, warm
> and fortified against the storm
> by nightly nips you once adored,
> though never going overboard,
> Harriet, when you used to play
> your chosen Nadia Boulanger
> Monteverdi, Purcell, and Bach's
> precursors on the Magnavox.

None of these musical personages are of New England: the culture is imported, distant in time and place. Only the setting is native, and in the end, only whiskey offers an immutable consolation, inherent and unchanging, a poor compensation for the loss of "God the Logos." It would be unchanging, too, in life as well as in art: Philip Booth in his elegant memoir reports that Lowell, like Harriet, over his whiskey on cool summer evenings listened to Nadia Boulanger on the same old Magnavox.[18]

The momentary joy of the poem is the presence of the younger Harriet, the poet's daughter, who "cartwheels in the blue." Her innocence extends to her pets, two "angora guinea pigs" that are "so humble, giving, idle and sensitive / few animals will let them live." These poor creatures unwittingly parody the impossible, impractical Christian ideal. Their presence in the poem undercuts Lowell's prayer for his daughter, his hope that she live "through the millennial year / Two Thousand," since to do so she would have to surrender the innocence portrayed here, symbolically devour her guinea pigs, and enter the disillusioned and declining world of her father's wry adulthood.

In the windy late-summer night, the voice of Joan Baez on the gramophone, another dedicated but hopeless idealist unable to grow or change, repeats and repeats itself. Unlike Boulanger, but like Lowell, Baez lived in New England and began her career there. Invoking a past that perhaps never existed, anachronistic yet appealing to the America of the early 1960s, her folk music represents a cultural decline from Bach and Monteverdi. Perhaps identifying with her, Lowell puts his hands out to the fire, mocking his own (and his wife's) frustrations, vain as Baez's reiterated song:

> And here in your converted barn
> we burn our hands a moment, borne,
> by energies that never tire
> of piling fuel on the fire;
> monologue that will not hear,
> logic turning its deaf ear,
> wild spirits and old sores in league
> with inexhaustible fatigue.

Lowell muses on a distant time, the early days of creation, but this leads to nothing except a more faintly elegiac note, a "diminuendo." As the fire dies, so does the ego, the sense of self, the soul. Out of fire and ash the phoenix-like spirit is supposed to rise, but in the poem's final four lines, a parody of the Lord's Prayer, the poet asks only for enough warmth to survive another day—a warmth, the poem concludes, he receives not from culture, not from faith, not from all that the sun and the fire and freedom and innocence represent, but from the same whiskey that once "fortified" Cousin Harriet:

> Great ash and sun of freedom, give
> us this day the warmth to live,
> and face the household fire. We turn
> our backs, and feel the whiskey burn.

Maine in this poem is a microcosm of New England collapsed under the weight of its own imperative. The attempt to "command the infinite" was fatal; the brittle old culture unraveled from the "dark design/ spun by God and Cotton Mather" could not survive because its obsession with mortality fated it to ebb with Calvinism itself. "Only fossils" know the names of those who have perished for the sake of this culture, and soon everyone, like cousin Harriet, will be "gone, as the Christians say, for good." The poem offers no reason why the younger Harriet should be exempt from this fate. In fact, assuming that the Baez record is hers, Harriet is apparently already caught up in the difficulties and frustrations of this bleak world. That Baez's voice is a new one, in many ways opposed to the cultural establishment Lowell represents, makes little difference. The "lethargy of Russian peasantry" self-renews and deepens, generation after generation, and is both political and cultural, condemned to repetition rather than revolution. "World-losers elsewhere," the "scions of the good old strain," including Lowell himself, find no comfort in the civilization they and their ancestors have created, so they turn their backs on their household fires and numb themselves with whiskey.

"Long Summer," though, to some extent corrects the bleak picture drawn by "Fourth of July in Maine." This sequence of sonnets is one of Lowell's most beguiling creations, though unfortunately the poet disassembled it when he rewrote *Notebook* into *History* and *For Lizzie and Harriet.* Allen Tate, on receiving proofs of *Notebook 1967–68,* wrote to Lowell in 1969, "Until my next reading, and perhaps after it, this is your finest work to date—uneven, of course, but most impressive. Not at all uneven is 'Long Summer,' the entire sequence of fourteen 'sonnets.' I'm inclined to think this is your finest work to date: not a word out of place, the 'confessional' material controlled and formal."[19] "Long Summer" is an impressive sequence that according to Alex Calder's account Lowell composed in the summer of 1967, beginning with a shorter sequence entitled "Ages," to which he added poems over a three- or four-month period.[20] It is too long and complex to be fully summarized here, but briefly, as the sequence opens at the beginning of summer, poet and wife, exhausted presumably by their city lives and caught in a deteriorating marriage, are uncertain of their future, though "each day more poignantly resolved to stay" (sonnet 1).[21] The second sonnet (its revised version is discussed in the chapter 8) depicts Lowell, in the aftermath of a lobster-bake, as almost preternaturally alert to the ancestral precedents of his life, calling himself "elfin, stonefoot." The third and fourth sonnets, which dramatize two months of fog, provide the landscape-emblem of the married couple's muddled attempt to focus their lives and bring coherence to their relationship. Ironically, they do so, to some extent, by imagining a renewal (sonnet 13) in the context of an Eden (sonnet 12) that the Maine landscape suggests though only ironically approximates. Caught up in the vision of the ideal, they "hunger for the ancient fruit,/marriage with its naked artifice," though they are old, nearly "widower/and widow" (sonnet 13). But summer by then has fled, and friends are "crowding everyone /to put off leaving till the Indian Summer," each couple hoping to be left alone with the revitalizing landscape. It is too late; the poet and his wife will return to the glacial marriage so familiar to them: "Ice over soon; it's nothing; we're used to sickness" (sonnet 14). The cyclical wheel has turned, and like the "circus poodles dancing on a ball" (sonnet 1) they find once again "something inhuman always rising" on them. The sequence concludes by wryly noting that "this life" is "too long for comfort and too brief/for perfection," the poet and his wife being compared to "surgeons' apprentices studying their own skeletons,/old friends and mammoth flesh preserved in ice."

Here the Maine seascape and human society perform complex and paradoxical functions. The two months' fog forms "an inarticulate mist so thick" the couple has "turned invisible" to face each other, so disoriented that the poet can't stand upright: "I have to brace my hand against a wall/to keep from swaying—swaying wall . . ." and he drifts into cruel associations of the mental hospitals he has so often endured: "straitjacket, hypodermic, helmeted/doctors" (sonnet 3). But the fog reminds him of, "thirty-five summers back, the brightest summer," a summer that in his memory now seems very much like this one. This is the first sign of renewal, the older, inarticulate, fogbound adult re-identifying with his youthful self. Though the fog disorients, it makes available an exhilarating vision by displacing the poet's ordinarily uncompromising quotidian seeing.

This vision of an earlier time lasts through sonnet 5, with its memory of a time when "all girls then [were] under twenty, and the boys/unearthly with the white blond hair of girls." But in sonnet 6 this vision is displaced by the noises of the Castine of 1967: "Shake of the electric fan above our village;/oil truck, refrigerator, or just man,/nightly reloading of the village flesh—"; and the poet concludes, with his rediscovered sense of proportion, that "there are worse things than marriage." Waking to the actual world of the present reminds him that the young summer people of the Castine noising about him differ from the romantic figures of his remembered youth:

> They come, each year more gallant, playing chicken,
> then braking to a standstill for a girl;
> soft bullets hitting bottles, spars and gulls,
> echo and ricochet across the bay—
> hardy perennials.

The young men are "hardy perennials" because each year a new or renewed crop of them appears. Nevertheless, generations pass, individuals mature and assume the stance of old age and the slightly prurient
relationship to youth attributed to Kokoschka, at eighty, saying, "If you
last,/you'll see your reputation die three times,/and even three cultures;
young girls are always here."

The next sonnet, eighth in the sequence, focuses on the seashore,
"pebbled with eroding brick," and in its richly inscribed texture detects
"the mangle and mash of the monotonous frontier,/bottles of dirt and
lighted gasoline." The idea of the frontier is one that permeates Lowell's
vision of Maine, a boundary between society and nature at which both
realms surrender certain qualities (nature surrenders some beauty, society surrenders some order) and forms a "land of unlikeness" in which
metaphor is a necessary and implicit presence in every apparent fact.

Unlikeness requires the poet to conquer it by fusing apparently disparate things through metaphor and juxtaposition, so in Maine as well
as in Boston landscapes become other places as well. To free himself
from the exhausted actualities of the landscape, in the ninth sonnet
Lowell imagines that the Maine islands are Greek and Homeric, and
counts again the catalog of ships in the *Iliad*. Freeing the mind from the
immediacy of perception by paying homage to antiquity allows the
imagination to drift still further and associate the actual harbor lying
before the poet with more distant yet equally palpable landscapes
drawn from reading:

> The iron bell is rocking like a baby,
> the high tide's turning on its back exhausted,
> the colored, dreaming, silken spinnakers
> shove through the patches in the island pine,
> as if vegetating millennia of lizards fed
> on fern and cropped the treetops . . . or nation of gazelles,
> straw-chewers in the African siesta. . . .

And like so much contemplated in the course of this sequence, this associative vision holds some degree of healing power, leading to the

mild concluding epiphany, "I never thought scorn of things; struck fear in no man."

The momentary easing of the poet's angst extends into the tenth sonnet, which begins, "Up north here, in my own country, and free," as if to assert a relatively comfortable sense of place; but the poem then turns ironic and satirizes the summer crowd from "the sallowing south" (Boston and New York, presumably). The freedom to satirize is embraced with mild exuberance, so that in sonnet 11 the poet can look wryly upon himself, "both . . . legs hinged on the foreshortened bathtub," and realize how small his world is, how "the scene confines," and how far from the heroism of "someone, Custer, leaping with his windgold/scalplock," how quickly he is aging. Aging dominates the concluding three sonnets, but unlike the opening poems of the sequence, these enjoy a sense of place and context, and the poet seems to have a stronger if still melancholy awareness of himself and his wife. Though the summer, by his account, has been rich with epiphany, he understands how ironic is the desire to "linger on past fall in Eden," the pun telling us all we need to know about such futile and ahistorical aspirations.

"Long Summer" most vividly interweaves the poet's sense of place and self, but some of its leaps and associations are difficult to follow. Like so much of *Notebook 1967–68,* this sequence seems tentative yet direct in a new way, as if making the reader privy to a more primitive act of composition in which the seams still show, transitions are omitted, syntax sometimes rough or incomplete. But the sense of place is strong, and firmly binds the individual sonnets and the sequence together. The development depends on the poet's eye for landscape, for the associations places stimulate. The Maine of the tourists plays little role here, though Castine as yachting center becomes the shore of Ilion with its crowd of warships. Rather, it is the Maine of bleak and lovely seascape, the Maine of blighted New England puritanism, and the Maine of oppressive but impure wilderness that lies behind this fragmentary but rich poem.

Lowell in each of these poems makes Maine his "own country," reading it with an eye that, while not Wordsworth's equal in natural observation, shares the nineteenth-century poet's sense of both the otherness of the world and its metaphorical imperative. In "Water," Lowell momentarily considers domestic submission, but the cold hostility of the sea, expressing that loss of self, deters him. "Soft Wood" entertains a gentler view of nature, embodied in the seals, but concludes as it begins with a rhetorical distance between Lowell's consciousness and the physical world. "Fourth of July in Maine" finds the late frontier society of small-town Maine decayed and untenable, largely because of the decline of New England's religious and social ideals. "Long Summer," on the other hand, most clearly elevates the poet's imagination over a more empirical view of landscape and offers a glimpse of a more transcendent, though vague and elusive, vision.

At the interface of nature and society, landscape and self, Lowell finds instead of a pastoral setting a frontier where language is primal but metaphor is more easeful than unmediated actuality. To explore this frontier in some of these poems—particularly "Water" and "Waking Early Sunday Morning"—is rhetorically to manipulate the relationship between the voice of a detached self in an empirical landscape and a self alert to the power and will of the mind to modify what it perceives and make landscape a metaphor of its own processes. Knowledge is not a still point for Lowell, and in the flux of weather, the sea, the fog, as these phenomena shape and are shaped by perception, he finds opportunity for a rhetoric of self-awareness and feeling, and comes close to fully expressing and therefore gaining some control over awkward human complexities.

8 | Vision, Landscape, and the Ineffable

WITH GREAT COMPRESSION, ECCENTRIC phrasing and syntax, and often sensuous language, the sonnets of *History* embrace an epic range of concerns. Some deal with imaginative vision and physical seeing, some with the relationship between perception and landscape, some with the seductive difficulties of abstract statement, philosophical absolutes, and the ineffable. The commonality of these closely related and often overlapping topics lies in Lowell's passion to work out warring tensions and reconcile the differing terms of life and art. As other commentators have pointed out, many of the poems in *History* pose great figures in an allegorical struggle between light and dark forces, and these famous figures, in wielding power, usually succumb to it and become forces of evil like those they attempted to subdue. This explains the less manic aspect of Lowell's attraction to Hitler, Napoleon, Mussolini, and other historically vivid but morally despicable personages. Lowell's revision of *Notebook* into *History* is not so much a matter of honoring linear chronology and moving personal experience from the center of concern to the periphery, as Steven Axelrod argues,[1] as it is of finding a way to expand personal experience to engage and thus overcome chronology. The individual sonnets, regardless of how they are ordered, are spatial rather than linear in movement. With lyric indifference to the dimensions of the bodily senses, they repeatedly expose the power of individual sensibility to overcome historical chronology by imposing itself between the event and the record of it. The poet's lyric sensibility, by cumulative effect, delineates a larger shape and structure that, while drawing upon narrative linearity, frames it in accordance with the poet's sense of purpose.

My concern here is with the structural and aesthetic consequences of Lowell's thematic and genre strategies, rather than with the psycho-allegorical impulses others have discovered in the construction of *History*.[2] The formal difficulties of the sonnets, including what Lowell calls their "cramping and military beat,"[3] derive from the attempt to reconcile the fragmentary lyric particulars of personal experience, the allegorical dialectics of history, and the cultural and visionary fruition of epic. The balance is tenuous, only half successful at best, and the poet comes to recognize the achievement of his writing more often through the depiction of tyranny, megalomania, and cultural blindness than through expressions of visionary triumph.

History proposes an aesthetic that would reconcile ordinary acts of perception with a visionary self that exists, for the most part, only in poems. Rather than a mass of immutable facts encased in unstoppable narrative, history becomes a mess of fragments to sift through. Writing history is a matter of discovering what illuminates the individual life. The grandeur of Alexander or Hannibal disappears and their sonnets find them painfully human: "His sweet moist eye missed nothing," Lowell notes of Alexander, and how sadly organic is that "sweet moist eye."[4] Both the material and the spiritual conditions of life, *History* suggests, render it poignant, unduplicable, and difficult to represent to ourselves and to others. Only poetry can help Lowell catch a full sense of selfhood. "Our insoluble lives sometimes come clearer in writing," he muses.[5] This clarification makes available a modest version of the sublime but refutes the grandeur of social and political romanticism. It precipitates the sighting of the "half-fledged robin" in "Under the Moon" and the "bright sky" envisioned in "End of a Year,"[6] but warns that "the laws of history tell us/irrelevant things that happen never happened"[7] and "if the steamroller goes over the flower, the flower dies."[8]

The three elements of the healing aesthetic of *History* are a comfortable affinity of imaginative vision and physical seeing, a clear view of the landscape-theater of the poem, and an illumination of absolutes and the ineffable by particulars. In this volume, however, by drawing the most compelling of those particulars from the traditional materials of history, Lowell claims a fuller aesthetic, social, political range. He also makes available the experience and perceptions of heroes, poets, kings, and tyrants, whose accomplishments are fixed in bronze but whose material weaknesses retain personal resonance. Before examining sonnets of vision and landscape that explore an aesthetic that blends personal with historical resonances, I want to discuss two sonnets that exemplify Lowell's attitude toward the artifacts of history, including the artifact of poetry. We must understand his skeptical approach to conventional narratives and historical themes in order to appreciate the mournful tone and occasional despair that characterize the poems about personal life and the ordinary objects and places of his world.

History demonstrates how Lowell's aesthetic concerns with the particulars of the world derive from his involvement with the past—how his poems bear the accumulated weight of all those before him, the historical and poetic forebears he has previously acknowledged and sometimes rejected. This weight of the past becomes manifest in concrete images of enduring significance. "1930's 5" is a particularly eloquent example:

> Timid in victory, chivalrous in defeat,
> almost, almost . . . . I bow and watch the ashes
> reflect the heraldry of an age less humbled,
> though hardened with its nobles, serfs and faith—
> (my once faith?) The fires men build live after them,
> this night, this night, I elfking, I stonehands sit
> feeding the wildfire wildrose of the fire

clouding the cottage window with my lust's
alluring emptiness. I hear the moon
simmer the mildew on a pile of shells,
the fruits of my banquet . . . a boiled lobster,
red shell and hollow foreclaw, cracked, sucked dry,
flung on the ash-heap of a soggy carton—
it eyes me, two pinhead, burnt-out popping eyes.[9]

Seated by the embers of a cooking fire and the ruins of a boiled lobster, Lowell registers the socio-historical-psychological significance of fire. In this primal situation, he consoles himself for loss of faith with a "bent generalization" (as he calls these abstracts in the "Afterthought" to *Notebook*)[10] derived from the homily, "the deeds men do live after them." As usual with generalizations or homilies in Lowell's late work, this remark assumes a more elevated register of diction than the rest of the sonnet. People survive in their works, and Lowell, though lacking religious faith, may survive in his poetry. But how significant would this survival be? Himself a primitive, an "elfking" and "stonehands," Lowell is one with his predecessors, who live through him as well as through their fires. As it rises over Stevens's dump, the moon simmers in the ruins of the immediate past, illuminating clamshells and a lobster husk, the poems of everyday. The lobster eyeing Lowell becomes a Yorick's skull, a *memento mori*, to remind us that the illuminating fire is reductive, that people die, leaving as artifacts mere excrescences, exoskeletons, of what they were.

This sonnet rationalizes Lowell's hierarchical concern with objects that function as synecdoches and symbols when subjected to the reductive fires of art. If fires, not deeds, remain to assert that we have lived, we must subject ourselves and our works to the flames. We and our works, whatever is left of them, will survive as popeyed fossils, like the remains of the lobster. This distorted ruin in Lowell's case is his poetry, though it could be any monument: a triumphal arch, a painting, a list of exploits in a history textbook. This degrading image of human works typifies Lowell's skepticism toward products, while acknowledging that artifacts speak both to and for us. *History* itself, as a commemorative work of art, is both a product or artifact and an example of the fire that reduces and petrifies the lives and works of others.

Another sonnet, "History," provides another instance of Lowell's acceptance of limitations. This is the opening poem of the volume, and it announces two primary concerns running throughout: that limited vision is the poet's necessary means rather than a hindrance, and that chronology will serve as a simple framework to support Lowell's lengthy sequence in the absence of narrative or dramatic movement. The poem begins with a personification of history:

> History has to live with what was here,
> clutching and close to fumbling all we had—
> it is so dull and gruesome how we die,
> unlike writing, life never finishes.[11]

Granting sentience to history aligns it with Lowell's imaginative vision and the unstated limitations of subjectivity. By arguing from those limitations the poem stresses a dichotomy: that individually we die in a "dull and gruesome" manner and our peculiar visions die with us, while life, in the aggregate and in the Emersonian sense, continues. Working from the limitations of history (tied to the particular and transient) and the discrepancy between life and writing as differing but closely linked processes, Lowell ruptures archetypes to make characteristic metaphors:

> Abel was finished; death is not remote,
> a flash-in-the-pan electrifies the skeptic,
> his cows crowding like skulls against high-voltage wire,
> his baby crying all night like a new machine.

The shock of the momentary sublime jolts the unbeliever; his animal passions push against the unknowable that can kill, while his weaker self protests his paradoxical affinity for and fear of power and sublimity. For what sublimity was Abel sacrificed? Life—the larger abstraction—never finishes, never succumbs to terror and vision, but individuals do. Death inheres in every visionary experience, coming as close to the seeker as the "high-voltage" wire that corrals the cows. But the "flash-in-the-pan" of sublime vision is so momentary that it can only startle, not convert the skeptic, who could be anyone from Adam (the father of Abel), a victim of Eve's infidelity with Satan, to Lowell's Castine neighbor with his herd of Holsteins.

Asserting the continuity of myth with life, Lowell centers himself in the night landscape, linking and equating himself with the moon (though a child's idea of the moon), an extreme projection of the visionary self into a natural sublime, a landscape of death:

> As in our Bibles, white-faced, predatory,
> the beautiful, mist-drunken hunter's moon ascends—
> a child could give it a face: two holes, two holes,
> my eyes, my mouth, between them a skull's no-nose—

The homiletic phrase "As in our Bibles" refers back to the opening two lines and the fifth line, and registers a continuity between the written word and the perceived experience. The ascent of the moon signals the rise of the ineffable in the figure of the natural sublime; it reflects the light of the poet's consciousness and refracts it as art, softened with mist. To a child, the full moon following the harvest moon does not signify sublimity or the muse, but a jack o'lantern. The skull-face, a characteristic New England graveyard icon, signifies death as the most drastic manifestation of the sublime. These four lines compress aesthetics, myth, and a child's imaginative visual naivete to capture the limitations decried earlier in the poem and resolve them through a unifying metaphor. But limited and limiting, imaginative vision dies with the visualizing mind. The hunter's moon is "predatory" not only because it signals the beginning of deer season but because it reminds Lowell of death and couples that absolute with beauty, mirroring in this grotesque pairing (derived from Stevens's "Sunday Morning")[12] the mortality of individual vision.

Complex modifiers and oxymorons empower the closing couplet:

"O there's a terrifying innocence in my face/drenched with the silver salvage of the mornfrost." Here both the innocence of the face and the metallic but ethereal fragility of the frosty dawn appear as passing states—one blending into the other, both to fade in the glare of daylight, in guilt and knowledge. The oxymoron "terrifying innocence" commemorates the guilt of Cain and acknowledges the most serious consequence of original sin—the ability to commit evil with full moral understanding of the deed and probable consequences. The jack o'lantern face, bearing Lowell's features, mirrors the description of the cows in the seventh line (bestial mindlessness) and points to Abel, who proved that "death is not remote" by becoming the first murder victim and first individual to die. Lowell thus begins his history by invoking the first killing to identify that loss of innocence with his visionary insistence on projecting the self into the landscape, an act of innocence deadly to himself and others. The "silver salvage"—rescued treasure; that is, the "mornfrost"—tints that innocence, but in melting will denude the self of its camouflage of metaphor; the poet will have to resolve the same problem over and over again.

The thematic organization of this sonnet-epic demonstrates the unity of past and present in terms of individual perceptions. "History" embodies Emerson's dictum that "all public facts are to be individualized, all private facts are to be generalized. Then at once History becomes fluid and true, and Biography deep and sublime."[13] This union of history and the individual resembles the more inclusive unity Lowell desires. Though his central concern—to heal the rift between life and art—remains nebulous and abstract, in the performance of the poem he takes concrete steps to achieve his ends. "History" projects the introspective self over the materials of traditional epic. The "innocence" in Lowell's face signifies the naïveté of this venture. Closing the volume with "End of a Year," Lowell more insistently asserts this, calling himself a *hero demens*, a crazed poet who thought that through compressed and straining sonnets he could unite the ideal with the quotidian.[14] The means, Lowell admits, are inadequate. A Rosetta stone—a "kind of verbal ruin," as Robert Pinsky calls it—is too crude, too eroded for his purpose.[15] History as such is an illusion, and Lowell's epic, as Pinsky argues, is actually elegiac, and mourns the unrealized possibilities of Lowell's "typescript," which instead of an epic that would heal all aesthetic, cultural, and moral disparities is only a year's worth of messy poems.

But in the three key poems following "History," Lowell traces an approach to this aesthetic ideal of a fully realized unifying vision. What Emerson calls "private facts," mingled with the archetypes of creation and the "public facts" of history, haunt these poems. Though in the end Lowell concedes that his sonnets are too crude to embody the ideal—the "bright sky" contrasted with the "carbon scarred with ciphers"[16]—his exploration of means clarifies his goals (to make the lucid self-realization of "End of a Year" plausible) and produces a sequence exciting in its struggle for aesthetic self-realization expressed in tense and energetic poems.

These poems show Lowell individualizing public facts, generalizing self-awareness, and challenging personal concerns with social complexities. "Man and Woman" deals with the problems of both poetic vision and physical seeing, as do many of the poems discussed here. Vision for Lowell always assumes metaphorical and literal dimensions. In "Man and Woman" he depicts the way his vision distances him from the world and directs his eccentric, myopic seeing, and the way his outrageous sensibility contrasts with his wife's calm. The peculiarity of Lowell's vision has distanced him from the myth of the Golden Age, the pastoral world of shepherd-poets, here trivialized in the banality of counting sheep in order to fall asleep. Problems of vision and seeing haunt the poem: even the sheep apparently suffer from imaginative or actual myopia, while Galileo's "eye," his telescope, is pointedly "glass," and the poet himself bears an "outrageous eye":

> The sheep start galloping in moon-blind wheels
> shedding a dozen ewes—is it faulty vision?
> Will we get them back . . . and everything,
> marriage and departure, departure and marriage,

village to family, family to village—
all the sheep's parents in geometric progression?
It's too much heart-ache to go back to that—
not life-enhancing like the hour a student
first discovers the unblemished Mother
on the Tuscan hills of Berenson,
or of Galileo, his great glass eye
admiring the spots on the erroneous moon. . . .
I watch this night out grateful to be alone
with my wife—your slow pulse, my outrageous eye.[17]

The poem links ordinary social and marital structures with the discoveries of astronomy, which are as mystical as religious visions, since they afford glimpses of inexplicable sublimity. Sitting up all night beside his sleeping wife, Lowell compares her calm with his vision, which in the face of the ordinary seems "outrageous"—violent, offensive, unrestrained, and self-tormenting. This closure reempowers a basic unit of force: the elementary motif of man and woman: her "slow pulse" the counter to his "outrageous eye." Though alienated from the pastoral myth, Lowell reasserts the importance of one of its central motifs to his vision, flawed though that vision may be.

"Bird?"—like Thoreau's parable of the hound, horse, and turtledove—casts the problem of the ineffable into animal imagery. Lowell finds the ineffable especially difficult to bring into focus because of his skepticism; he has to invent peculiarly harsh symbols, then in an almost juvenile way desecrate them. This desecration has characterized Lowell's poetry since *Land of Unlikeness*, and serves to help him avoid a fatuous embrace of the natural sublime. In Lowell's aesthetic, such a Wordsworthian gesture would diminish the role of the senses in encompassing the quotidian. Consequently, in "Bird?" (and hence the question mark) his symbol of the ineffable drops "excretions like a frightened snake."[18] The question is not whether this is actually a bird, but whether the ineffable it represents is real or a figment of metaphor.

Lowell in this poem assumes the role of a savage in nature. In a

dream he hunts a large ugly bird, hoping to divest it of symbolic qualities—its "crest, the crown"—so that he may "cross/ the perilous passage" between earthly and visionary states. By the end of the poem,
Lowell's "thoughts/stream on the water" as momentarily he becomes
one with nature—his actions and ideas, now that he has transcended
that passage and bridged the gap between art and life, having become
harmonious enough for "cleaning fish," harvesting nature for human
use. This last simile is ironic, though, and reminds us that this narrative bears the illogic of a dream, as noted in the poem's opening line,
"Adrift in my sweet sleep . . . ."

"Bird?" offers a myopic view of human relationships with beasts
and all they represent in the natural sublime, just as "Man and Woman"
presents an angular vision of a basic unit of force and commitment, distorted by the poet's self-limited vision and myopic sight. "Dawn," the
third poem in this trio, explores the landscape that man, woman, and
beast share, and attacks another important problem, the function of
landscape as a projection of the unconscious, the imagination, the
mind's eye. Though "Dawn" speaks in the first person, Lowell's voice
and ego are muted, represented as much by someone else's "crimson
blazer" than by dramatic presence. Yet Lowell creates, not merely reports, the scene:

> The building's color is penny-postcard pale
> as new wood—thirty stories, or a hundred?
> The distant view-windows glisten like little cells;
> on a wafer balcony, too thin to sit on,
> a crimson blazer hangs, a replica
> of my own from Harvard—hollow, blowing,
> shining its Harvard shield to the fall air. . . .
> Eve and Adam, adventuring from the ache
> of the first sleep, met forms less primitive
> and functional, when they gazed on the stone-ax
> and Hawaiian fig-leaf hanging from their fig-tree. . . .
> Nothing more established, pure and lonely,

> than the early Sunday morning in New York—
> the sun on high burning, and most cars dead.[19]

Primal Eden, the poem suggests, was less primitive and more practical than New York on Sunday morning, the cityscape insistently symbolic but devoid of human presence. This diminution of the actual present in favor of a mythic past creates a landscape of absence, rich with metaphor, that reminds Lowell of the emptiness and therefore the opportunities of the world at the time of creation. Here, though, creation does not function through God but through Lowell's perception. His adjectives—"penny-postcard pale," "hollow, blowing"—and imaginative juxtapositions give life to a mundane scene. Like Adam and Eve waking from nonexistence, Lowell, by perceiving and describing what is "established," whether by God or humanity, lends meaning to the scene. The Harvard blazer suggests the vacant potential of the unrealized self and unperceived scene. Where is the owner of the blazer? He cannot safely step onto the tiny, flimsy balcony, but has sent his clothing where he cannot go. Lowell, on the other hand, from a distance freely enters the scene. But however rich the symbols seem, they apparently remain empty as the blazer: New York stands as lifeless as Eden before Adam and Eve, the sun a powerful but pointless emblem of a sublimity no longer (or not yet) relevant to this violated landscape. Complex and ambiguous, this poem draws the imaginative self into the landscape that it may invest the scene with meaning. Cultural primitivism does not serve this process, since it fails to fully enlist the material reality—which is more than metaphorical—that engrosses Lowell's seeing.

Lowell's reliance on vision and the attempt to shape seeing to imagination determine both the structure (the associations, the metaphorical leaps, the narration) and the scale of these sonnets. Myopia limits the sweep of his seeing, while the requirement for concrete, fully felt images forces his imaginative vision to correspond to his physically limited seeing. Thus even poems about biblical subjects, which are conventionally allegorical, depend on sensory imagery not merely for rhetorical effect but as the aesthetic and dramatic fulcrums of the poems. For Lowell, not only the generative impulse but the essential substance of the poems comes from what he once called "some little image."[20]

"In Genesis" demonstrates how the "little image" shapes Lowell's sonnets and, more importantly, demonstrates how the intensity of his seeing infuses his imagination, here lending an eccentric tone to his replay of biblical drama. This is one of Lowell's principal methods of individualizing "public facts." "In Genesis" demonstrates the power of detail in dramatic movement by using imagery as another poem might use narrative:

> Blank. A camel blotting up the water.
> God with whom nothing is design or intention.
> In the Beginning, the Sabbath could last a week,
> God grumbling secrecies behind Blue Hill. . . .
> The serpent walked on foot like us in Eden;
> glorified by the perfect Northern exposure,
> Eve and Adam knew their nakedness,
> a discovery to be repeated many times . . .
> in joyless stupor? . . . Orpheus in Genesis
> hacked words from brute sound, and taught men English,
> plucked all the flowers, deflowered all the girls
> with the overemphasis of a father.
> He used too many words, his sons killed him,
> dancing with grateful gaiety round the cookout.[21]

"In Genesis" compares the shapelessness and subjectivity of God to the human discovery of the power to imitate the subjectivity and shape the world with words. Thus it places imaginative vision over the ineffable as a means to knowledge. The key images embody Lowell's concept of creation, both as the poet's act and as God's. Following the emphatic "Blank."—the birth of consciousness—the presence of the dirty and bestial camel underscores the material miracle of nature and creation, while the minor drama of its appearance suggests the essential role of seeing. Creation, after all, is what is *seen*. The water, possibly a mirage (like so much vision), disappears as the camel (the product of seeing) attempts to make use of it, calling into question the relationship between seeing (the actuality of the camel) and vision (the idea rather than the actuality of creation), while undermining those very categories.

The phrase "taught men English" points to the allegorical dimension of the poem. Here Lowell unfolds the brutal relationship among poets, which is the opposite of that between Cronus and his children. The ephebes devour the pioneer poet and delight in their cannibalism. But the original poet, though he goes too far and gets eaten, bears the honor of breaking new ground, deflowering all the young women. The poet of genesis, the first cause, enjoys a new world in which reality, vision, creation, and seeing are freshly defined. Eden, Lowell suggests, is Maine, and he is Orpheus, who will be cannibalized by his followers, his children, his fellow poets, and, as it were, his critics.

This bleak if comic view of the poet's fate accords with Lowell's skepticism and the negative emotional impulse from which he almost always writes. It also concurs with his practice. Lowell, himself a cannibal poet practicing textual ingestion, does not, despite the claims of some critics, dine off portions of his own body; instead he dines deeply, lovingly, and even with gaiety on the poems of others, digesting and disgorging them as his own. This is of course a process sanctioned by the major modernist poets, Pound and Eliot. He who eats Orpheus becomes Orpheus. Lowell maintains his position as the poet of Genesis by re-creating in his "imitations" the poems of those who have preceded him. He imposes his imaginative vision on theirs, as he imposes it on biblical imagery, and reduces mystery to the deceptively simple imagery of physical seeing.

But Lowell is not readily convinced that what he sees corresponds to anything. The problem of "description without significance" and the complexities of verbatim transcription and its contrast with a more audacious and inspired directness haunts the poems of *History*, most notably the sonnet on Albert Ryder. Ryder's paintings confound imaginative vision and seeing in a shifting, uneasy flux of ideal and concrete forms. His overworked, thickly painted canvases embalm a vision that sharply contrasts with the quickly painted if often similarly tortured abstractions of more contemporary art. Lowell's poem on Ryder occurs in a sequence addressed to Elizabeth Bishop. Her poetic vision resembles the new painting to the extent that it is casual, but she takes care to make "the casual perfect." But like Ryder, she retains her work for years, reworking and revising. Like his, her smallest creations bear heavy significance:

> The new painting must live on iron rations,
> rushed brushstrokes, indestructible paint-mix,
> fluorescent lofts instead of French *plein air.*
> Albert Ryder let his crackled amber moonscapes
> ripen in sunlight. His painting was repainting,
> his tiniest work weighs heavy in the hand.
> Who is killed if the horseman never cry halt?
> Have you seen an inchworm crawl on a leaf,
> cling to the very end, revolve in air,
> feeling for something to reach to something? Do
> you still hang your words in air, ten years
> unfinished, glued to your notice board, with gaps
> or empties for the unimaginable phrase—
> unerring Muse who makes the casual perfect?[22]

By naming Bishop "unerring Muse," the final line makes her inspirer as well as inspired. Whether she functions as Lowell's muse or solely as her own remains unclear. The compliment, however, interestingly contrasts with Eliot's description of Pound as *"il miglior fabbro."* Lowell honors Bishop's craft, but credits inspiration with making "the casual perfect." Vision, then, is manufactured as well as intuited, but only the Muse (in this instance, the spark of inspiration in Bishop, the Muse of her own poetry) brings perfection (a vision of the ideal poem) to craft.

Without inspiration, and without accommodating the gap between the ideal and the actual work of art, all artists, like Ryder, would leave their work unfinished. The poem strikes a warning note. Does making "the casual perfect" justify allowing poems to lie around unfinished for ten years? Lowell refuses such insouciance. Further, in refusing to prolong his work to make it perfect, he resists trying to make it conform to his vision of the ideal poem. Even more dependent on physical seeing than Ryder, more committed to immediacy than Bishop, he avoids the trap of the ideal.

The ideal usually ensnares visionaries who abandon the quotidian and lack a footing in the natural world. Like most romantics, as James McIntosh and others have pointed out in discussing the nineteenth-century American Renaissance, Lowell loves his own imagination more than nature.[23] The imagination characteristically yearns for the ineffable ideal, for absolutes. But like Thoreau, Lowell detects the trap, and will succumb to neither absorption into nature nor the vicissitudes of the imagination. His concern with what is physically seen, within the limitations of his myopia, helps him check his imaginative vision short of untenable abstraction. While he remains alert to the ideal poem of the mind, he will not allow it to refute the actual poems he can write, gather in books, and publish. Like Wallace Stevens, Lowell seems to believe that "one of the essential conditions to the writing of poetry is impetus. That is a reason for thinking that to be a poet at all one ought to be a poet constantly."[24] Lowell's idea of inspiration is not the axiomatic bolt of lightning striking at random intervals. What good is that lightning unless when it strikes one is sitting at one's desk in front of a blank sheet of paper with pencil in hand? The poet needs to work constantly, regularly at his trade, as Lowell worked daily and furiously to write the sonnets that became *History*.

The process of linking and comparing differing artistic sensibilities points to Lowell's central concern with resolving dichotomies: history and art, life and art, vision and seeing, his life and the art of others, his poems and other people's lives. The poems that deal with the problems of vision—like "Dante 1," "Thoreau 2," "Orestes' Dream," and "Under the Moon"—examine the role of individual sensibility in Lowell's lyric history and Emersonian theories of subjective history.

"Fears of Going Blind (for Wyndham Lewis)" is one of the key poems on the relationship between the two kinds of vision that obsess Lowell. This sonnet confounds the threat of the loss of poetic vision with that of going blind:

> El Greco could paint a thunderstorm reflected
> on a cufflink; Americans reflect
> the space they peopled. . . . I see non sequitur:
> *Watch the stoplights, they are leopards' eyes;*
> *what's the word for God, if he has four legs? . . .*
> Even the artist's vision picks up dirt,
> the jelly behind the eyeball will leak out,
> you will live with constellations of flusters,
> comet-flashes from the outer corners;
> see the failed surgeon exit with a smile,
> they will not let you move your head for weeks,
> your wife will hold up gin in a teacup to your mouth,
> you will suck from a crooked straw—what depresses
> me is they'll actually take my eyeball out.[25]

Wyndham Lewis, the writer and painter to whom this sonnet is dedicated and addressed (and who speaks the last line and a half), was one of the most independent and eccentric of the great modernists. His early painting, with its fractured, hard-edged style, might exemplify the "non sequitur" Lowell sees. "Even the artist's vision picks up dirt," but Lowell refers both to imaginative vision and a serious physical problem; as if Lewis, who had relied on the inner eye of inspiration, were forced by the material world to examine his psyche with the failing physical eye.

A similar difficulty with dirt in the eye figures in a key poem in *For the Union Dead*. "Eye and Tooth," in its self-conscious but effective symbolism, is one of Lowell's most Rimbaud-like poems. Like "Fears of

Going Blind," it confounds the problem of failing eyesight with murky or fading artistic vision. As Vereen Bell argues, "Lowell is as ready to deglamorize the artist's vision as he is history, that vision's subject matter, and to conclude that the vision is necessarily flawed or doomed."[26] In the earlier poems, Lowell equates this failing vision with a faltering memory and inspiration. The opening stanza of "Eye and Tooth," with its allusion to Saint Paul, its careful alternation of consonance and assonance, seems hard and formal compared with the equally apocalyptic but more conversational sonnet:

> My whole eye was sunset red,
> the old cut cornea throbbed,
> I saw things darkly,
> as through an unwashed goldfish globe.[27]

Explaining this poem's background and its reference to 1 Corinthians 13:12, Lowell emphasizes the connection between physical seeing and imaginative vision: "I tried contact lenses. . . . But they were absolute hell in New York because little bits of filth, grit, would get under them. . . . The cornea was all red from being cut. . . . And the whole poem is about sight, really, seeing that way—and Saint Paul's thing of seeing through a glass darkly, and so forth—seeing things as they are."[28] Paul actually said (in the King James Version) that "now we see in a mirror, darkly; but then face to face; now I know in part, but then shall I know even as also I am known." So seeing things as they are becomes seeing one's self and attaining a simultaneous self-knowledge and larger knowledge.

Paul's visionary self-knowledge is difficult to obtain, though, and many competing forms of vision and seeing exist. The early lines of "Fears of Going Blind" present opposed ways of seeing: El Greco's obsession with perfection represents one; the other is the American hunger for the oversized in life and landscape. Lowell confides his own situation; he sees in a disorderly, illogical manner. In italicized quotations, he offers two examples of the "artist's vision," which materializes but distorts objects and concepts, and sees in riddles. From the general idea of artistic vision Lowell derives the particulars of his own problems, and finally, Lewis's genuine physical dilemma. The personal and bald statement with which the poem concludes resembles conventional prose in cadence and syntax, but is a glimpse of the actuality empowered by the poem as a whole.

In this climactic moment of clear vision and physical fear, Lewis abandons his "artist's vision" and looks ahead, without illusion, to the forthcoming surgery. "Eye and Tooth," similarly withholding its moment of self-realization, remains committed to its symbolist approach until the last line, "I'm tired. Everyone's tired of my turmoil." With naked assertions of fear and defeat, these poems attempt through the exigencies of drama to justify their fascination with physical problems. The ending of "Eye and Tooth," while psychologically effective, is apologetic and self-effacing, while the sonnet shifts unexpectedly into a plaintive tone. Also surprisingly, it shifts in the penultimate line from second-person address to the first person, as Lowell and Lewis seem almost to merge their voices. In a shock of dramatic recognition, this merger facilitates the poem's confrontation with the physical horror of the situation; but it perhaps calls too much attention to the randomness that has led to this climactic statement, leaving the greater part of the human drama undepicted, unexplored. Fear of blindness is universal. Confounding fears for physical sight with the fear of the loss of mental or imaginative vision intensely dramatizes Lowell's commitment to the vision that makes poetry possible and revises histories into *History*.

Imaginative vision and physical seeing together penetrate the surfaces of particulars to expose their hierarchical relationships. Lowell is a romantic in the narrow but useful terms James McIntosh has applied to Thoreau: "He is continually fascinated by the relation of the poetic mind to the external world."[29] The consequent relationship with nature is complex and problematical. By contending that Lowell rejects sublimity in favor of a vision of myopic but concrete poetic realism, I do not mean that he rejects it once and for all. On the contrary, sublimity and the ineffable frequently tempt him as he detects them in nature and the ethereal complexities of the imagination, just as they once tempted him to become a Roman Catholic and confront the problem of the Incarnation, which, he once claimed, "under examination . . . becomes more probable, after a while you believe."[30]

Historians of American art in recent years have found luminism the visual arts counterpart of transcendentalism in literature. Luminism manifests a certain distrust of nature, revealed by its tendency toward simplified and linear structure; but like Thoreau's writing it paradoxically counterpoints this distrust with a fresh regard for the elements of nature, especially the sea, rocks, and the clear light of the sky. In "Shipwreck Party" Lowell contrasts luminist painting—a direct aesthetic approach to the sublime—with the harsh mechanics of the modern quotidian. To resolve the contrast, the poem offers Lowell's own aesthetic of abrupt contrast, angular vision, and odd modifiers attuned to the flux and ugliness of modern life and art:

> One misses Emerson drowned in Luminism,
> his vast serenity of emptiness;
> and FitzHugh Lane painting a schooner moored in Castine,
> its bright flywings fixed in the topographical
> severity of a world reworked as glass.
> Tools are honest functions, and even toys;
> you puzzled out small devices, mini-motors,
> set children and parents trotting in your trash,
> you danced dressed as a beercan, crosscut, zany thing—
> wit and too much contrivance for our yacht club brawl.
> After the party, I heard your unmuffled car
> loop the town, ten or twelve laps a minute—
> a village is too small to lose a date
> or need a hatchet to split hairs.[31]

Like luminism, Lowell's poem recognizes the ineffable in terms of silence, emptiness, and horizontality, and suggests that although these qualities have aesthetic merit, they stifle the individual voice, drowning Emerson in the very art that embodies his directives. In dramatic contrast, modern mechanical life fends off the ineffable with beercan costumes and unmuffled cars. Neither the cold aesthetic nor the new technology allows sufficient scope to depict the "distinctiveness of [the] human state." The "unmuffled car," unbridled technology, speaks for the extremes of the modernist aesthetic. The noise of machines has filled "the serenity of emptiness," demonstrating that the luminist aesthetic fails to account for everything. These artists who rework the world as "glass" ignore flux and change, and therefore become its victims. "Tools are honest functions, even toys": they require intelligent use, not "wit and too much contrivance." The village doesn't need a hatchet to "split hairs" because its modest scale magnifies insignificant events, and it is easy to go "too far." Insults to "honest function" give outsized, exaggerated offense. One unmuffled car encompasses the whole village in its swath of disturbance.

Some of this sonnet's power comes from the contrast between the high mimetic tone of the first five lines and the low mimetic of "you danced dressed as a beercan." But its larger effect derives from the richly humorous confrontation of life and art in which life literally imitates art. The person addressed by the poem is an artwork manqué, a comic personification of modernism to contrast with the serenity and severity of luminism. The latter's "emptiness" clashes with the landscape of modern Castine, disrupted and yet defined by the looping, noisy car; silence characterizes the luminist landscape, while reckless individualism, expressed as noise, generates the modernist artwork. Of course neither modernism nor luminism accurately represents Emerson's strong individualism—they smother it, one with noise, the other with silence. This for Lowell is the irony of the aesthetic of Emerson and luminism. High modernism doesn't argue for subjectivity but condemns it, though in practice modernist aesthetics foster the most outlandish and unsupportable forms of individualism. This confusion of principle and practice helps give the poem its comic air.

In various poems, Lowell questions and tests the capabilities of his aesthetic, but in "Shipwreck Party" he extends his doubts to other aesthetics of widely differing characteristics. Despite the self-confidence that keeps him writing, Lowell worries about his dependence on the innate limitations and mechanical qualities of language and poetry. In several poems (besides those discussed here, see, for example, "Off Central Park") he uses painting as a metaphor for the "description without significance"—an impossibility that frightens and attracts him. Painting, like language, imposes considerable mechanical hindrances to realizing a vision. "Lévi-Strauss in London" argues that in the light of this technical problem the artist cannot and should not attempt unattainable perfection. Like Lowell, Lévi-Strauss sees the world imaginatively, metaphorically. And again like Lowell, Lévi-Strauss encounters difficulties in expressing his perceptions. The resultant structuralist theory and the jargon it generates remind Lowell of the artificiality and mechanical difficulties of art. The complexity of the linguistic situation generated by encountering Lévi-Strauss exemplifies the confusion and imperfection of the world. Lowell personified this flaw in the world order as a case of "severed head":

> Lévi-Straus[s], seeing two green plants in a cleft
> of a cliff choosing diverse ammonites,
> imagined a crevasse of millennia spanned—
> when he told me this in English, our hostess spoke French;
> I left the party with a severed head.
> Since France gave the English their tongue, most civilized
> Englishmen can muck along in French. . . .
> I was so tired of camp and decoration,
> so dog-tired of wanting social hope—
> is *structuralism* the bridge from Marx to death?
> Cézanne left his spine sticking in the landscape,
> his slow brush sucked the resin from the pines;
> Picasso's bullfighter's wrist for foil and flare—
> they cannot fill the crack in everything God made.[32]

In "The Severed Head" (in *For the Union Dead*) Lowell explores his poetic career, following this visionary chronicle through an allegory of sleep and dreaming. A dream-figure (or "alter ego," as some critics have termed it) serves as Lowell's instructor and speaks for the repressed self. R. K. Meiners argues that the "confrontation with the alter ego" of which "The Severed Head" is an example is "obsessive" with Lowell and Allen Tate.[33] Such insistence on the psychological significance of the dream-figure obscures its aesthetic function. The freedom the dream-figure embodies is to create, not to run amok. Stephen Yenser respects the complexity of the poem and understands it (correctly, I believe) to be about the "poet-artist and his relationship to his material."[34] Whether he is the poet Lowell wants to be, or the one he fears becoming, is hard to decide. The dream-figure suggests the desirability of creative freedom, yet the image of

> a pen
> that left no markings on the page, yet dripped
> a red ink dribble on us, as he pressed
> the little strip of plastic tubing clipped
> to feed it from his heart[35]

depicts an undisciplined sentimentalism rather than a generous emotional reach like Whitman's. Indecision shapes the poem by imposing a greater emotional uncertainty than the formal gestures of the poem can contain or resolve. Lowell cannot free himself from the aesthetic consequences of his inhibitions and rescue the poem from self-constriction.

"Lévi-Strauss in London" presents a different problem, but Lowell's reaction to the tension between his visionary and his quotidian egos—metaphorically to lop off his own head—is similar. The problem is the world's imperfection, "the crack in everything God made." Neither Picasso nor Cézanne could fill that crack. Structuralism, Lévi-Strauss's intellectual systemization of anthropological data (long since extended to the humanities) offers little more than a way to correlate theory and prophecy with inevitability. The act of auto-decapitation speaks both for Lowell's confusion and for the imperfections and dissociations of the larger world.

The sonnet enjoys a colloquial, broadly referential freedom unavailable to the rather cramped though much longer "Severed Head." Its concern with the proper entry to landscape, exemplified by Cézanne and distorted by Lévi-Strauss's reductive science, opens the poem to larger problems of vision and creation. Neither Cézanne's intimacy with reality nor Picasso's radical, fluent style can represent perfection, since their visions necessarily reflect the flawed landscape they recreate or mirror. Their imperfections and greatness support Lowell's claim that "a poem should be imperfect" to remain open to all possibilities.[36] This unavoidable imperfection partly explains how and why Lowell's poetry distances the ineffable to which it is drawn. Imperfect art cannot and should not attempt to embody the ideal, while an obsessively perfected creation dies of fixed and glassy-eyed vision, cut off from the world. But Lowell does acknowledge the existence and attraction of the ideal, characteristically if naively, by contrasting the social or individual sensibility with nature.

"For Frank Parker 2" contrasts the sea with Lowell's bombastic juvenilia: natural chaos shrugging off his immature efforts to impose order on it. Chaos triumphs when the ocean dies (withdrawing its winds) and Lowell and his prep-school friend Frank Parker, a pair of amateur sailors, find themselves becalmed, stranded, caught in a current, and threatened with shipwreck. The last threat, however, is a metaphor for full commitment to art, the equivalent of Rimbaud's *bateau-ivre*. Lowell's juvenile lines are merely decorative: they describe the seascape, but fail to engage its actual dangers. Emphasizing danger rather than pleasure, shipwreck will impose a stark lesson in the ineffable's powerful link to reality. Echoing "Down the Nile," "Achilles to the Dying Lykaon," and "Helen,"[37] the poem engages the difficult relationship between the poet's vision and the landscape, and the consequences of effective art:

> The *Pisspot,* our sailing dory, could be moved
> by sail and oar in tune . . . immovable
> by either singly. The ocean died. We rocked
> debating who was skipper, then shipped oars;
> as we drifted I tried to put our rapture in verse:
> *When sunset rouged the sun-embittered surf.*
> This was the nearest we got to Melville's Nantucket,
> though we'd been artist cottagers a month. . . .
> The channel gripped our hull, we could not veer,
> the boat swam shoreward flying our wet shirts,
> like a birchlog shaking off loose bark and shooting:
> *And the surf thundered fireworks on the dunes.*
> This was the moment to choose, as school warned us,
> whether to wreck or ride in tow to port.[38]

The echoes of other poems from *History* are partly ironic, but all the more vivid for their tonal contrast with Lowell's novice work, which derives from and unintentionally parodies classical models (Lowell majored in classics at Kenyon College). The structure of this sonnet turns on shifts in tone and imagery marked by the absurd quotations. After the bombastic "*When sunset . . .*" the poem shifts to a deadpan narrative. Following five conversational, unrhetorical lines, the even worse line "*And the surf thundered fireworks on the dunes*" introduces the comically didactic and homiletic closure. The foolishly rhetorical quotations, which mark structural and tonal shifts, provide further evidence of how autobiography becomes exemplary in recapitulating and summarizing the history of poetic vision and human feeling.

In the penultimate line, the phase "the moment to choose" links the sailing metaphor to Baudelaire's *Invitation au Voyage* and Rimbaud's *le bateau ivre* as expressions of the romantic identification of a voyage with the devotion of one's life to art. "For Frank Parker 2" suggests that while at St. Mark's School Parker and Lowell were warned that to choose art would mean to "wreck," while a safer life would mean "riding in tow to port." Instead they, like Rimbaud, chose to ride the drunken boat of art and romanticism. Lowell extends his borrowed metaphor by juxtaposing it with his inept early verse to reveal the gulf between his youthful ideals of art and his actual skills. The allusion to Rimbaud reveals Lowell's commitment to the freedom and anarchy of art; Rimbaud chose to "wreck" and ended his career at an age when Lowell had scarcely begun. But the shared metaphor does not merely denigrate Lowell in comparison to Rimbaud. It strategically yokes together allusions to Melville, Rimbaud, and other voyagers to assert the essential unity and continuance of the arts.

Frank Parker's role in Lowell's life and poetry is important and still unexplored. Parker's title-page drawing for *History* is startling and recondite. It points to Lowell's obsession with the ineffable in various manifestations materially relevant to historical subject matter. Death, a skeleton, is part of that experience with the unknown. The moon and sun, the natural muse and the absorption of the self in reductive and fossilizing flames (as in "1930's 5"), contrast with the artificial sublimity of classical ruins, which never attain the status of the ineffable. The passage of time, the chasm between humanity and nature, the mutability of works, the inevitability of death are all present, but the theme of the picture is meditation; the living figure centers the composition, his consciousness dominates the scene. Lowell's book is an act of meditation, and its method is its substance as well. The man who has shed his breastplate and dropped his sword stands on the edge of the ineffable, his defenses put behind him. Whether his apparent resolution would solve his dilemma and heal the gap between life and art remains uncertain, but in Lowell's world seems doubtful.

Skill, as "Frank Parker 2" and other poems about artist and writer friends of Lowell argue, is a tool for survival, which in Lowell's case requires making effective if imperfect poems. The poem that most fully engages its subject foils the temptations of nature, avoids the trap of the ineffable, overcomes the limitations of both vision and seeing. In the various concerns of *History,* that engagement assumes many shapes and wields innumerable strategies within the constricted means Lowell has chosen. In the poems discussed here, chosen because they work close to the essential center of *History*—its obsession with the relationship between life and art—that engagement is self-conscious, self-reflexive, shaped by the problems of perception and the making of art. Lowell is alert to these problems. In "End of a Year," one of the most beautiful poems of his career, he draws together the three problems I have been discussing, and in vividly metaphorical terms bemoans the necessity of art's imperfection and the impossibility of resolving infinite problems with finite language wielded by semicrazed poets:

> These conquered kings pass furiously away;
> gods die in flesh and spirit and live in print,
> each library a misquoted tyrant's home.
> A year runs out in the movies, must be written
> in bad, straightforward, unscanning sentences—
> stamped, trampled, branded on backs of carbons,
> lines, words, letters nailed to letters, words, lines—
> the typescript looks like a Rosetta Stone. . . .
> One more annus mirabilis, its hero *hero demens,*
> ill-starred of men and crossed by his fixed stars,
> running his ship past sound-spar on the rocks. . . .
> The slush-ice on the east bank of the Hudson
> is rose-heather in the New Year sunset;
> bright sky, bright sky, carbon scarred with ciphers.[39]

The complexities and limitations of imagination and seeing, Lowell notes, impose limitations on writing. His poetry cannot adequately capture the movie-like passage of history—cannot, even with a Rosetta stone, translate history into the living tissue of a poem. Lowell, a mad hero, finds his attempt to make an epic merely foolish. But the landscape and the temptation of the sublime stimulate his imagination and his seeing, and engage the reader with the complexity rather than simply the bald fact of significance. The "conquered kings," the facts of history, are not, as Lowell now makes clear, the real issue of *History*.

Writing is his real subject—writing and the year of writing just past. In its final poem, *History* funnels down to a confrontation among the passing actualities of history, Lowell's limited vision and writing, the phenomenal fact of his life, and the sublime landscape of the ineffable.

Lowell concedes that his own poems are flawed and in many ways inadequate. Like the Rosetta stone they contain a key to knowledge; but like Ryder's canvases they are overworked, and their artifice wryly contrasts with the natural world that duplicates or imitates those same scarred carbons in the sensuous winter sunset. No more than Cézanne's landscapes can these "bad, straightforward, unscanning sentences" cure the world's or even the poet's woes. Instead, they construct a parallel world, necessarily as flawed as the real one. Rosetta stones enable us to read what is otherwise unintelligible, so the simile qualifies Lowell's self-criticism by asserting the interpretive power of his vision. Though the Rosetta stone is badly eroded and difficult to read, its corruption is its message—a sad comment on history and landscape and language, yet a viable emblem of the survival of literacy.

The palimpsest embodies Lowell's accomplishment in an unfinished but vital arrangement. It remains flexible, unfixed, forever subject to further revision. By embracing the palimpsest as a literary-historical archetype he can claim not only his own poems but all of history, including the work of poets before him, as drafts to rewrite, translate, reinterpret. Imaginative vision, coupled with rough and energetic language, reshapes and even revises history. By making the entire breadth of history part of his life and poetry, Lowell chooses Emersonian inclusiveness over Thoreau's requirement for a "simple and sincere account of his own life"; but he adheres to Thoreau's plain-style aesthetic admonition: "It is, after all, always the first person that is speaking," acknowledging that regardless of his ambitions the author must be the *hero demens* of his own life.[40]

The despair of "End of a Year" is the realization that an enterprise begun as a projection of individual consciousness over all human thought and history has narrowed to the naked fact of a year's struggle over imperfect poems. Looking back at that year, Lowell now sees himself a madman for making such a grandiose gesture. Still later (in 1977) he comments on these sonnets: "Obscurity and confusion came when I tried to cram too much in the short space. Quite often I wasn't obscure or discontinuous. I had a chance such as I had never had before, or probably will again, to snatch up and verse the marvelous varieties of the moment. I think perfection (I mean outward coherence not inspiration) was never so difficult."[41] Struggling with the limits of form, the difficulty of making his materials cohere and ordering his vision, Lowell still honors the ideal embodied in the sunset, the healing wholeness to which his poems aspire, which signifies the union of art and life as disparities and dualisms of all sorts disappear.

Focusing vision and seeing, finding concrete expression for unwieldy and insistent abstractions, and scaling drama to landscape concern all poets. Lowell's special difficulty lies in valuing process over product, inspiration over coherence. *History*, in Lowell's unsurprising estimation, fails to cohere. In the end, it remains what Lowell called the first version of his sonnet sequence, a "notebook of a year."[42] Yet as I have tried to show here, *History* engages in a brave and exciting aesthetic struggle with both ancient and contemporary problems and materials. In its frequent flashes of brilliance, and especially in its final poem, in which despair and vision so eloquently coexist, *History*, of all of Lowell's works, most fully engages his humanistic concerns, his aesthetic commitment, and even his corrosive skepticism. And it most fully delineates his faith in poetry as source of personal engagement and social values, tempering that skepticism to render in modestly visionary terms the debased and dehumanizing culture he so clearly sees.

9 | Borrowed Visions

ACENTRAL PROBLEM IN *HISTORY*, ONE THAT PER-
tains to Lowell's use of "imitations" derived from Horace,
Dante, Baudelaire, and other non-English-language poets, is
to define a relationship between the world and the poet larger
than the problematic one between his art and his life. This wider vision,
which could be called epic, resists the autobiographical thrust of Lowell's poetry. Although he has successfully engaged American historical
themes in "For the Union Dead" and "After the Surprising Conversions," and confronted the political moment in "Waking Early Sunday
Morning" and "Fall 1961," he has yet to fulfill his desire for a poetry as
wholly inclusive as Dante's theologically anchored vision, or Homer's
martial grasp of emotional and political struggle.

Merely reading the work of poets with differing historical senses
doesn't satisfy Lowell. He has to appropriate their voices and stances
and merge his sensibility with theirs. Fully to assimilate them, he requires the poems of the past to correspond with some shade or tone of
his own voice. With a frankly utilitarian poetic, he imposes himself on
these poems in an approach to translation that is both critical and creative, and makes them "something living . . . a Person," his own flesh,

his own poems.[1] The personal anthology of imitations in *History*, like that in *Imitations*, resuscitates as personae some of the poets who have contributed to Lowell's historical vision and mental image of the ideal poem. The difference between the earlier collection and the new one is the degree of assimilation. Instead of at least roughly honoring the versification of the original, Lowell now slots every poet, every poem, into the same form or formulation: the unrhymed sonnet. Asking what he gains from these poets—in aesthetic exemplar and subject matter—reveals the ways in which he traces the minutiae of history threaded through each poet's self-created life. Baudelaire, Rimbaud, Dante, and certain other poets express more fully, in terms unavailable to Lowell except through rewriting their work, worlds of experience and imagination vital to the fulfillment of his aesthetic and to the completion of his vision of history.

Baudelaire, in Lowell's versions, confronts his distrust of the romantic sublime and his narcissism. His delicate balance of intuition and craft, ego and the phenomenal world, generates a poetry empowered, like Lowell's, by the tensions between sublimity and corruption, spirit and flesh. These conflicting and coexistent poles define Baudelaire's aesthetic as well as his subject matter. In his journals, Baudelaire asks himself, "What is the modern conception of art," and answers himself, "To create a suggestive magic including at the same time object and subject, the world outside the artist and the artist himself," then concludes, "What is a poet if not a translator, a decipherer?"[2] This chimes with Emerson's idea that the poet of the past has written "a confession true for one and true for all."[3]

Though he shares many concerns with his immediate predecessor, Rimbaud with his brashness rejects Baudelaire's self-doubting posture. With his heroic and reckless descent into hell, Rimbaud embraces the role of visionary poet, aloof from yet critically engaged with the world. For him this role is the only viable reply to social, religious, and cultural decay. Given this stance, the dissociation of the poet from society is a simple necessity, not a cause for intellectual dismay. To overcome this dissociation, in his most famous poem he centers the poet in the world through the consuming metaphor of the voyage, a vision of sensuous freedom and emotional fulfillment.

By including these sonnets in a context (unlike that of *Imitations*) that is an autobiographical recasting of history, Lowell allows them to speak wholly for himself. That is, they are fictional versions of the originals, and insofar as they represent Baudelaire or Rimbaud they do so not in a literary-historical context but in the self-created historical fiction of *History*. Therefore I will not consider which parts of these poems are analogous (and they are never more than that) to the French originals and which are entirely of Lowell's devising. His imitations are allusive rather than schematic in their reference to their models. Critics who complain about his lack of fidelity or respect have to consider where to draw the line between originality and revision. For instance, when Eliot quotes Baudelaire in *The Waste Land* he is clearly alluding; but when he rewrites Baudelaire in English (lines 60–75, ending with the quotation in French), he is incorporating Baudelaire's sensibility into his own through a kind of ventriloquism in which the spirit of the nineteenth-century poet has entered Eliot. Lowell works in a similar way, incorporating what in *Imitations* strikes some critics merely as confusion between translation and creation into a context as absorptive, original, and ambitious as Eliot's poem. To condemn Lowell's freewheeling versions in *Imitations* on the grounds that he presents them under the names of their original authors and therefore raises certain expectations is one thing; but in claiming these poems more wholly for himself in *History*, Lowell commits himself to the same principle of reclamation-through-context by which Eliot makes Baudelaire his own. Lowell now asks that this material be considered as part of a whole for which he, not Baudelaire, Dante, Horace, or any other poet, is responsible.

To accommodate the ego of the poet and the stubborn phenomenal world in a single expansive vision is Lowell's Baudelairean goal. Early, in many of the poems of *Land of Unlikeness* and *Lord Weary's Castle*,

Lowell echoes Baudelaire's simultaneous visions of urban corruption and the romantic sublime. Now in the two Baudelaire sonnets of *History* he embraces the French poet's terror of the insensate void, the "nightmare" of the absolute that disrupts the tensions that make poetry possible by engulfing the poet in a protective insensibility. "Baudelaire 1: The Abyss," a version of Baudelaire's "Le gouffre," identifies that void as "Pascal's Abyss" and imagines Pascal to be a romantic contemplating the nothingness beyond individual sensibility:

> Pascal's abyss moved with him as he moved—
> all void, alas—activity, desires, words!
> above, below me, only space and shoal,
> the spaces, the bat-wing of insanity.
> I cuddle the insensible blank air,
> I envy the void insensibility
> and fear to sleep as one fears a great hole.
> On my mind the raised hand of the Ultimate
> traces his nightmare, truceless, uniform.
> I have cultivated this hysteria
> with terror and enjoyment till I see
> only the infinite at every window,
> vague, captivating, dropping who knows where . . .
> Ah never to escape from being and number![4]

The infinite, however "captivating," assumes a fearful aspect here. Large abstractions—the Ultimate, the infinite, the romantic sublime, the ineffable—attract Lowell's Baudelaire, but in their presence he fears sleep, the great surrender, "as one fears a great hole." Partly, it is vagueness, an aesthetic taboo, that distresses him. He requires "activity, desires, words." This Baudelaire, contemplating his difficulty on Lowell's behalf, cannot afford to escape being and number, regardless of how alluring the prospect, any more than he can afford to escape his own emotions.

"Baudelaire 2. Recollection," a version of "Recueillement," opens with an apostrophe to emotion. This is another instance of a poetic strategy, like the appeal to the Ultimate, above, that Lowell would not use on his own. In the guise of an "imitation," he can embrace a solipsism that otherwise, despite his autobiographical bent, is alien to his sensibility:

> Be calm, my Sorrow, you must move with care.
> You asked for evening, it descends, it's here;
> Paris is coffined in its atmosphere,
> bringing some relief and others care.
> Now while the common multitude strips bare,
> feels pleasure's cat o'nine tails on its back,
> accumulating remorse at the great bazaar—
> give me your hand, my Sorrow. Let's stand back,
> back from these people. Look, the defunct years, dressed
> in period costume crowd the balconies of the sky.
> Regret emerges smiling from the river,
> the sun, worked overtime, sleeps beneath an arch . . .
> and like a long shroud stretched from east to west—
> listen, my Dearest, hear the sweet night march![5]

In addressing sorrow as he would a lover, Lowell as Baudelaire endears his grief to himself. Negative emotions typically engender Lowell's best poems, as he acknowledged by remarking that "in remembering, in recording, thanks to the gift of the Muse, it is the pain,"[6] a genuinely Baudelairean sentiment. Evening, the conventional setting of this emotion, has "coffined" Paris in a gloom that fosters the apposite reactions of hedonism and remorse. Baudelaire thrives on the paradox, withholding himself to maintain, despite his narcissism, the objectivity required of the poet. A vision of prophetic proportions rewards him for remaining aloof from the pleasure-seeking mob. He sees time, the great abstraction, dressed in "period costumes" in the sky, much as Hamlet saw entities—camels, weasels, whales—in the clouds, while Polonius could see nothing without the aid of verbal suggestion. Surely the sound of the marching night is ineffable, yet the poet, thanks to his nurture of his sorrow, gains a transcendent vision that promotes the possibility—even if the poet chooses for now to withhold himself—of linking self and the ineffable in a single embrace.

This abstract version of what Northrop Frye calls the "poem of imaginative confrontation" occurs often in nineteenth-century French poetry; Keats's "To Autumn" exemplifies the genre in English. It is a genre that does not seem amenable to Lowell's perceptual aesthetic and dense textures (though Keats's example is magnificently concrete), which may explain why he has not more thoroughly revised "Recollections" from its *Imitations* version—perhaps finding it more difficult to reenter than a poem that more clearly places itself in the phenomenal world. Yet it serves a purpose in *History* by giving voice to an important, influential aesthetic stance that helped foster the modernism in which Lowell first matured as a poet. Baudelaire's version of the romantic sublime, though abstract or personified in a manner uncongenial to Lowell's aesthetic, marks one of the important boundaries of Lowell's poetic world.

While Baudelaire finds himself emotionally drawn into the urban abyss he loathes, and at times loathes himself for it, Rimbaud insists on the poet's superiority to a corrupt and disintegrating society. The five Rimbaud poems in *History* explore the poet's relationship to society through the traditional motif of the journey, and through Rimbaud's defiant claim to the role of outlaw. Lowell, despite some violent episodes in his past, could hardly claim this role for himself. These Rimbaud imitations serve an important purpose in Lowell's book by exposing an aspect of his poetic personality otherwise rarely seen. Rimbaud fearlessly committed himself to the romantic role of outlaw and outcast, and separated himself from society, first psychologically in the bohemian circles of Paris literary life, then geographically when he surrendered his career as poet and exiled himself in Africa. If Rimbaud sometimes treats the Muse with undue familiarity, he enjoys with her an intimacy available only to the greatest poets. With a ferocity unavailable to Lowell even in his rebellious youth, Rimbaud dedicates himself to the inspired life of the prophet in the urban wilderness.

Numerous critics have remarked upon Lowell's affinity with Rimbaud. John Baley argues that Rimbaud's *dérèglement* "seems in accord with Lowell's own poetic temper,"[7] while Irvin Ehrenpreis comments that "if in artistic sensibility Lowell seems peculiarly at home with Baudelaire, he seems as a person still more at ease with Rimbaud . . . [who] brings out attitudes toward childhood and corrupted innocence that remind us of *Life Studies*."[8] Richard Fein further develops this notion by observing that "in the versions of Rimbaud we witness the child's lust for freedom, the wise boy tortured by his knowledge and a desire to escape, the weights of which we feel in '91 Revere Street' and in some of the poems from *Life Studies*."[9] Even John Simon, in an otherwise hostile review of *Imitations*, seems to concede that Rimbaud, along with Rilke, is Lowell's "major kinsman"; on the other hand, Elizabeth Bishop, writing to Lowell about *Imitations*, argues that "Baudelaire is more sympathetic to you verbally (and probably emotionally) than Rimbaud—at least those early Rimbauds you've chosen."[10] Regardless of whether Simon or Bishop is correct, even Lowell's immature work displays something akin to Rimbaud's defiance of conventional religious pieties, as in this uncollected early 1940s poem, which seems to echo Rimbaud's "Les Pauvres *à* l'église" (among other sources):

> One Night in Johns Hopkins
> I made these gallows, God. Pushed to the wall,
> With splintered hands and knees and splintered blood,
> I pieced together scaffolding, O God,
> To lift my wooden heels into the tall
> Third Heaven of that myopic blockhead, Paul,
> Who preached that Heaven's pillars are the wood
> Of Christ the Goat, whose hanging was too good

For my unseasoned heart, gone wooden, all
Splinters. Lord of Libanus, so it was:
Now morning smites the jaded city mist
And wooden shrubbery of Baltimore;
From the white stoops the men of Sodom pass
Whispering through Johns Hopkins where the Christ
Swings from the wooden belfries of the poor.[11]

Marjorie Perloff argues that "Lowell and Rimbaud are in fact very different poetic sensibilities"—that Lowell has, in contrast to Rimbaud, a "historical" rather than a "visionary imagination."[12] I think this comparison errs in suggesting that these are mutually exclusive forms of imagination. Lowell's earlier poetry had a strongly mystical element, and his later historicism still displays a visionary dimension. And Rimbaud is as much a social satirist as a visionary. But my point is that Lowell in these versions of Baudelaire and Rimbaud makes good use of sensibilities different from his own. Of course, no two poets, let alone poets in different centuries, writing in different languages, will have identical sensibilities. Taking advantage of those differences, Lowell engages aesthetic and social positions distinct from his own not to vitiate but to incorporate them into a poetic world large enough for mutual accommodation.

All five of the Rimbaud versions in *History* previously appeared in *Imitations*, but were revised for their new context.[13] "Bohemia," first of the group in *History*, appeared in *Imitations* as "On the Road." Under either title it exemplifies the rhetoric of self-assertion and defiance Lowell finds so engaging in the youthful outlaw:

I walked on the great roads, my two fists lost
in my coat's slashed pockets; my overcoat too
was the ghost of a coat. Under the sky—
I was your student, Muses. What an affair
we had together! My only trousers were a big hole.Tom

> Thumb, the stargazer. I brightened my steps with
>   rhymes.
> My inn was at the Sign of the Great Bear;
> the stars sang like silver in my hands.
> I listened to them and squatted on my heels,
> September twilights and September twilights,
> rhyming into the monster-crowded dark,
> the rain splashing on my face like cheap wine.
> I plucked the elastics on my clobbered boots
> like lyrestrings, one foot squeezed tight against my heart.[14]

Though the poem occurs in early autumn, a season associated with maturation rather than adolescent wanderlust, Lowell's Rimbaud roams the world with the careless bravado of youth, flaunting his poverty, risking dark infinities with his poems. In the totality of his commitment, even his boots become an intimate part of the poetic experience, their elastics "like lyrestrings," a sign of a self so purposeful that one foot touches his heart. That is, the soul or center of his vision—the heart—inspirits the otherwise ordinary parts of the body, like his feet, to manifest this vision in the phenomenal world. The poem defines Rimbaud's dedication to a romantic sublime that externally expresses his psychic unity. Unlike Baudelaire, he is not usually skeptical about that sublime, perhaps because his poetry in its confident symbolism rarely loses touch with imagery even when exploring abstract concepts. He exemplifies a courage and recklessness Lowell as Baudelaire cannot find in himself—or if he does, he subsumes by questioning the actuality of the experience and invoking fear of absorption and loss of identity.

Baudelaire suffers an introverted skepticism, while Rimbaud's self-doubts turn almost entirely outward to satirize the French bourgeoisie he abhors and has abandoned. His self-portrait (or Lowell's portrait of him) as romantic vagabond represents a role otherwise unavailable to Lowell—the visionary outlaw-poet free of ordinary human relationships. This is hardly a complete picture of Rimbaud or his poetic, but besides working the outlaw role into *History* it makes possible the depiction of contrasting social roles, such as that of the young soldier, portrayed in "Sleeper in the Valley," who sacrifices more than Rimbaud the outlaw has. It also introduces a careless sexuality perhaps not totally alien to Lowell's sensibility.

"Rimbaud 2. A Knowing Girl" furthers the exploration of the poetic life by illustrating the careless amorality of his relationships with others. The housemaid recognizes in the poet one whose moral attitudes accord with her own, and her playfulness suggests that these casual encounters need entail no serious consequences:

> In the cigar-brown dining room perfumed
> with a smell of fruitbowls and shellac,
> I was wolfing my plate of God knows what
> Belgian dish. I sprawled in a huge chair,
> I listened to the clock tock while I ate.
> Then the kitchen door opened with a bang,
> the housemaid came in . . . who knows why . . . her blouse
> half-open and her hair wickedly set. She passed
> her little finger trembling across her cheek,
> pink and white peach bloom, and made a grimace
> with her childish mouth, and coming near me
> tidied my plates to make me free . . .
> then—just like that, to get a kiss of course—
> whispered, "Feel this, my cheek has caught a cold."[15]

Lowell portrays Rimbaud's muse as a whore, and the poet as a tramp, so the poem assumes a tone and register of diction appropriate to the ethos of their shared world. The poet has the opportunity to link visionary with sexual prowess, to possess, if even for a moment, the sublimity of her bold and playful rhetoric. Rimbaud's wanderlust represents a dedication to the uneasy life of the poet, but in his time the romantic quest already has come to seem a chimera. Lowell as Rimbaud doubts the stability and even the reality of the ineffable, but quells this skepticism to assert the importance of vision in contrast with the social quotidian.

Rhetorically these sonnets, in common with the bulk of postindustrial poetry, impose an aesthetic order to repudiate social amorphism. They also personify this order in the most disorderly sort of lifestyle. Rimbaud's bohemian tramp, "rhyming into the monster-crowded dark," walking "the great roads," is the poet-hero chronicling a life of shabby poverty. His "two fists lost /in [his] coat's slashed pockets" comically foreshadow Ernest Hemingway's literary manliness while suggesting the futility of his defiance. This five-poem sequence argues that to be a poet one must take an aggressively self-defining stand against history, whatever the cost. It graphically demonstrates how poems about poetry are poems about how poetry is life, a poem "a person," as Lowell remarks elsewhere.[16] To be a poet in Rimbaud's politically tormented France requires transgressing natural and social law, as Lowell satirically views himself doing in youth:

> I was a fire-breathing Catholic C.O.,
> and made my manic statement,
> telling off the state and president, and then
> sat waiting sentence in the bull pen
> beside a Negro boy with curlicues
> of marijuana in his hair.[17]

And in any number of ways, Lowell has said, "I was your student Muses, What an affair/we had together." This linking of sexual and literary unlawfulness could stand as epigraph for *The Dolphin*.

In the two Rimbaud antiwar sonnets, color and sensuous imagery compete with the critique of unreasonable social demands and the dark visual sublimity of death. These poems derive much of their effect from the complexity and vividness of their texture and a wry emotional stance. Other than in their apostrophes to nature, they consist of almost documentary description. Like Stephen Crane in *The Red Badge of Courage,* Lowell uses color to illuminate a battlefield:

> The river sings and cuts a hole in the meadow,
> madly hooking white tatters on the rushes.
> Light escalades the strong hills. The small
> valley bubbles with sunbeams like a beerglass.
> The young conscript bareheaded and open-mouthed,
> his neck cooling in blue watercress;
> he's sleeping. The grass soothes his heaviness,
> the sunlight is raining in his green bed,
> baking away the aches of his body. He smiles,
> as a sick child might smile himself asleep.
> O Nature, rock him warmly, he is cold.
> The fields no longer make his hot eyes weep.
> He sleeps in the sun, a hand on his breast lies open,
> at peace. He has two red holes in his left side.[18]

"Cuts," "hooking," "tatters," and "escalade," words of consonantal and tactile vigor, enhance the sublimity of the scene as Lowell invokes the language of slaughter to describe an ordinary topographical process. The word "escalades" usually refers to the scaling of a fortification, but Lowell uses it to describe daylight creeping over the landscape. This prepares the scene for the emotionally draining depiction of the corpse in a language of natural plenitude. Nature, which readily accept the dead soldier, isn't violent after all. The first four lines, with their linguistic violence and military metaphor, have misled. The artificial notes of rhetoric fade in the presence of the cadaver, demonstrating how tentative a link language makes with the actual. The arch construct of metaphor can't compete with the ultimate sublimity of death. Like the soldier, the language finds ease only in submitting to the aesthetic unity of the poem, which occurs not despite but because of the failure of metaphor and rhetoric.

"Rimbaud 4. The Evil," like the preceding poem, deals with both worldly and aesthetic conflicts. The blood streaming into the sky re-proaches the infinite, which later in the poem Rimbaud personifies as the conventional but misunderstood Catholic god of his era, a being who promotes real evil and cynically robs the poor:

> All day the red spit of the grapeshot smears
> whistling across the infinite blue sky;
> before the Emperor, in blue and scarlet,
> the massed battalions flounder into fire.
> The criminal folly that conspires and rules us
> lays a hundred thousand corpses end on end—
> O Nature, in your summer, your grass, your joy—
> you made them, these poor dead men, in holiness! . . .
> There's a God who laughs at damask altarcloths,
> the great gold chalice, the fuming frankincense.
> He dozes exhausted through our grand hosannah,
> and wakes when mothers, brought together in pain,
> and weeping underneath their old black hat,
> give him the big penny they tied in their handkerchief.[19]

As in "Sleeper in the Valley," the poet here challenges the conventional romantic sublime and the benign religiosity of the bourgeoisie with the phenomenal actuality of war. The god of Rimbaud's poem, like the poet himself, rejects the trappings of ritual. Altar decorations and incense fail to rouse him from his indifference—only money, even in minute quantities, and the accompanying misery excite interest. In some of the poems in *Land of Unlikeness* and *Lord Weary's Castle*, Lowell expresses a similarly harsh approach to conventional religious practices, suggest-ing, as he does in the guise of Rimbaud, that Christianity has degener-ated into casual idolatry, as these lines from "Christmas in Black Rock" illustrate:

> Christ Child, your lips are lean and evergreen
> Tonight in Black Rock, and the moon

Sidles outside into the needle-screen
And strikes the hand that feeds you with a spoon
Tonight, as drunken Polish night-shifts walk
Over the causeway and their juke-box booms
Hosannah in excelsis Domino.[20]

This acculturated industrial-era god, not the merciful father of Jesus but an idol erected by bourgeois social necessity, presides over corruption that Rimbaud/Lowell finds epitomized in Napoleon, whose evil is matched only by his foolishness. The emperor, like Rimbaud, is an outlaw; but while the poet-vagabond's rejection of society derives from his unquenchable idealism, Napoleon in his cynicism has lost touch with the humanity consumed by needless and unceasing wars, as the fifth of Lowell's Rimbaud sonnets, "Napoleon after Sedan," illustrates:

(Rimbaud, the servant of the France he saved,
feared the predestined flow of his aesthetic
energies was to use the wrong direction;
he was looking for writing he needn't hate—)
Napoleon is waxy, and walks the barrack's unflowering
garden, a black cigar between his teeth . . .
a hand once able to stub out liberty.
His twenty years orgy has made him drunk.
Liberty jogs on, the great man stands,
he's captured. O what name is quaking on
his lip? What plebiscites? What Robespierre?
His shark's eye on the horses, the Grand Prix,
soirées at Saint Cloud, their manly vapor . . .
watching his cigar blue out in smoke.[21]

Extensively revised from the *Imitations* version, this poem more candidly than the other four mixes Rimbaud's and Lowell's voices. In the parenthetical opening, Lowell suggests the particular significance of Rimbaud. Continually rewriting his poems and rethinking his aesthetic (as Lowell imagines him), Rimbaud searched for a mode of writing that wouldn't promote illicit social aims, like Napoleon's. This is both a political and an aesthetic stance, appropriate for a poet placing his verse at the service of history, as Rimbaud imagines himself doing, and as Lowell might have done if he could have escaped the imperatives of his introspective vision, lyric-meditative aesthetic, and autobiographical obsessions. Rimbaud faced much the same problem as Lowell: an obsession with epic scale and a commitment to a lyric voice. Perhaps under the pressure of this self-imposed imperative, he abandoned poetry and chose a life as explorer, trader, and arms dealer. Lowell, however, permanently committed to poetry, enlists Rimbaud's literary remains in an effort to solve this mutual romantic dilemma.

Napoleon with cigar in hand, waiting while the forces of history plow ahead, personifies the "wrong direction" Rimbaud fears. The emperor misjudged the direction and strength of historical forces he thought he controlled, and fell into disgrace, "waxy" now, like one of Madame Tussaud's figures. The smoke of his cigar enshrouds him, obliterating his countenance and his individuality. Rimbaud feared the same fate, worried that his obsession with poetry had doomed him; yet his motive was as innocent as Lowell's when (in "Shifting Colors") while fishing and watching a white horse graze he flashes on the efficacy of an inspiration so pure it would obviate the need to write.

Lowell's Rimbaud sonnets present the poet as a wanderer independent of society, engaged in it only through perception of its corruption. This role might tempt any poet, and is one that along with Rimbaud's satire and mysticism attracted Lowell in his early years, as shown by another uncollected poem from his early notebooks:

> Rimbaud sprawled among cocktails . . .
> Olive his sockets as trawler balls . . .
> Deep, drenching green his glass—
> The hour-glass's abstracted force.
>
> The Frenchman's chaotic, vivid verse
> —Sensitive, insensible, a voice

> Eccentric in its chaotic fury
> To the rhetorician's simplicity
>
> Wrang lordly rhetoric by the neck,
> That bushy tail-plume of the cock,
> And quarried its surly paradise
> From dazzling, unrealistic dives,
>
> Lord, on thy servant have mercy!
> Rhetoric fathers rarity![22]

Thematically and contextually, this poem asserts the inspired force of intense language—"chaotic, vivid"—coupled with a life wrung dry by experience and sin. Lowell in the early stages of his religious phase finds Rimbaud's youthful dissipation fascinating because it seems necessary to the success of his verse. In the conclusion, Lowell pairs supplication and apology, assuming a stance he would maintain till the end of his career:

> How often have my antics
> and insupportable, trespassing tongue
> gone astray and led me to prison . . .
> to lying . . . kneeling . . . standing.[23]

For Lowell, the adolescent breeziness of Rimbaud counters Baudelaire's timidity on the brink of the abyss. While Lowell/Baudelaire fears even sleep because of its absorbing visions, Lowell/Rimbaud gladly, sardonically, steps into the dark, as the actual Rimbaud did by retreating to Africa to live out a renunciation that began as a metaphor.

What part of Lowell's vision resembles Rimbaud's? Certainly the restlessness, the urge for change, and his role as impassioned witness to political folly and social decay complement Rimbaud's sensibility, though Lowell is not as relentlessly visionary and his language isn't so buoyant. The self-conscious observer role assumes new importance in the later poems of *History*, such as "The March 1," in which the sardonic sequence of "fear, glory, chaos, rout" and the savage picture of the "Martian, the ape" echo Rimbaud's disgust with militarism and its distorted values, while the opening lines invoke Lowell's own meditative vocabulary to capture the overstated landscape:

> Under the too white marmoreal Lincoln Memorial,
> the too tall marmoreal Washington Obelisk,
> gazing into the too long reflecting pool,
> the reddish trees, the withering autumn sky,
> the remorseless, amplified harangues for peace—
> lovely to lock arms, to march absurdly locked
> (unlocking to keep my wet glasses from slipping)
> to see the cigarette match quaking in my fingers,
> then to step off like green Union Army recruits
> for the first Bull Run, sped by photographers,
> the notables, the girls . . . fear, glory, chaos, rout . . .
> our green army staggered out on the miles-long green fields,
> met by the other army, the Martian, the ape, the hero,
> his new-fangled rifle, his green new steel helmet.[24]

The shriveled vegetation, the withered society, the false heroism, the overstated monuments, visionary as well as historical in Lowell's language of deprivation and excess, are Rimbaud-like; even the empathy of trees and sky with the war-theme completes a Rimbaud-like visual unity. Furthermore, Lowell assumes the role of an outlaw happy in his admittedly mild defiance. Comforted by the presence of others (the poem is dedicated to Dwight Macdonald, who stood next to Lowell in the actual march), but self-defined by apprehension and infirmities, he asserts his individual vision by unlocking arms to adjust his glasses. After that moment of self-assertion, the poem speaks not only in a historical but a prophetic voice, conjuring both the Civil War and the "Martian," the potential enemy of the future. In Rimbaud, Lowell finds confirmed the essential otherness of the poet, defining his own role as a critical observer who participates only through a rhetoric of perception. To this degree, many of Lowell's early poems owe much to Rimbaud, as the richly but self-consciously symbolic second stanza of "Aunt Hecuba" (c. 1938) shows:

> Full-blooded shadows
> Of a viennese husband, wedded
> To a gory slavic chants and psalters,
> And a hundred unmarried daughters
> Corrupt and corrode the jaundiced shallows
> Of her sea-weedish house.[25]

Baudelaire, on the other hand, aggravates Lowell's suspicion of the stock romantic stance through which the first-person speaker resolves a problematic relationship to otherness by means of a vision of natural or spiritual unity. Baudelaire's mistrust of transcendence shapes much of the last third of *History*, particularly those poems like "Flaw (Flying to Chicago)" that through Lowell's myopic or angular eccentricities expose limits to his perception that compromise his ability to carry out some of the ordinary functions of living:

> My old eye-flaw sprouting bits and strings
> gliding like dragon-kites in the Midwestern sky—
> I am afraid to look closely, and count them;
> today I am exhausted and afraid.
> I look through the window at unbroken white cloud,
> and see in it my many flaws are one,
> a flaw with a tail the color of shed skin,
> inaudible rattle of the rattler's disks.
> God is design, even our ugliness
> is the goodness of his will. It gives me warning,
> the first scrape of the Thunderer's fingernail. . . .
> Faust's soul-sale was perhaps to leave the earth,
> yet death is sweeter, weariness almost lets
> me taste its sweetness none will ever taste.[26]

From Baudelaire, Lowell learned to subsume fears and self-doubts in the very design of poetry, integrating these negatives into the affirmation of a poetic. The perfection of God's design reproaches, but Baudelaire's admission of human weakness into the aesthetic construct of his imaginative world suggests the humility of voice Lowell needed in this and other poems. This humility enabled him not only to recognize his limitations as aesthetic opportunities but to realize the contributions predecessor poets could make to his autobiographical epic.

10 | "Lightning on an Open Field"

D
AY BY DAY, LOWELL'S LAST COLLECTION, appeared in August 1977, a few weeks before his death. Despite suggestions of plot and sequence, the book coheres primarily through aesthetic commonality and a tight nexus of themes and concerns. These poems benefit from Lowell's experiments with unrhymed sonnets in that their language is freer, more limpid and yet more boldly associative than in the free-verse poems of *Life Studies* and *For the Union Dead.* No longer haunted by fractured syllable-stress meter, Lowell's rhythms seem less insistent, more relaxed, though perhaps less urgent and forceful. The poems in *Life Studies* regularly refer to the iambic pentameter line from which they derive; their freedom is deviation, like Milton's deviations from blank verse in *Samson Agonistes.* The poems in *For the Union Dead*, metrically more varied, are not structurally but more casually associative; their structures consist of clearly developed metaphors unfolded in a restrained, wiry syntax. Compared with these earlier volumes, *Day by Day* seems slack in rhythm and more open to narrative, yet usually less beholden to prose logic. More generously than in his earlier free verse, Lowell has opened the very structures of his poems to the free play of the imagination. Because he respects and usually maintains the in-

tegrity of the individual stanza (that is, each stanza is a complete, end-stopped sentence or verse paragraph) the poems at a glance seem more logical than they actually are.

In the collection's weakest moments, however, some poems invert the overall aesthetic of the collection and accept prose logic at both the level of the sentence and of the paragraph. These weaker poems embrace without fulfilling prose strengths, particularly those of prose narrative, and attempt the orderly dramatic vignettes of the *Life Studies* poems without the underlying rhythmic imperative. Lacking Lowell's early, more baroque rhetorical strategies, this compromise cannot sustain poems of such limpidity. Most notable, perhaps, is the retreat from the historical and epic concerns that shaped *Notebook* into *History*. *Day by Day* is Lowell's most personal book and offers the fewest examples of the confluence of public and private voices. For this reason, much of the thematic tension that made *Life Studies* and *For the Union Dead* so memorable is lacking.

Lowell refers to these last poems as "simple autobiography,"[1] and suggests that they have no "plot" except insofar as his poetic meditation could supply one. But the conventions of lyric or meditative poetry and of the prose autobiography are difficult to reconcile. The modern poem is recondite, more introspective than life, and substitutes association for logic, chronology, and traditional narrative; though the prose autobiography occasionally shares these characteristics, it more often proposes a chronology that excludes or minimizes the associative method typical of poetry. The poem and the prose autobiography, written from differing aesthetic motives, engage distinctly different areas of experience and the psyche. *Life Studies*, much of it versified from prose drafts, tentatively reconciles these motives, but *Day by Day*, more freely associative, rejects the compromise in favor of more documentary techniques. While Lowell has pared down his rhetoric to suggest versified prose, he retains many aesthetic and associative strategies, and now writes from what William Carlos Williams calls the "crystallization of the imagination."[2] Many of Lowell's last poems, refusing the complex juxtapositions of his sonnets and early work, leap out of enraptured moments in which landscape and mood find mutual focus. These concentrated perceptions are not visionary opportunities but aesthetic ones. They occur at an actual time of day (or other perceptible time-unit), or represent a unity of time and place that engenders the sort of perception that empowers a poem. They might suggest Wordsworthian epiphanies, glimpses of the natural or socio-cultural sublime, or they may simply offer a heightened sense of landscape and mental acuity. These perceptions do not derive from history, the use of mythopoeic language, or the intellectual self-discernment that empowers much of Lowell's previous poetry. They occur in ordinary domestic actuality, resulting in poems that at their best seem unusually disarming, frank, and freshly conceived.

Lowell's instincts, however, remain resolutely poetical. As his work becomes less dependent on conventional literary expectations, it delves more directly into inspiration and the immediacy of perception. Grasping these propitious moments—loci of perception and imagination—Lowell creates an illusion of spontaneity; but this is the work of a hand guided equally by the eye and by the unconscious, welded together by years of study and effort. It is also the result of hundreds of hours of revision. Comparing earlier published versions of the *Day by Day* poems with the final book versions demonstrates that they have received the same reconsideration Lowell gave all of his work. Pairing the opening stanza of "Since 1939" as published in the *New York Review of Books* (29 May 1975, under the title "1938–1975") with the version published in *Day by Day* will demonstrate that Lowell eased the tone and juggled the rhythm in the later version to create a greater illusion of spontaneity and more wieldy syntax:

> 1938, our honeymoon train west,
> Munich, the boy beside us
> leafing the revolutionary Thirties'
> poems of Auden till our heads fell down,
> swaying with the comfortable
> ungainly gait of obsolescence . . .
> I miss more things now,
> am more consciously mistaken—

I see a girl reading Auden's last book.
She must be very modern,
she diagnoses him in the past tense.

(*New York Review of Books*)

We missed the declaration of war,
we were on our honeymoon train west;
we leafed through the revolutionary thirties'
Poems of Auden, till our heads fell down
swaying with the comfortable
ungainly gait of obsolescence . . .
I miss more things now,
am more consciously mistaken.
I see another girl reading Auden's last book.
She must be very modern,
she dissects him in the past tense.

(*Day by Day*)

The deep irony of this poem is the confrontation between Auden's vividly political poems of the thirties, poems that Lowell's more public voice in many respects echoes, and the private moment of the honeymoon. Auden's poems are soporific to the drowsy lovers, whose purpose, after all, is not to read poems but to sleep with each other. Sleeping in the seats of a train is not the sort of sleeping together that defines a honeymoon. Rather it uneasily compromises their public presences, represented by the declaration of war, with their private and therefore unstated passion for each other. The irony, however, lies in the relationship of this poem to the bulk of the poems that follow. In them, Lowell utterly ignores most public matters and states quite explicitly his passions, private difficulties, fears, and doubts.

Perhaps this is what being "more consciously mistaken" means—to voice the previously unspoken and to displace a more public mode of discourse with one so private that in poems like "Unwanted" he is able to say about himself that which he has never before said. That this occurs at the expense of the public voice he has so assiduously devel-

oped and so successfully incorporated into the personal lyric or meditative poem suggests that, despite some wonderful writing, *Day by
Day* represented a kind of writing that "makes writing impossible" and
therefore a dead-end in Lowell's development. While "Unwanted" succeeds in part through the sheer bravado of its confession, "St. Mark's,
1933" shows how aesthetically lifeless this mode of writing can become:

> "Cal doesn't like everyone."
> "Everyone doesn't like Cal."
> "Cal,
> who is your best friend at this table?"
> "Low-ell, Low-ell"
> (to the tune of Noël, Noël).[3]

This impressionistic rendering of dialogue catches the flavor of the
boys' cruelty, but like most of the rest of the poem fails to generate
rhythmic interest and syntactical tension. In the end, the poem fades
away in self-analysis and a halfhearted Latin tag. Its defeatism fairly
represents the exhausted moments of self-derision and exhaustion that
Bell and other critics find central to *Day by Day*; but the genuine
drama of "Unwanted" and other poems and the aesthetic satisfactions,
however muted, of much of the rest of the book prove that Lowell has
not entirely collapsed into negation.

And Lowell the craftsperson has not entirely given up, either. The
revision of "Since 1939" thematically moves toward the exposure of
private concerns, but it avoids the debilitating flatness of "St. Mark's,
1933" and some of the other poems in the later part of the collection.
Instead of relaxing into narrative, it works toward compression and
the dramatic impact of brevity and focus. The boy beside Lowell has
disappeared; he was a superfluous character. By eliminating him and
placing Auden's books in his and his wife's hands, Lowell clarified the
opening lines and placed Auden's book firmly into the center of the
poem, which is Lowell's consciousness. The simplification of the rhythmic structure is obvious, especially in the first two lines and the last

one. Changing the title, too, adds to the immediacy of the poem. "Since 1939" places the poem in a continuum, while "1938-1975" locates the poem in a definite, bounded past. Open-ended experience and open form constitute the psychological and aesthetic framework of *Day by Day*. Lowell in his later work usually revised to increase this openness, as well as to sharpen and clarify imagery and syntax.

This openness, however, does not indicate any simplification of Lowell's thematic concerns. The complexity of the relationships among art, nature, and individuals is the dominant topic of *Day by Day*. Its ambitious and only partly realized aesthetic goal is what Harold Bloom has called the "saving transformation" that through the creation of an alternative world (as close as possible to phenomenal actuality) facilitates fresher and more satisfying encounters between literature and life.[4] The social and aesthetic potential of the quotidian (attained through the "crystallization of the imagination") and the need to reconcile abstract and concrete elements (assertions and imagery) shape Lowell's verse tactics and rhetorical strategies: associative freedom; imaginative-perceptual, rather than rhetorically logical ordering; a language that adheres to the informality of realist fiction; and a distinct verse cadence to distinguish the verse from good prose. The integrity of individual stanzas, syntactical and grammatical orthodoxy, and a respect for the individuality and wholeness of phenomena, characterize Lowell's devotion to landscape, domestic drama, and the quotidian event.

By identifying a juncture of landscape and mood as the engendering moment of these poems, I do not intend to invoke what M. H. Abrams calls the Romantic Moment.[5] He refers to a revealed insight, akin to an epiphany, while the locus I perceive in Lowell's poems is more tentative, an aesthetic opportunity, not a metaphysical revelation, embodied in a specific convergence of time and place. The two moments share the illumination of phenomenal objects or situations, but the Romantic Moment is committed to a "significance beyond itself," one belonging to the otherworldly or subliminal revelation, while Lowell's crystallized moments of perception engender poems that are more domestic than symbolic. Closer to the spirit of the poems of *Day by Day* is Abrams's description of the Greater Romantic Lyric:

> [the poems in question] present a determinate speaker in a particularized, and usually a localized, outdoor setting, whom we overhear as he carries on, in a fluent vernacular which easily rises to a more formal speech, a sustained colloquy, sometimes with himself or with the outer scene, but more frequently with a silent human auditor, present or absent. The speaker begins with a description of the landscape; an aspect or change of aspect in the landscape evokes a varied but integral process of memory, thought, anticipation, and feeling which remains closely intervolved with the outer scene. In the course of this meditation the lyric achieves an insight, faces up to a tragic loss, comes to a moral decision, or resolves an emotional problem.[6]

This amply describes the roles of landscape and presence and the overall structure of many of the poems in *Day by Day* and helps explain the sometimes startling continuities of tone and mood between some of Lowell's poems and certain poems by Wordsworth and Coleridge. It also suggests why stylistic lapses mar much of the book as Lowell gropes through elegiac romanticism toward a further revision of his aesthetic.

Lowell's earlier poems do not display such continuities with romantic causality; they often begin with a self-conscious melding of history and the present, as in the opening of "For the Union Dead," in which Lowell perceives the present landscape of the broken-windowed aquarium as contiguous with the past. The partial continuity of the past in the present, which heightens the failure of the contemporary world to maintain heroic ideals, is a central motif in that poem, which shuttles between personal and societal concerns. Other poems begin with generalizations, later parsed and modified, as in "Law":

> Under one law,
>
> or two,
>
> to lie unsleeping,
>
> still sleeping on the battlefield . . .[7]

Still others open with complex metaphors to distance the present and assert the significance of the speaking voice and the imagination before establishing the setting, as in "Waking Early Sunday Morning," "The Flaw," and in these lines from "The Neo-Classical Urn":

> I rub my head and find a turtle-shell
>
> stuck on a pole,
>
> each hair electrical
>
> with charges, and the juice alive
>
> with ferment.[8]

The poems in *History* and *The Dolphin* that open with an encouraging conflux of time and place, such as "Summer between Terms,"[9] do not develop the possibilities of this locus because the sonnet's cramped structure requires abrupt associative leaps that create stunning aporia rather than the more leisurely development afforded by the more open *Day by Day* poems.

In contrast, many of the best poems in *Day by Day* open with crystallized moments of perception from which they expand with relatively conversational ease. These are brief moments, caught like snapshots from life, not distilled from the extended life of the mind. These powerful openings occur in poem after poem:

> For the last two minutes, the retiring monarchy
>
> of the full moon looks down on the chirping sparrow . . .[10]

> Only today and just for this minute,
>
> when the sunslant finds its true angle . . .[11]

Characteristically, Lowell acknowledges an efficacy of setting as well as of time and mood:

> Here indeed, here for a moment,
> here ended—that's new.[12]

> The airy, going house grows small
> tonight, and soft enough to be crumpled up
> like a handkerchief in my hand.[13]

When heightened by the apparent simplicity and syntactical ease of Lowell's most eloquent late free verse, which is burdened by few of the rhetorical devices common to his previous work, these intersections of setting and emotion are critical to *Day by Day*. Gratefully perceived intersections of setting and situation—not revealed by glimpses of sublimity but assembled from familiar elements—make these poems possible, and Lowell acknowledges the efficacy of such an everyday idiom. He relies on the illusion of finding poems in daily life the way a sculptor finds a bust in a block of stone. Certain poems emphasize these loci not only by relying on them for emotional intensity and aesthetic direction, but by referring subsequently to the lucky and fruitful moments that make writing possible. These poems extend Lowell's challenge to autobiographical conventions by centering such moments in ordinary life—in the aggregate, arguing that the true center of life is not great insight itself but the moment when perception and imagination crystallize, making such knowledge possible. To move from such a moment to the point at which aesthetic exploration brushes against metaphysical speculation is to write a poem.

The difficulties come when Lowell relies on the reader's knowledge of his life, overvalues autobiographical content, or undervalues poetry as an end in itself, as he seems to do in "Notice":

> "These days of only poems and depression—
> what can I do with them?

> Will they help me to notice
> what I cannot bear to look at?"

To ask a "resident doctor" the purpose of art (as he does here) is to abandon the poet's sense of vocation, and too many of the poems in *Day by Day* are pervaded by this sense of lost purpose. The result is writing that fails to enact itself dramatically and instead mutters aimlessly without much engagement, as in the opening stanzas of "Grass Fires" or much of "Phillips House Revisited."

Other poems, however, successfully catch and dramatize the elegiac moment as one of poetic empowerment. "The Day," the first poem in the "Day by Day" section of the larger volume, honors the enduring presence of the twenty-four-hour solar circuit and attempts to reconcile this recurrence with the particular days of shared lives. It opens by expressing surprise at the eternal day's persistence, and evokes but simultaneously diminishes or localizes the sublime. Fresh and vivid and momentary as lightning, the day is both earthen and sublime, and has maintained this duality—as recurrence and as singular entity—since creation:

> It's amazing
> the day is still here
> like lightning on an open field,
> terra firma and transient
> swimming in variation,
> fresh as when man first broke
> like the crocus all over the earth.[14]

Lightning, earth, man, flowers: these images lend themselves to the making of archetypes and symbols. Permanent in its self-succession, and therefore best characterized by such global imagery, the day mirrors its own ideal, renewing image-creation like a new poem. As the title of Lowell's book suggests, the day exemplifies his current aesthetic. Each day, each poem, arrives fraught with possibilities, yet each one varies, and consequently seems fresh. To seize the day means to perceive the locus of landscape and mood and generate a poem. *Day by Day* has an air of carpe diem, though uncommitted to that genre's conventional obsession with lovemaking ("Suburban Surf," below, does, however, offer a distinctive slant on that subject). Sex certainly threads its way through these poems, but doesn't shape them as it does many of the *Dolphin* sonnets. Along with daily opportunities for poetry, *Day by Day* finds occasion for healing old wounds, revising old relationships, and reconciling the ordinary difficulties of living with hopes for love and domestic intimacy.

The second stanza of "The Day" moves from generalized imagery to a particular image of the present instance: cows on a hillside, illuminated by the strong light, and glimpsed from a moving train—the agrarian past seen from the peculiar angle of the industrial present. The poem, though, has shifted to the past tense, severing the first stanza relationship between the eternal day and the present one. In its negotiations between the sensuous and the cognitive, it is an instance of the fresh aesthetic Lowell is trying, with only partial success, to invent for himself. Tillinghast describes this process as an attempt "to enunciate a visually based aesthetic that is only partially substantiated in his practice."[15] "The Day," however, demonstrates how beguiling even the attempt can be:

> From a train, we saw cows
> strung out on a hill
> at differing heights,
> one sex, one herd,
> replicas in hierarchy—
> the sun had turned
> them noonday bright.

"Replicas in hierarchy," the cows, like the day itself, live in pastoral time, which is neither present nor past but a human and animal state of primitive innocence. They existed for Lowell before he became fully conscious of his intellect: "They were child's daubs in a book / I read before I could read" and therefore offer a particular challenge to the adult cognitive process. Since Lowell typically renders his experience as archetype, his childhood becomes that of the race, as the particular day is also the ideal one, and his attempt to intellectually categorize also represents the general human desire for order.

The cows, the innocence of the new, and the attractions of the primitive dissipate in the rush of time, technology, and particularity. The "we" here is critical: Lowell argues for an ideal intimacy as well as an understanding of the individual's place in the hierarchy of time. The cows, not the train, "fly by" because time and change, not the individual lives of cows, are the verities. The pastoral idyll, in which Lowell and his new wife lived at ease with themselves and each other, expired because they believed in it; they expected to enter the ineffable—nothingness—while retaining their dangerous human passions. Because Lowell has rejected the notion of actualizing the ideal, the many replications of the day now pass as quickly as the glimpse of the cows. Their love affair, although it occurred on the Great Day, and should have transcended time, nonetheless terminated because it could not thrive in paradox:

> They flash by like a train window:
> flash-in-the-pan moments
> of the Great Day,
> the *dies illa,*
> when we lived momently
> together forever
> in love with our nature—
>
> as if, in the end,
> in the marriage with nothingness,
> we could ever escape
> being absolutely safe.

The train ride as metaphor of the passing of personal or historical time occurs in various Lowell poems ("Beyond the Alps" is the obvious example). Here the train provides a quickly shifting vantage point, a height that clarifies hierarchies but obscures the individual. Although the cows loom with unnatural vividness, they "flash by" like the days ("They," a craftily ambiguous pronoun referring back to the cows and forward to the "moments") and present themselves as a hierarchy, a metaphor, rather than as individuals. This distinctive point of view provides an essential but elusive and sometimes distorting knowledge, one that can conceal private passions as well as reveal the structures of relationships.

It is important that Lowell's acquaintance with cows began not with nature but with art. Both art and nature, however, reveal themselves to the emotions rather than to the intellect, which is why Lowell could "read" the cow book before he could read. The cows, like creatures in cave paintings, are prehistoric; they belong to a time in which he could neither understand nor record his feelings or ideas. Whether nostalgically or with primitivist longing, his art often takes this prehistoric innocence as its topic. The *Life Studies* poems look back at the child-beast with horror and nostalgia, and in *Day by Day*, "Ten Minutes," "Turtle," and "Unwanted," among others, dwell as Wordsworth often does on primitive innocence as a prelude to aesthetic consciousness. This awaking from innocence to aesthetic awareness is a lifelong theme in Lowell's work. For instance, an early poem (c. 1938) finds the self-absorbed innocence of adolescent lust mirrored and challenged by natural process through mutual if corrupting illumination:

EROSION

> The sunlit waves dolloped and dropped
> Along the long and scalloped sands;
> Erosive chaffering chafed and rubbed
> My wounded groin with brutal thumbs
> And humid palms and pads of hands—
> My navel groaned as a bruited drum.

> The summer months I flowed and ebbed
> On sunlit gusts of love and lust,
> Until the bruised numbness spread
> My nerves burning and sloughed as rust.[16]

"Erosion" demonstrates that while early sexual desire and mature nature are both entropic, their mutuality generates a grim beauty that would otherwise go unnoticed. Written from a similar conviction of the inseparability of the beholder and the beholden, the last two stanzas of "The Day" suggest that the banal dualism of self and other may falsely distinguish art from knowledge. To live "momently together" is to acknowledge that nature (human or otherwise) bonds people because it does not recognize their individualism, only the species. The final stanza suggests that any attempt to merge the individual into nature fosters delusion, since for the sake of unity nature sacrifices individual consciousness. In death, "the marriage with nothingness," one suffers absolute safety, no longer free to err or to choose. One no longer enjoys access to the Great Day and its individual manifestations. The empowerment of landscape and mood, after facilitating access to the ideal, has faded in the stress of the rather mixed epiphany it has engendered. But the poet retains the aesthetic opportunity afforded by the rich conception of the day as both temporal and eternal. Despite the loss of the pastoral idyll and the consequent disillusionment, the vision of the poem momentarily unites life and art by revealing the child and the man to each other, linking childhood with the present, linking art to Lowell's ideal of living "together forever" with his wife in a humanized and yet idealized landscape.

The perception that empowers "This Golden Summer" opens a further glimpse of mythic possibilities. Lowell detects an emblematic landscape overlaid on the particular facts of a dry English summer. The depicted episode affords a renewal of his love relationship by paralleling it with historically privileged encounters, uniting biblical patriarchs, Jonathan Edwards (through allusion to the spider essay, previously used in "Mr. Edwards and the Spider"), and Lowell and his wife. The two opening stanzas depict a concentration of mood and landscape, and metaphorically link the moment to the biblical or archetypal past:

> This golden summer,
> this bountiful drought,
> this crusting bread—
> nothing in it is gold.

> Its fields have the yellow-white hair
> of Patriarchs who lived
> on two goats and no tomorrow—
> a fertility too rich to breathe.[17]

The drama unfolds when Lowell, carrying a tray, steps on the paw of his cat, whose recent maternity should have entitled her to special consideration:

> Our cat, a new mother, put a paw
> under my foot, as I held a tray;
> her face went white, she streaked screaming
> through an open window, an affronted woman.

This dramatic but premature climax contrasts in tone and tense (shifting, as in "The Day," into the past tense) with the depicted summer fields, and undermines the tranquil scene with low comedy, disruption and affront. Having demonstrated that even patriarchal tranquility is liable to unforeseen irruptions, the poem turns to the problematical marital relationship running through *Day by Day*, and compares it with the biblical stability of the second stanza, trying to account for the presence of anger and his perhaps unnecessary sense of fragility:

> Is our little season of being together
> so unprecarious, I must imagine
> the shadow around the corner . . .
> downstairs . . . behind the door?

I see even in golden summer
the wilted blowbell spiders
ruffling up impossible angers,
as they shake threads to the light.

We have plucked the illicit corn,
seen the Scriptural
fragility of flowers—
where is our pastoral adolescence?

I will leave earth
with my shoes tied,
as if the walk
could cut bare feet.

The lost or imperfectly realized pastoral adolescence shaped Lowell's aesthetic bond with his wife and was a type of the first relationship between man and woman, an alliance begun in innocence but soiled by knowledge. This flawed summer, a specific summer, not an eternal one, cannot admit the ideal: "nothing in it is gold." Everything is golden, but that is a temporary state, different from possessing the actual substance of gold. Beyond appearances, nothing of the old pastoral survives. The fertility of the patriarchs now chokes off life rather than engendering it; they are too consecrated to literary and social convention to enlighten the recalcitrant present.

Lowell acknowledges the failure of his husbandry—both his animal care and his marital situation—when he steps on the cat's paw and sends her screaming through the window. This comic mishap decisively redirects the tone of the poem, shifting its registers of diction to suit a more personal, though still mythopoeic experience. Now in that landscape of golden effects, he notices imperfections—the "impossible angers" ruffled up by the "wilted blowbell spiders." These byproducts of evolution, fated by the terms of their existence, ominously suggest the pointless or unexplainable angers that can wreck a marriage. However Lowell and his wife, having plucked the "illicit corn" (a wry allusion to Ruth exiled in the alien corn), have alienated themselves from nature. Too old and knowledgeable for their own good, they've grown beyond youthful and primal innocence and therefore cannot be touched by the natural world however closely they observe it.

In the closing stanza, Lowell, rejecting the role of Huckleberry Finn or Saint Francis, refuses to go barefoot into the unknown. Rather than strip himself of twentieth-century values, however inadequate they may be, he will enter the ineffable—if he must—with shoes tied, "as if the walk / could cut bare feet." Lowell cannot transcend a preference for concrete actuality, which, once invoked, renders his poetry earthbound and nonmythic. Having abandoned pastoral illusions (as in "The Day"), which in "This Golden Summer" seem to derive in part from the Old Testament, he accepts his exclusion from nature, his inability even to coexist with his cat, yet defiantly expects to retain his shoes, even in death, as vestigial human values and acknowledgment of the possible hazards of whatever lies beyond. Leaving earth, for Lowell, doesn't entail a flight into the abstract sublime of Paradise; it means merely taking a walk. Though Pasternak (in Lowell's imitation) said "to live a life is not to cross a field,"[18] to die in "This Golden Summer" requires proceeding on foot. In particularizing the universal, archetypal "golden summer," Lowell deprives it of mythopoeic efficacy, demonstrating how badly the power of the pastoral convention has faded. In the resolute but practical closure, he resigns himself to a finite life in an uncertain universe, where it is always safer to wear shoes.

"Ants" examines a familiar natural synecdoche to parse some of the lessons learned in poems like "The Day" and "This Golden Summer." "Ants" thrusts forth a lengthy prologue, deferring its powerful juncture of landscape and mood until late in its development. The first lesson is aphoristic:

> Ants
> are not under anathema to make it new—

they are too small and penny-proud
to harm us much or hold the human eye
looking downward on them,
like a Goth watching a game of chess.[19]

Unlike second-generation modernist poets following the example of Ezra Pound, ants are not doomed to originality. Nor are they likely to cause harm or require undivided attention. The difference in scale is too great for the familiar synecdoche, in which ant culture somehow parallels the human. Lowell wonders, as some wonder about modern poetry, if what cannot "harm us much" should even catch our attention. Yet clearly, as Pound's unpalatable radio broadcasts caught the attention of the Federal Bureau of Investigation, so the ants have caught Lowell's attention and kept it, though like "the day" they surprise rather than instruct, another reason they cannot function as metaphors or allegory: "Ants are amazing but not exemplary;/their beehive hurry excludes romance."

This exclusion of romance—a dominant factor in Lowell's world —helps explain the nonhuman regularity and purpose of ant-lives. Fragile, unreflective, and single-minded, but empowered by their intimacy with the landscape, they function with minimal complexity, "one tactic" serving for multitudinous instances. But long before history, ants must have *created* this society they now perpetuate. Though their state is primal, archetypal, each anthill is the individual expression of a particular group of ants and, like all temporal creations, requires constant upkeep. The anthill resembles art that expresses a tradition rather than one that strains for originality: "like the Chinese traditional painter/renewing his repertory flowers—/each touch a stroke for tradition." Traditional art is reinforced by each new example, but it represents an aesthetic alien to Lowell, who possesses the modern mind.

Despite his resistance to the ants as exemplary or allegorical, Lowell does find them emblematic of social origin. Their invention of the state is recurrent, continuous, "before and after/Plato's grim arithmetic." That this state remains unchanging, despite its multiple instances, places it outside of the human paradigm, renders it nonallegorical; yet its actual history (unrecorded, of course) is annual, traditional, and in that way comparable to the human use of tradition. If "They are the lost case of the mind," that case remains unavailable for use. They may represent the state the human mind would invent if left to its own devices, but such a society would be so traditional and unchanging it would fail to interest the modern mind.

The engendering perception occurs in the last verse paragraph of the poem as Lowell lies looking up into an oak catacombed with ants, "more of a mop than a tree." He remains there despite fearing that branches may fall, and notes that the trunk is so rotten it probably wouldn't bear his weight. In childhood, he "found the sky too close," lived, like the young Wordsworth, uncomfortably near the natural sublime, but now, "uneasily" himself in maturity, fears that both he and his means of access to the ineffable have decayed past redemption. Does a desire to recover this sense of the ineffable, or merely memory, explain his present childishness, his desire to return to thoughtless times ("pastoral adolescence") when he attempted to earn love by reading the ant-war section of *Walden* (a forthright allegory) to his lover? Much as Thoreau revised the *Iliad* into the low spectacle of an ant-war, Lowell revises his romantic past into "daffy days" associated with immaturity. This remembered past and Thoreau's ant-war, a work of literature, not of nature, have shaped Lowell's resisting response to the present landscape. As a mature possessor of the modern mind he cannot accept Thoreau's allegorizing or his previous use of it, yet he yearns for a more innocent time when he accepted this means of linking nature and culture. Ants still inspire, but Lowell's experience with literature prevents him from accepting their world as a parallel to his own. With some subtlety, he argues that the aesthetic modernism resists romanticism and the natural sublime in the same way that the mature modern mind resists nineteenth-century allegories. That some part of the psyche resists maturity (by asking for "daffy days") complicates the argument of the poem but does not negate it.

Like "Unwanted" (discussed below), "Ants" suggests that not only means but ends change as Lowell refines his aesthetic. Primal elements assume fresh significance, shedding the old, as he reviews the use of natural emblems in terms of human needs and passions. The ants, enslaved to a social and political ideal, embrace their own archetype. They can teach nothing about the natural sublime because their traditional state excludes all but quotidian concerns. Only persons with leisure to read and meditate can concern themselves with the ineffable, even if to reject it. And Lowell again prefers to reject it rather than risk losing touch with worldly concerns. Instead of climbing the rotten tree, risking all, he daydreams about the time when he read Thoreau's earthy and reassuring allegory with the expectation of being rewarded with earthbound but satisfying love.

Climbing the tree, like wrecking the *Pisspot,* requires a greater trusting of imaginative vision than Lowell is now willing to employ. Extended metaphors or allegories are tricky means, and Lowell's aesthetic, which has become more and more that of the "snapshot" (as "Epilogue" notes),[20] resists such self-conscious literary constructions. They seem too flimsy to support his weight. Yet trees remain sensitive natural emblems of his mood, stance, and temper. They respond to a variety of needs and passions, assuming forms, shapes, and colors that reveal the direction and tone of his poems. A tree-omen sensitively responds in "Ulysses and Circe," for instance ("On his walk to the ship, / a solitary tree suddenly / drops half its leaves."),[21] while in "Ants" the decay of the oak corresponds to the waning of Lowell's interest in the ineffable and natural sublime, though both remain intact, if dilapidated.

In the instance of "The Withdrawal," the initial empowering image of the tree changes from a "gentle, fluffy" one to an ominous "patched-up oak," flanked by "indelible pines," as Lowell turns from a calm observation of the scene to reveal a less benign situation. In the end, the poem fades in Kafkaesque images from the past and a chilling synecdoche of death. "The Withdrawal" parallels the change of seasons with the sale of Lowell's house, then links those events to the more drastic shift between Lowell as a young man and Lowell as corpse. The poem gains in pathos through the contrast of differing loci of scene and mood. Its closure, especially when read in the light of Lowell's actual death a month after the publication of *Day by Day*, is one of the bleakest and saddest in his poetry.

The poem opens by commemorating an instantaneous conjunction of natural beauty and human perception, offering a glimpse of Keatsian truth particularized by modernist exactitude:

> Only today and just for this minute,
> when the sunslant finds its true angle,
> you can see yellow and pinkish leaves spangle
> our gentle, fluffy tree—[22]

Though this tree is friendly it is vaguely ineffectual, as Lowell feels himself to be. The perceptual moment is necessarily brief. The moment Lowell directs his wife's attention to it, everything changes: summer has passed, and now his house fills with strangers considering purchase. However, not only has the summer revealed its temporal limitations but autumn is also already preparing its departure:

> suddenly the green summer is momentary . . .
> Autumn is my favorite season—
> why does it change clothes and withdraw?

When Lowell turns his attention to the interior of the house he realizes that his perception precipitates change: "when I go into a room, it moves / with embarrassment, and joins another room." The rooms move only in his imagination (though the people in the rooms may well move about), but both the movement and the embarrassment are real. This autumn Lowell is selling his house—changing clothes, like the season. Condemned by perception to change, like the tree, the house assumes new and unfriendly characteristics. Perhaps it feels rejected, or reflects Lowell's sense of dislocation, so the rooms unite against him, silently protesting the breakup of the household. The psychological actuality is the literal movement and bonding of the alienated rooms.

Psychological and physical actualities merge in the ethos of the poem, in which persons move in space and time and environments do the same.

The aura of change and disruption challenges Lowell to rethink his own needs, and to minimize them:

> I don't need conversation, but you to laugh with—
> you and a room and a fire,
> cold starlight blowing through an open window—
> whither?

Mere talk will not comfort when intimacy is required. Further, Lowell craves a distant view of the ineffable, a sense of infinity and immortality. He wants his ambition and his domesticity to merge in the catalytic context of a home and secure relationships. But how does one generate so comfortable and unburdened a relationship?

Part 2 opens with another perception of rich and ominous potential. In the waning light, the sky is "a temporary, puckering, burning green," the trees, oak and pine, stand barren as backbones. This macabre landscape mocks sublimity and yet faintly replicates it. Overtly allegorical, this terse vision stimulates a deeper response, a miniature *L'Allegro,* a more detailed explanation of what Lowell needs for happiness:

> One wishes heaven had less solemnity:
> a sensual table
> with five half-filled bottles of red wine
> set round the hectic carved roast—
> Bohemia for ourselves
> and the familiars of a lifetime
> charmed to communion by resurrection—
> running together in the rain to mail a single letter.

This Bohemia, hardly an impoverished one, echoes Ford Madox Ford's image of heaven as a place much like Provence, where one can eat and drink and enjoy intimate conversation with friends. As the vision of the green sky and bony trees is to a larger sublimity, so this modest heaven is to the heaven of youthful piety.

The weird and meager oak and pines shadow this section, however. Heaven does not actually offer a "sensual table"; it sets a stage for melodrama, framed by the black and naked trees, which like the masks of comedy and tragedy represent Lowell's uneasy moods. His vision of a better heaven lasts only seven lines. The eschatological closing image of Lowell and his friends "running together in the rain" suggests that like ants they have found the ability to unite in a single daffy gesture. Clearly this balmy but pleasant heaven offers more than the persistent despondency that sours Lowell's vision.

This souring precipitates parts 3 and 4. Part 3 interjects, from some remote part of the psyche, a plea for a childlike vision of the ideal: *"Yet for a moment, the children / could play truant from their tuition."* Childish impulses in Lowell, his wife, and his friends would direct them to evade their responsibilities and defer the regret and self-deprecation that follow almost any mature undertaking. These negative feelings precipitate a vision of hell as the failure to appreciate available happiness. But first Lowell introduces his youthful self, whose restlessness and ignorance made this present failure inevitable:

> When I look back, I see a collapsing
> accordion of my receding houses,
> and myself receding
> to a boy of twenty-five or thirty,
> too shopworn for less, too impressionable for more—
> blackmaned, illmade
> in a washed blue workshirt and coalblack trousers,
> moving from house to house,
> still seeking a boy's license
> to see the countryside without arrival.

Though this boy stands distant in time, a surreal figure intruding into a cubist painting, Lowell in his unease still resembles him. Once again he leaves a house behind and refuses the settled, committed life he professes to desire. The difference is that the adult Lowell knows what hell is; as he argued in "Skunk Hour," it is an ill-conceived response to one's own life: restlessness, resistance to happiness, unending complaint. In "The Withdrawal" he links his earthly hell to his impending death:

> Hell?

> Darling,
>   terror in happiness may not cure the hungry future,
>   the time when any illness is chronic,
>   and the years of discretion are spent on complaint—

> until the wristwatch is taken from the wrist.

If heaven is red wine, a roast, and friends, hell is being homeless, rootless, self-destructive, and willfully insecure and unhappy. The stability of heaven contrasts with the geometric, primary-toned depiction of Lowell's past, the "receding houses . . . / the boy . . . / in a washed blue workshirt and coalblack trousers." This boy resembles a figure by Faulkner or Kafka, but the movement of the verse, imitating the boy's "movement from house to house," engenders what Lowell in the "Afterword" of *Notebook* calls "unrealism."[23] The "collapsing accordion of . . . receding houses" recesses in time as well as architecture, making an image that embodies both the act and the substance of memory. Hell is suspension in time and space, which links Lowell indelibly to his rootless past. He now warns his wife that the future, when illness becomes chronic, cannot be delayed by worry. His wandering, after all, has always been chronic, his complaints habitual, and together they presage a future of illness. Though in late middle age he has learned to imagine alternatives, he will nonetheless suffer willfully till he dies. The poem holds no hope. It prophesies continued failure to find permanent and lasting intimacy in landscape and in love—a life doomed, like the seasons, to mutability as an axiom of existence.

Suffering, as nearly every possible critic has remarked, serves as one of the central motifs of Lowell's poetry. It may assume cosmic proportions or, more commonly, may occur in small-scale instances in poems like "Myopia: A Night," "Between the Porch and the Altar," "During Fever," and "Night Sweat." As I have previously mentioned, Lowell speculated that his poetry might attract some readers because of his awkwardness, pain, and difficulties. "The Withdrawal" concludes with the extremity of that impracticality: Lowell's inability to find ease in happiness. The two concentrations of landscape and mood, each centering on tree imagery, lead into despairing self-reflection, with no compensation available in transcendence of self or nature, no acceptance of actual if transitory pleasure.

Perhaps with this perpetual unease in mind, "Suburban Surf" describes and dwells on a sexually charged juncture of setting and mood, traces it through the dramatic unfolding of lovemaking and the dawn of a new day, but rejects the extreme implications of metaphors that pose the animal spirit of Lowell's wife, the meditative self, and the sexual act against an impersonal, technological environment. This poem embodies the "last, failed erotic dream" that Vereen Bell places at the heart of *Day by Day*.[24] Refusing the implications of intimacy in a mechanistic world, Lowell prefers to dwell on the tension that makes a poem possible. The poem opens with a moment of stasis: "You lie in my insomniac arms / as if you drank sleep like coffee."[25] Lowell cannot sleep, but Caroline, his wife, can. In fact she sleeps as if she were mildly addicted to it. This opening echoes the second section of "Ulysses and Circe," in which Ulysses, reveling in the early hour, wakes beside a still-sleeping Circe: "He sees the familiar bluish-brown river / dangle down her flat young forearm, / then crisscross."[26] As "Suburban Surf" continues, Caroline herself wakes to indulge another appetite: "Then, / like a bear tipping a hive for honey, / you shake the pillow for French cigarettes."

Having bestialized Caroline's appetites, Lowell turns away from the silence between them, still unbroken, to compare the suburban traffic to cows. He then discovers the title image, and compares the whitecaps of the surf (the chrome trim of the passing automobiles) to the brilliance of Caroline's eye. Yet he undercuts that brilliance by describing the diamond facets of the surf as "glassy, staring lights / lighting the way they cannot see," allowing the ambiguity of reference to impute this mechanical blindness to his wife. These lights illuminate without revelation. Mechanical and mindless, they cannot compete with genuine vision. The limitations of the aesthetic of technology (if an aesthetic is a way of reshaping the world to fit our image of it) are specific—"friction, construction, etc. / the racket killing / gas like alcohol"—and include an addictive appetite like Caroline's, but noisy.

Mechanical limitations, including too much reliance on technique (sexual, literary), noise, and addiction, prevent those auto headlights, like ordinary sight, from achieving vision. But Lowell does not further explore the implied distance between his own vision and Caroline's more restricted seeing, and refuses to climax the poem with a predictably epiphanic image or statement distinguishing watchful waking from the animal indulgence of sleep and other appetites. Instead, he traces the aesthetic implications of noise and traffic back to himself and Caroline and fulfills them in sexual gratification:

> Long, unequal whooshing waves
> break in volume,
> always very loud enough to hear—
>
> *méchants,* mechanical—
>
> soothe, delay, divert
> the crescendo always surprisingly attained
> in a panic of breathlessness—
>
> too much assertion and skipping
> of the heart to greet the day . . .
> the truce with uncertain heaven.

Lowell and Caroline make love with an excitement and rhythm too assertive and jolting to ease them into the ordinary particulars of the new day, but the pleasure of the act precipitates a "truce" with an ill-defined, perhaps unattainable ideal. In their moment of release, the automobiles represent all things—like passion—that in bright light seem less exciting than in the dark:

> In noonday light,
> the cars are tin, stereotype and bright,
> a farce
> of their former selves at night—
> invisible as exhaust,
> personal as animals.

Although Lowell joins the rhythms of traffic and lovemaking, and establishes with the "glassy, staring lights" a link between Caroline and the mindless technology revealed by noonday glare, he does not trace the full implications of this analogy concerning the relationship between sex and technology. His refusal to follow the opening afforded by the locus of landscape and mood in which he distinguishes himself (despite momentary physical union) from Caroline gives "Suburban Surf" a calculated air of dangling possibilities. The brief verse paragraphs seem tentative and disconnected, each suggesting a new direction to follow, new opportunities never realized yet exposed by this satisfying and unusual poem.

The major poem "Unwanted" is the most aggressively autobiographical in the book. Flat in affect, disconcertingly prosaic, it nevertheless allows Lowell the necessary expanse of space in which to tell his "own story" (his "one story," as Jarrell called it) not in an unassailably factual version but as it seems in a particularly efficacious moment. This is the most cogent of Lowell's insistently personal poems, since it most directly engages the aesthetic possibilities of verse autobiography; that is, it pushes as closely as possible to the illusion of an unmediated, nonfictional, literally presented narrative, while honoring a poetics of vision and inspiration. Perhaps the stark poetics as well as the subject matter prompted Helen Vendler to note (surely thinking of this poem) that *Day by Day* includes "the very worst memories suppressed from *Life Studies*."²⁷ Such naked self-presentation, such lack of poetic masking, would not have suited the more ambiguously oedipal drama of the earlier book, which was carefully linked to a variety of social critique largely absent from *Day by Day*. Bell notes that in the poems of personal memory in *Day by Day* "the language at the poet's command is not allowed to ritualize and therefore transcend the banal truth of its subject matter."²⁸ Such ritualizing is part of the poetics of *Life Studies*, though it is less apparent than the greater formalities of *Lord Weary's Castle*. *Day by Day* does without, however, and "Unwanted" refuses even the faint memories of former ritual that linger nostalgically in poems like "Ulysses and Circe" and "The Day." "Unwanted" opens with an awareness of physical deprivation and inadvertent self-realization, expressed in a language of self-mocking penance:

> Too late, all shops closed—
> I alone here tonight on *Antabuse*,
> surrounded only by iced white wine and beer,
> like a sailor dying of thirst on the Atlantic—
> one sip of alcohol might be death,
> death for joy.
> Yet in this tempting leisure,
> good thoughts drive out bad;
> causes for my misadventure, considered
> for forty years too obvious to name,
> come jumbling out
> to give my simple autobiography a plot.²⁹

For some unstated or unknown reason, overcoming the self-destructive desire to drink inspires Lowell not to indulge in self-congratulation but to explore painful memories now freely faced. This affords him aesthetic as well as psychological satisfaction. Now he can plot his autobiography, which he hasn't satisfactorily accomplished since he formally began it in the mid-1950s. Perhaps although his previous poems had exposed and explored his oedipal relationship, he hadn't yet squarely faced it, hadn't sufficiently armed himself with Freudian understanding. As the poem explains, he has never before attempted to fill the gaps; he has ignored or concealed the very memories, speculations, and emotions the work (indeed the career) should explicate. Lowell implies a connection between alcohol abuse and a previous lack of self-honesty. The artificial deprivation imposed by an anti-alcohol drug prevents self-indulgence, and late on this particular night privation and self-pity have triggered a monumental self-revelation.

In the past (Lowell both asserts and doubts) he possessed a dubious confidence, a clear aesthetic goal, so by juxtaposing incongruous phenomena through metaphor he shielded himself and transformed what now seems evasion into poetic knowledge:

> I was surer, wasn't I, once . . .
> and had flashes when I first found
> a humor for myself in images,
> farfetched misalliance
> that made evasion a revelation?

No longer dependent on "farfetched misalliance," now empowered by unprecedented circumstance and mood, Lowell unfolds apparently spontaneous but carefully patterned revelations that weave the mythopoeic roles of seducer-lover-healer through his oedipal (mythic and Freudian) intimacy with his eccentric mother. The seducer-lover-healer roles belong to Merrill Moore, who carried out a possibly actual but probably figurative seduction of Lowell's mother. Not only does he fuel Lowell's own incestuous fantasies, but he is a poet as well as a therapist, and therefore embodies the link between poetry and the unconscious. Lowell and Moore become intimate and in some ways one person, in the peculiar way that therapists and their patients share or exchange identities. Attempting to demonstrate the efficacy of candor, Moore tells Lowell he was an unwanted child. Though an inconsequential writer, Moore, in violating medical ethics and revealing to the patient a difficult, unwelcome truth, becomes Lowell's first model for the confessional poet. If Moore has become Charlotte Lowell's lover to save her son, as the poem suggests, that is no more dramatic than what Lowell is doing: preying on his mother and her secrets to save himself.

The poem now depicts Lowell's struggle with his mother, torn between indulgent love and the urge to shrug off unwanted burdens. Charlotte was unhappy, but unlike her son she had no audience for her confession. She wanted to die when she found herself pregnant, and found no one to absorb that sad fact except her child. Her rage to hurt him mingled with her passion to share her life with him. The poem by this point seems more case study than literature; it rejects efforts to analyze its language, refuses metaphor and imagery, and insists on emotional content rather than form. Yet as Priscilla Paton has pointed out, "Unwanted" corresponds in character and plot to the most self-consciously literary poem in *Day by Day*, "Ulysses and Circe."[30] The deliberate construction of the poem becomes apparent in the powerful and central contrast between the New York landscape, with its conventionally domestic opportunities for "good views," and Charlotte's rejection of vision and home as she faces the romantic, chaotic sea. She is elemental, and so is her son, as he reveals by associating fire with religion:

> . . . mother saw me poking strips of paper
> down a floor-grate to the central heating.
> "Oh Bobby, do you want to set us on fire?"
> "Yes . . . that's where Jesus is." I smiled.

Charlotte considers sacrificing her identity to the elements: "yearning seaward, far from any home, and saying / 'I wish I were dead, I wish I were dead'"; while the young Lowell, however naively, chooses a visionary life.[31] His mother's suicidal urge negates her capacity for vision and self-knowledge, which is one reason that death, as far as Lowell is concerned, is unforgivable, as he suggests in describing a depleted landscape in "The Mouth of the Hudson":

Across the river,
ledges of suburban factories tan
in the sulphur-yellow sun
of the unforgivable landscape.[32]

But self-destruction, an ultimate and "consuming love," constitutes part of Charlotte's "dowry for her children," a psychological burden Lowell carries into "Unwanted," an obsession with self-loathing and death.

In concluding, Lowell wonders if his worst sin hasn't been his self-torment over being an unwanted child. For this preoccupation, he asks himself, should he doom his mother in his mind to the demeaning image of shrew and obsessive house-cleaner making life unbearable for husband and child? Can indulgence in confession become art, and if so will such art heal him, justifying what he has done by exposing his mother?

Is the one unpardonable sin
our fear of not being wanted?
For this, will mother go on cleaning house
for eternity, and making it unlivable?
Is getting well ever an art,
or art a way to get well?

The psychic wound, then, is not the actual content of the past but Lowell's preoccupation with it, which amounts to a clinging and destructive self-love. Empowered by circumstance, the "simple autobiography" he tries to plot would provide an invigorating aesthetic and psychological perspective, an opportunity to write with candor and self-honesty—qualities represented by his recognition of his present situation. Surrounded by the trappings of physical obsession—"iced white wine and beer"—Lowell for the first time can tell the worst, explaining the "cause" of his problems. That is, indulgence in alcohol signifies his obsession with the past, and its present inaccessibility forces him soberly to confront that past. But the situation occurs because Lowell has revised his aesthetic and prepared himself for a more documentary kind of writing. His "snapshot" aesthetic, described in "Epilogue"—despite often presenting his subjects as "lurid, rapid, grouped," and hardly the ultimate style that makes "writing impossible"[33]—sustains "Unwanted" and makes available whatever psychological healing the poem offers.

Previously, Lowell had avoided explicit self-revelation while giving the impression of writing straightforward autobiography. Besides freely engaging in the fiction-making implicit in poetry, *Life Studies* and *The Dolphin* withhold far more than they reveal, depicting events so disconnected from each other that coherent narrative eludes the reader. "Unwanted," however, tells more than we often know about close friends—immediately disclosing, for example, that Lowell suffers such a predisposition to alcohol that he has to take Antabuse (although we know from other sources that Lowell's difficulty with alcohol was due more to a potentially dangerous combination of necessary medication and alcohol than to ordinary alcoholism). More painfully, the poem unleashes years of suppressed hatred and oedipal yearning for his mother. This candor does not derive from psychotherapy but from the poet's fresh confidence in his aesthetic, engendered by a "crystallization of the imagination" and expressed through the relaxation not only of psychic defenses but of rhetorical artifice.

Though *Day by Day* contains terser and more unified poems, "Unwanted," the most explicitly oedipal of Lowell's published works, echoes all the mother-son-lover dramas of the ages and achieves a level of tragic expression that compensates for its undisciplined narrative. It maintains considerable dramatic tension while pushing metrical and rhetorical freedom to the very limits of verse form. "Unwanted," rather than the *Life Studies* poems, most closely approaches the cadences and narrative logic of "91 Revere Street" and most explicitly considers the tension between Lowell the son and Lowell the potential lover. But the simplicity of its compact syntax and the rhythmic ease of its line-breaks are deceptive. "Unwanted," like most poetry, is constructed in lines, not sentences, and maintains its integrity as verse through attention to the nuances of its rhythms. Whether this impure and flexible aesthetic would suffice for Lowell's present needs remains, in the poem, an open question: "Is getting well ever an art/or art a way to get well?" To declaim in verse for the first time (Lowell had long before attempted to explore some of this material in prose) one's most intimate problems with minimal dramatization may or may not help Lowell free himself and his poetry from psychological burdens and lifelong aesthetic difficulties. The poem does not answer itself, but its candor suggests that learning how to ask such questions is a victory.

Intrinsic to the success of "Unwanted" and many of Lowell's other late poems is the poet's recognition of enabling perceptions of setting and emotion, coupled with a newfound ease in dealing with aesthetic problems and psychological concerns. In writing *Day by Day*, Lowell reaffirms his allegiance to a modernist respect for the immediate dramatic situation, the finite argument, and the telling visual detail. He has abandoned, for the moment, the declamatory public voice of "The Quaker Graveyard in Nantucket," "For the Union Dead," and "Waking Early Sunday Morning," the historical voices of "After the Surprising Conversions," "Beyond the Alps," and much of *History*, and the religious symbolism of his early work. Further, he refuses the temptation of exploring the natural or religious sublime even when his poems bring him face to face with it. "Summer Tides," Lowell's last published poem, embraces a moment of natural sublimity as an opportunity to further meditate upon domestic problems:

> Tonight
> I watch the incoming moon swim
> under three agate veins of cloud,
> casting crisps of false silver-plate
> to the thirsty granite fringe of the shore.[34]

Characteristically, Lowell's Wordsworthian moment of pictorial clarity succumbs to the murk of self-reproach and puzzlement over the collapse of a relationship:

> Last year
> our drunken quarrels had no explanation,
> except everything, except everything.
> Did the oak provoke the lightning,
> when we heard its boughs and foliage fall? . . .

The sublime loses dimension, the domestic drama reshapes perception, and culture remakes nature in its own image. The ending of the
poem, referring to Lowell's children of two marriages, leaves him
perched on a "wooden beach-ladder" that like his emotional world is
on the verge of collapse: "Their father's unmotherly touch / trembles
on a loosened rail." That flimsy structure is an aesthetic one, its "one
bolt" barely sufficient to keep it erect. Yet like everything else Lowell
has built, it functions.

With trembling touch and palpable sigh of acceptance, Lowell has
distilled and simplified from the temptation of a new romanticism
what "Epilogue" calls a "snapshot" aesthetic. This documentary mode
of art is consistent with his earlier work insofar as it confounds the immutable with the harshly textured present, an occurrence found even
in *Land of Unlikeness*. Lowell in his last years renews a commitment
made in writing *Life Studies* to a poetry of the domestic quotidian, but
brings to it a fresh conviction of the primacy of individual vision while
honoring Emerson's more mimetic assertion that "the eye is the best of
artists."[35]

Conclusion

"I F A POEM IS AUTOBIOGRAPHICAL," LOWELL argues, "—and this is true of any kind of autobiographical writing and of historical writing—you want the reader to say, this is true."[1] Though inadequate as a basis for defining the autobiographical lyric or meditative poem, this remark suggests one reason why Lowell frequently attempted to invent alternative styles of discourse. The creation of the illusion of truth engages the reader to a greater degree than other rhetorical strategies, especially in the case of the contemporary American audience and its palpable bias toward documentary naturalism. No genre study or psychoschematic examination of autobiography can fully illuminate Lowell's practice because of the individuality of his shaping voice, but some of his poems attempt to define, in dramatic context, the nature of autobiography and its relationship to the historical and public dimensions of his poetics. James Olney, in the frustration of attempting to define autobiography, argues that "a man's lifework is his fullest autobiography,"[2] and this bond between the work and the person is what Lowell invokes in calling his *Selected Poems* a "small-scale Prelude."[3] From the mid-1950s, when he began his never-completed prose autobiography, his poetry moved haltingly but inevitably toward the starkness of "Unwanted," a confrontation between aesthetic and ego that would expose if not resolve the dichotomy of visionary epic historicism and a compelling aesthetic of commonplace perception. In less metaphysical terms, this is the dichotomy of public and private experience, but by now I hope I have demonstrated that for Lowell it was the metaphysical or aesthetic terms that shaped his sense of the personal and the public, not the other way around.[4] His attempts to symbolically resolve such tensions through aesthetic experiment reveal him not as Narcissus, as some critics have thought him to be, but as Orpheus, devoured not by ego but by devotion to his art.

In examining one more sonnet from the inexhaustible mine of *History*, I wish to demonstrate how Lowell saw work and life, public and private worlds, coalesce. More precisely, this poem illustrates how the ego and the meditative sensibility mutually engage the chimera of the imperishable work only to reject, in reflexive self-criticism, the possibility of lasting achievement when life and art have intimately bonded. However he worried over his status and limitations, Lowell understood better than his critics what those limitations were. In "Reading Myself," as in numerous other poems, he makes those limitations his subject and the basis for his aesthetic strategies. He didn't claim to be a critic of his own poems "except in the most pressing and urgent way."[5] The ingenuousness of this claim mocks the critic with the supremacy of the poet and the poem. To suggest that the effort behind the poem gives the poet an intimacy with the work no critic can share, he invents in a late essay an elaborate metaphor of identification, asserting that after "hundreds of hours shaping, extending, and changing hopeless or defective work," the parts of the poem, "the fragmentary and scattered limbs become by a wild extended figure of speech, something living . . . a person."[6] What more eloquent and subtle argument against reading a poem as "about" its author, as if a person could be "about" a person?

Lowell, in this conjoining of author and poem, echoes Williams's masterful identification of Paterson (the city and the poem) with Dr. Paterson, the half-present hero of his epic. But the goal for Lowell was to merge the poem-person and the poet-person, and thereby mend whole worlds of duality. His autobiography, the entire body of his poetry, is "not a lesson and example" but an act of accretion and resolution.[7] In "Reading Myself," in which the honeycomb eloquently represents the work that remains after death, Lowell in magisterial summation again demonstrates how radically his aesthetic qualifies the relationship between autobiography and history:

> Like thousands, I took just pride and more than just,
> struck matches that brought my blood to a boil;
> I memorized the tricks to set the river on fire—
> somehow never wrote something to go back to.
> Can I suppose I am finished with wax flowers
> and have earned my grass on the minor slopes of
>   Parnassus. . . .
> No honeycomb is built without a bee
> adding circle to circle, cell to cell,
> the wax and honey of a mausoleum—
> this round dome proves its maker is alive;
> the corpse of the insect lives embalmed in honey,
> prays that its perishable work live long
> enough for the sweet-tooth bear to desecrate—
> this open book . . . my open coffin.[8]

I cannot agree with Lawrence Lipking that Lowell in this poem "repudiate[s] his life as a poet."[9] That his "open book" should be his "open coffin" (compare with Basil Bunting's comment, "A man who collects his poems screws together the boards of his coffin")[10] results from the poet's drive not toward completion but toward further accumulation, as the bee adds to its honeycomb until death, when hive and book become mausoleums. Certainly, Lowell supposes that only the vision of the living artist vitalizes his poems. He "never wrote something to go back to" because setting "the river on fire" and making "wax flowers" violate nature and indicate a lack of understanding of poetry as amalgamative process. The honeycomb, the dominant metaphor of this poem, not only demonstrates a better, more natural use of wax but illustrates the actual relationship between the poet and his body of work. Rereading his poems, Lowell does repudiate the "wax flowers," but this affirms rather than rejects his "life as a poet," which derives from the conception of poetry as a living process rather than an accumulation of museum pieces. As the maker vitalizes his work by his presence, so it "proves its maker is alive," keeping him preserved—if embalmed—long enough for the judgment of literary history—the "sweet-toothed bear"—to desecrate the mausoleum-hive by devouring its contents, including the bee-poet.

Lowell has indeed cared a great deal about "building a great career," but the process itself was enjoyable, consisting of "heavenly hours of absorption and idleness."[11] Building the mausoleum required the labor of love and, as with the bee, the powers of instinct and intuition. Where in this late work is the "bitterness" toward the critics and the public "he believed had misunderstood him," which Helene Flanzbaum detects?[12] Lowell has not closed the book; since he cannot close the coffin on himself, cannot seal his own mausoleum, he adds to his life-work even as he admits its failure. He blames this failure on no one but himself—it is the inevitable result of clinging to a poetics of process, of trying to write himself into his work. As the work accumulates, he becomes more aware that his work is "perishable," that the attempt to unite his life and his work implies mutual extinction. Yet he will not shrink from considering his mortality, since it generates new responsibilities, fresh tasks that stimulate an increase in aesthetic awareness and, as "Epilogue," the poem at the end of *Day by Day,* records, a sense of the limitations of history and of the pathos of simple accuracy:

> We are poor passing facts,
> warned by that to give
> each figure in the photograph
> his living name.[13]

The lyric pathos of the detached individual and the perception of the fragility of life lend urgency to Lowell's aesthetic and frequently redirect his attention to the social quotidian, where occurs that "little image" of historical context, the "detail" that alone or more often in combination with other elements generates a union of personal perception and public utterance.[14] Because wedded to private perception as well as dedicated to public statement, the poem functions only as long as the generating cultural situation lingers. Beyond that cultural moment, the "living name" may survive, but the figure in the photograph persists only as image, the human fact terminated. All art is elegiac, and mourns both its subject and itself. Like a person, the "passing fact" of the poem requires style and inspiration to link its disparate concerns:

> the grace of accuracy
> Vermeer gave to the sun's illumination
> stealing like the tide across a map
> to his girl solid with yearning.

The rewards of art touch upon the ineffable and inflame the material world of the flesh. Art reaches out to the sublime, authenticates it, and then binds that sublimity to the palpable, emotional figure of a "girl solid with yearning"—an idealized sexuality Lowell also invokes in "Waking Early Sunday Morning": "All life's Grandeur / Is something with a girl in summer." Lowell's poem, like Vermeer's paintings, is real, is a "person" because a melange of personal vision and public concerns, much like Lowell himself: complex, rooted in fact, historical, obsessed but constrained by context, exposed to the mistakes and "impracticability" of living and writing.

How long Lowell's vision of a poem-person can "live embalmed in honey" remains to be seen: literary history has not yet determined Lowell's fate. But the vitality of his best poems attests that the "maker is alive" in them. The stymied progression of his life and his poetry is not embalmed as exemplary life-career but explicated through the interplay of aesthetic vision and historical and domestic realism through which, as he hoped, the reader may detect "increase of beauty, wisdom, tragedy, and all the blessings of this consuming chance."[15] Despite the imperfections of his work, often caused by his attempts to disburden himself of formalisms and conventions, Lowell's poetry will survive because it clarifies "our insoluble lives." Though it does not overcome its own despair, it effectively dramatizes it, and in doing so invests the individual with tragic dignity by illuminating the mutual implication of the psyche and the body politic. The dilemma Lowell chose to face, the conflict between his desire for a limitless art and the formal demands of a stubborn historicism, becomes in his work an allegory of the free will opposing the limitations of temporality, a central and defining human concern.

Appendix   The complete text of "Caron, Non Ti Crucciare,"
discussed in chapter 2, as it appears in *A New
Anthology of Modern Poetry,* Selden Rodman, ed.
(New York: Modern Library, 1946).

Caron, Non Ti Crucciare

*"And with Him they crucify two thieves, the one on
His right hand, the other on His left."*

I

My beauty is departed: they will square
My hands and feet, and Omar's coarse-hair tent
Towers above the Kedron's Torrent, Sent,
Ben Himnon and the hide-bound outlands where
The little fox runs shivering to its lair,
Fearful lest the short-sighted Orient
Mistake it for this shambles of dissent
Where the red victims of the gallows stare
And dazzle the trenched highways with their blood.
My brothers, if I call you brothers, see:
The blood of Abel, crying from the dead
Sticks to my shaven skull and eyes. What good
Are *lebensraum* and bread of Israel dead
And rotten on the cross-beams of the Tree?

II

This the hour of darkness and the clocks
Of Heaven bawl and falter and the Ram
Kicks over his loose traces, earthquake rocks
The stolid temple of Jerusalem,

Whose cornerstone is rocking with a will
To scatter Jew and Roman to the wind;
The wolves steal up on tiptoe for the kill.
Our beauty is departed. All have sinned.
We are a chosen people, Satan, be still;
We huddled against the gallows lest we die.
O why did God climb out on this bald hill,
That Young Man, worse than prodigal, and lie
Upon the gallows of our brotherhood?
The wolves go round in circles in the wood.

III

I wandered footloose in the wastes of Nod
And damned the day and age when I was born.
I weary of this curse, Almighty God,
Which solely falls on my cleft heel and horn;
My shepherd brother led the lepers back
To Jordan. Then I strayed to Babylon
Where gold-dust sands the sidewalks, lost the track
Of Abel through the fallow to thy Son.
Here merchants trim the sheep and goats in mills
Where woolen turns to gold and dollar bills:
The merchants snare us in the golden net
Of Mammon. O Jerusalem, I said,
If I forget thee, may my hand forget
Her cunning. Let the stranger eat my bread.

IV

"There is a woman, if you find her, Son,"
My worldly father whispered, "Where each street
Bubbles and bursts with houses of concrete,
There shall you know the whore of Babylon."
In this way Cain's instruction was begun,
Mother of God, before I could repeat
An *Ave* or know the fabulous clay feet
Of Babylon are dynamite and gun;
Mother of God, I lie here without bail.

Instruct a lasher of the sheep and goat
In Jonah, who three nights of midnights lay
Buried inside the belly of the whale,
Then, grappling Nineveh by its mule's throat,
Hauled a great city to the Scapegoat's hay.

V

Behind his sliding window, Dives sits
To turn out Lazarus, if he should knock;
Wealth is a weighty sorrow. But my wits
Are addled by the sepulchre, the rock,
By splinters of the Godhead in a head
That knows the devils Saul and Joshua smote
From Salem repossess their old homestead
And keep up open-house to feast the Goat;
O tame and uniform conceits of man
And human reason, you should light the night
By burning! Goat-foot Satan, I have lain,
Clutching my nothing close as death, tonight
And heard you hooting, when our women ran;
Your goat-horns rattle on the whited pane.

VI

We saw Mount Sinai and the Holy land
In Egypt, compound of black earth and green
Between a powdered mountain and red sand
Scoured by the silver air-lines: we have seen
The sworded Seraphim, the serpent-tree,
The apple, once more distant than light-years,
Falling like burning brands about our ears.
The hydra-headed delta choked with sea;
On that sarcophagus of the Nile's mud
And mummies, the Destroyer clamped a lid,
Weightier than King Cheops' pyramid,—
Coffin within a coffin. In whose blood,
Or Jordan, will our spiked and burdened hands
Cup water for a mummy and his lands?

VII

But peace, in Israel bearded elders keep
The peace as they have always kept it. No
Wolves break into these pastures where the sheep
Wait for the hireling hind to shear them. O
People, let us sleep out this night in peace.
Jehovah nods, the doors of Janus slam,
Cocks on the weathervanes will never cease
Crowing for our defilement of the Lamb.
Lamb in the manger, come into our house:
Here you may find and buy all you can eat,
Dirt cheap. On high, till cockcrow, Lord of Hosts,
The gallows' bird is singing to his spouse,
And mad-cap Lamb is gambolling in the street
And splatters blood on the polluted posts.

VIII

Virgil, who heralded this golden age,
Unctuous with olives of perpetual peace,
Had heard the cackle of the Capitol Geese,
And Caesar toss the sponge and patronage
Of Empire to his prostituted page.
The gold is tarnished and the geese are grease,
Jason has stripped the sheep for golden fleece,
The last brass hat has banged about the stage.
But who will pipe a new song? In our land
Caesar has given his scarlet coat away.
But who will pipe a new song? In our land
Caesar has given his crown of thorns away.
But who will pipe the young sheep back to fold?
Caesar has cut his throat to kill the cold.

IX

God is my shepherd and looks after me.
See how I hang. My bones eat through the skin
And flesh they carried here upon the chin
And lipping clutch of their cupidity;

Now here, now there, the sparrow and the sea
Gull splinter the groined eyeballs of my sin,
Caesar, more beaks of birds than needles in
The fathoms of the Bayeux Tapestry;
Our beauty is departed. Who'll discuss
Our scandal, for we are terror and speak:
"Remember how the Dove came down to us,
Broke through your armor of imperial bronze
And beat with olive-branch and bleeding beak
And picked the Lord's Annointed to the bones."

X
I made this Babel. Pushed against the wall,
With splintered hands and knees and sky-sick blood,
I pieced together scaffolding. O God,
To swing my cloven heels into the tall
Third heaven of heavens, where the Prophet Paul
Fathoms that Jacob's Ladder is the wood
Of Christ the Goat, whose hanging is too good
For my unnourished horns, gone wooden, all
Splintered. God even of the goats, that was:
The fearful night is over and the mist
Is clearing from the undemolished shore
Of Paradise, where homing angels pass
With the dunged sheep into the manger. Christ
Swings from this Tower of Babel to the floor.

Notes

Introduction

1. *Time,* 2 June 1967, 67.

2. Richard Tillinghast, *Robert Lowell's Life and Work: Damaged Grandeur* (Ann Arbor: University of Michigan Press, 1996), 29.

3. Monroe Spears, *Dionysus and the City* (New York: Oxford University Press, 1970), 240.

4. "Telling the Time," *Salmagundi* 1, no. 4 (1966–67): 23.

5. Norman Mailer, *The Armies of the Night* (New York: NAL, 1968), 44–45.

6. In his earliest work, Lowell was particularly drawn to ethical and moral concerns—addressed in "The True Light" and "Dante's Inferno" (*Vindex* 59 [1935]: 129–30, 130–31).

7. Vereen Bell, *Robert Lowell: The Nihilist as Hero* (Cambridge: Harvard University Press, 1983), 7.

8. Stanley Kunitz claims that "few realized that [Lowell] had first accepted the invitation and then rescinded his acceptance at the urgent solicitation of a few friends," but even if true, the fact remains that Lowell was open to such solicitation ("The Sense of a Life," in Jeffrey Meyers, ed., *Robert Lowell: Interviews and Memoirs* [Ann Arbor: University of Michigan Press, 1988], 235). Lowell's reply, published in the *New York Times,* admitted that he had "accepted somewhat rapidly and greedily," so he made no attempt to conceal the change of heart (*Collected Prose* [New York: Farrar, Straus, 1987], 370).

9. William Meredith, rev. of *Notebook 1967–1968, New York Times Book Review,* 15 June 1969, 1.

10. *Newsweek,* 26 September 1977, 81; *Time,* 2 June 1967, 67.

11. See Thomas Parkinson, "For the Union Dead," *Salmagundi* 1: no. 4 (1966–67): 87–95.

12. Lowell, *History* (New York: Farrar, Straus, 1973), 193, 194.

13. William Doreski, *The Years of Our Friendship: Robert Lowell and Allen Tate,* (Jackson: University of Mississippi Press, 1990), 9.

14. Neil Corcoran, "Lowell Retiarius: Towards *The Dolphin,*" *Agenda* 18, no.3 (1980) 76.

15. Wallace Stevens, *The Necessary Angel* (New York: Knopf, 1951), 77.

16. Lowell, "After Enjoying Six or Seven Essays on Me," *Salmagundi* 37 (spring 1977): 114.

17. Lowell, "Elizabeth Bishop," in *Collected Prose,* 77.

18. See Doreski, *The Years of Our Friendship,* chapters 3 and 4.

19. Harold Bloom, introduction to *Modern Critical Views: Robert Lowell,* Harold Bloom, ed. (New York: Chelsea, 1987), 2.

20. Lowell, "On Skunk Hour," in *Collected Prose,* 227.

21. "On Skunk Hour," 227. Lowell's friendly relationship with Ginsberg has never been carefully explored.

22. "In the Cage" and "Rebellion" in *Lord Weary's Castle* (New York: Harcourt, Brace, 1946) deal with highly personal subject matter, but the manner of the poems distances them from the reader.

23. David Kalstone, "The Uses of History," in Bloom, *Modern Critical Views: Robert Lowell,* 83.

24. Many reviewers, however, strongly disliked *Notebook 1967–68.* David Bromwich argued that "the style it invents is bad—really, because it is not in any accepted sense a style, but rather the flow of an unremittingly turbid subconscious" ("Notebook," in Bloom, *Modern Critical Views: Robert Lowell,* 35). This is nonsense, of course—the subconscious, if it exists, does not write sonnets of such syntactical elegance and complexity, or any sort of sonnet at all. Such commentary is only a step away from the childish—but once common—practice of dismissing all new writing styles as the products of insanity. But the general sense that Lowell had gone too far this time pervaded many of the reviews.

25. See William Doreski, "Lowell: Autobiography and Vulnerability" in *The Modern Voice in American Poetry* (Gainesville: University Press of Florida, 1995), 125–27, for a more concerted attempt to refute this critique of *The Dolphin.*

26. "Afterthought" to *Notebook 1967–68* (New York: Farrar, Straus, 1969), 159.

27. *Day by Day* (New York: Farrar, Straus, 1977), 120.

28. Kalstone, "The Uses of History," 83.

29. See Alan Williamson, *Pity the Monsters: The Political Vision of Robert Lowell* (New Haven: Yale University Press, 1974), and Bell, *Lowell: Nihilist as Hero.*

30. See Stephen Yenser, *Circle to Circle: The Poetry of Robert Lowell* (Berkeley: University of California Press, 1975).

31. Henry Hart, *Robert Lowell and the Sublime* (Syracuse: Syracuse University Press, 1995).

32. Though Hart demonstrates that Lowell remained strongly interested in the sublime, I do not agree that in his later work he became obsessed by it. Rather, I think it became one more element in an increasingly complex and increasingly skeptical poetic vision.

33. Lowell, interviewed by Frederick Seidel, *Paris Review* 25 (winter–spring 1961): 75.

34. *History,* 193.

1. War and Redemption

1. *Collected Prose,* 369.

2. Lowell's performance astonishes me, although Joanne Feit Diehl seems to think such authority is available to all male poets: "The male poet resolves his difficulties—the terrifying discontinuity in his selfhood—by aligning himself with the culturally assumed identity of the patriarchal voices of authority, thus at once reclaiming his own superiority without denying his access to the reciprocal relationship between the imagination and the natural world" ("In the Twilight of the Gods: Women Poets and the American Sublime," in *The American Sublime,* ed. Mary Arnesberg [Albany: SUNY Press, 1986], 177). If only it were so simple for all of us males—but most of us are not born into the cultural and social elite, and lack the confidence and standing to so readily engage the powers that be. Diehl's simplistic characterization of gender roles fails to convince, but it does suggest what the ideal function of such identification could be. Lowell, however, never resolved the "terrifying discontinuity in his selfhood," and he had far more access to power than do most poets, male or otherwise.

3. Anthony Hecht, "On Robert Lowell," interview with Nancy Schoenberger (New York: New York Center for Visual History, 1987), 7.

4. Lowell's politics could come from either divergent angle, and generally mingle in his poetry, as he confessed in conversation with Stanley Kunitz: "One side of me . . . is a conventional liberal, concerned with causes, agitated about peace and justice and equality, as so many people are. My other side is deeply conservative, wanting to get at the root of things, wanting to slow down the whole process of mechanization and dehumanization, knowing that liberalism can be a form of death too. In the writing of a poem all our compulsions and biases should get in, so that finally we don't know what we mean" ("Telling the Time," 22).

5. Hart, *Robert Lowell and the Sublime,* 75.

6. Unfortunately, *Land of Unlikeness* (Cummington, Mass.: Cummington Press, 1944), published in an edition of only 250 copies, is difficult to find. Few of its poems have been reprinted, except for the dozen or so (depending on how one counts fragmented and combined poems) Lowell revised for *Lord Weary's Castle.* Four, however—"A Suicidal Nightmare," "On the Eve of the Feast of the Immaculate Conception 1942," "Christmas Eve in the Time of War," and "Cistercians in Germany"—appear in *The Achievement of Robert Lowell: A Comprehensive Selection of His Poems with a Critical Introduction,* ed. William J. Martz (New York: Scott Foresman, 1966). For more bibliographical information, see Jerome Mazzaro, *The*

Achievement of Robert Lowell, 1939–1959 (Detroit: University of Detroit Press, 1960), or the less descriptive bibliography in Hugh Staples, *Robert Lowell: The First Twenty Years* (London: Faber & Faber, 1962).

7. The title derives from a passage in Etienne Gilson, *The Mystical Theology of Saint Bernard,* cited in Staples, *Lowell: The First Twenty Years,* 22.

8. Yenser, *Circle to Circle,* uses this opening stanza to argue that "at the same time that it affords a means of unifying a poem on one level, the submerged verbal pattern invites disorganization on other levels. Too great a concentration [on the poet's part] upon the intention of a poem is liable to involve disruption or obfuscation of its 'extension,' or abstracted logical structure, which depends upon denotation" (21). I would argue that the verbal pattern that causes this disruption is not at all "submerged," but is the very fabric of the poem. Staples, on the other hand, argues that the language of this poem "reflects in part a young poet's conscious striving for novelty; it is barely rescued from bathos by the dignity and strength of the religious emotion that produced it" (*Lowell: The First Twenty Years,* 25). I am not entirely convinced by the religious emotion, and would argue that even if entirely sincere the poem can rescue itself only by the effectiveness of its language, which Staples finds lacking.

9. *Land of Unlikeness* is unpaginated.

10. Other critics do not seem to find this poem as problematic as I do. Jerome Mazzaro, for example, comfortably describes it as a simple condemnation of war, elegy for lost human brotherhood, entreaty to Mary, and offering up of hope (*The Poetic Themes of Robert Lowell* [Ann Arbor: University of Michigan Press, 1965], 22–23). Such a reading, however, by taking Lowell's Catholicism and apparent intentions at face value, misses everything of interest in the poem.

11. Mazzaro, *The Poetic Themes of Robert Lowell,* 23.

12. Yenser, *Circle to Circle,* argues that "Lowell's use of the refrain ('The Bomber,' 'Concord Cemetery after the Tornado') . . . can only point up the isolation of stanzas from one another and thereby emphasize the lack of structural development" (23).

13. *Lord Weary's Castle,* 17.

14. Though the conclusion of "At the Indian Killer's Grave" is modified from "Cistercians in Germany," the germ of the poem derives from "The Park Street Cemetery," the first poem in *Land of Unlikeness.*

15. Lowell Papers, Houghton Library, Harvard University.

16. "Rebellion," *Lord Weary's Castle,* 29. Steven Gould Axelrod notes that the earliest draft of this poem appears in a notebook that is nearly contemporaneous with the event (*Robert Lowell: Life and Art* [Princeton: Princeton University Press, 1978], 59). Axelrod argues that the poem is "figural rather than representational," and claims that reading it autobiographically is "anachronistic"; but his reading of the later version (in *Lord Weary's Castle*) is based on the early drafts, which cer-

tainly attempt to transform the incident into a "figural" one, as these lines, later dropped, indicate: "The son, worse than prodigal, shall bear / The sacred stigma of Cain's brotherhood, / Renounce the earth's face and the face of God" (Lowell Papers). I would argue that the movement from a figural version to a representational—and autobiographical—version is an important part of Lowell's development from *Land of Unlikeness* to *Lord Weary's Castle* and beyond. Why should the existence of early drafts require us to read a later, much different version as though it still embodied the earlier, abandoned intent?

17. "Commander Lowell," *Life Studies* (New York: Farrar, Straus, 1959), 70.

18. T. S. Eliot, "The Three Voices of Poetry," *On Poetry and Poets* (New York: Farrar, Straus, 1957), 96.

19. Yenser, *Circle to Circle*, 25.

20. Yenser, *Circle to Circle*, rightly notes that the "allusion to Mark Antony's oration" is "distractingly superfluous," but the self-conscious irony does seem accurately to represent the speaker's state of mind (19). Mazzaro, on the other hand, sees the paraphrase of *Julius Caesar* as an extension of the irony embodied in the use of "burial" to challenge "Easter, a time of resurrection." He adds the observation that "As Mark Antony's funeral oration was deliberately geared to stress the good in Caesar's life—that which is 'oft interred with the bones,' the reader is led by analogy to believe that for Winslow this 'good' is not the humanity which Antony attributes to Caesar, but the materialistic pursuit of a million dollars" (*The Poetic Themes of Robert Lowell*, 15).

21. R. P. Blackmur was one of the first critics to note a certain disjunction between Lowell's profession of and expression of faith. In a profoundly observant 1945 review of *Land of Unlikeness* he wrote, "Lowell is distraught about religion; he does not seem to have decided whether his Roman Catholic belief is the form of a force or the sentiment of a form" ("Nothing Loved," in *Robert Lowell: A Portrait of the Artist in His Time*, Michael London and Robert Boyers, eds. [New York: David Lewis, 1970], 3).

22. *The Dolphin* (New York: Farrar, Straus, 1973), 68.

23. Later, in writing *History*, Lowell would find another way to focus those epic ambitions.

2. Crossing the Styx

1. Lowell, "Dylan Thomas," in *Collected Prose*, 101.

2. Randall Jarrell, "From the Kingdom of Necessity," in *Poetry and the Age* (New York: Knopf, 1953), 188.

3. Lowell, "Dylan Thomas," *Collected Prose*, 99.

4. *Dylan Thomas: The Poems*, Daniel Jones, ed. (London: Dent, 1971), 116. Subsequent quotations are from this edition.

5. *Dylan Thomas: The Poems,* Jones, ed., 262.

6. *Dylan Thomas: The Poems,* Jones, ed., 263.

7. Dylan Thomas, letter to the editor, *Sunday Times* (London), September 1936.

8. Charles S. Singleton, trans., *The Divine Comedy: Inferno: Text and Commentary* (Princeton: Princeton University Press, 1970), 31.

9. In Selden Rodman, ed., *A New Anthology of Modern Poetry* (New York: Modern Library, 1946), 413. Subsequent quotations are from this appearance.

10. Lowell, *Collected Prose,* 102.

11. Christopher Dawson, *Progress and Religion* (New York: Longmans, 1929), 158–59.

12. *Lord Weary's Castle,* 69.

13. Mary Jarrell, ed., *Randall Jarrell's Letters* (Boston: Houghton Mifflin, 1985), 138.

14. *Letters,* 139.

15. *Letters,* 146.

16. *Letters,* 147.

17. Staples points out that "France" is an adaptation of Francois Villon's ballade "L'Epitaphe" (*Lowell: The First Twenty Years,* 95). Not only sonnet IX but several other passages in "Caron" allude to Villon's poem. But without the title "France" the adaptation would be difficult to discern.

18. Hart, *Robert Lowell and the Sublime,* 131.

19. Lowell, *Life Studies,* 3. In sonnet VIII of "Caron, Non Ti Crucciare," in a strange parallelism, Caesar tosses the sponge of empire.

20. Berryman in his essay on "Skunk Hour" asks, "Who cares to hand grades to a writer who could first *make* the Ovid stanza in "Beyond the Alps" (I believe it appeared in the *Kenyon* version) and then delete it?" (*The Freedom of the Poet* [New York: Farrar, Straus, 1976], 318). The stanza did appear in the first published version (*Kenyon Review* 15 [1953], 398–401), but although it is a fine stanza, the poem moves more decisively without it.

21. Lowell, *For the Union Dead* (New York: Farrar, Straus, 1964), 56.

22. Lowell, "Three Poems for *Kaddish,*" *Ploughshares* 5, no. 2 (1979), 72–73.

3. "The Sudden Bridegroom"

1. Jarrell, "From the Kingdom of Necessity," 195.

2. Bloom, introduction to *Modern Critical Views: Robert Lowell,* 1.

3. Eliot defines tradition as involving "the historical sense," and argues that "the historical sense involves a perception not only of the pastness of the past, but of its presence." Further, "it is at the same time what makes a writer most acutely conscious of his place in time, of his contemporaneity" ("Tradition and the Indi-

vidual Talent," *The Sacred Wood* [London: Methuen, 1920], 49). Extrapolating from this, one might define postmodernism as the loss of the presence of the past and a sense of place in time combined with a heightened sense of contemporaneity, though some, differing with Eliot, have defined modernism itself in much the same way.

4. A peculiar expression of Lowell's later, more plainly secular view of Eliot's (and perhaps by implication his own) spiritual quest occurs in a consolatory letter Lowell wrote to Valerie Eliot in 1965: "Somehow I think, the long spiritual pilgrimage, that gruelling, heroic, and yet inwardly at peace exploration and purgation—all that shines through Ash Wednesday and the Quartets was inevitably going to end in the surprise reward of a joyfull marriage" (*Southern Review* 21 [autumn 1985]: 999).

5. Lowell, "T. S. Eliot," in *Collected Prose,* 47.

6. Much later in his life, no longer professing Catholicism, Lowell commented to Ian Hamilton on the religious conflicts in his early works: "I was born a non-believing Protestant New Englander; my parents and everyone I saw were nonbelieving Protestant New Englanders. They went to church, but faith was improper. In college, I began reading Hawthorne, Jonathan Edwards, English seventeenth-century preachers, Calvin himself, Gilson and others, some of them Catholics—Catholics and Calvinists I don't think opposites; they are rather alike compared to us in our sublunary, secular sprawl. From zealous, atheist Calvinist to a believing Catholic is no great leap. I overhammered the debating points. Yet Calvinism is ill-conceived, an abstract expressionist church of Rome" (interview with Ian Hamilton, in *The Review* 26 [summer 1971]: 19). Clearly, the Robert Lowell of 1971 has distanced himself from his more youthful and obviously conflicted persona, but the description of the "zealous, atheist Calvinist" echoes the critical attitude of the early poetry.

7. Typical of critics who take Lowell's professed Catholicism at face value, Irvin Ehrenpreis overlooks the vulgar sexuality and the psychological tensions of this passage. He argues that Lowell invokes "John, Matthew, Mark and Luke . . . to guide him towards the inclusive faith of the Roman Catholic church, to a vision of salvation that more than admits the Indian chief; for it promises Philip that the blessed Virgin herself will deck out his head with flowers" ("The Age of Lowell," in London and Boyers, *Robert Lowell: A Portrait of the Artist in His Time,* 167). Yenser sees this imagery as "compressing suggestions of rebirth, spiritual marriage, and Armageddon" (*Circle on Circle,* 58). Like Ehrenpreis, Yenser neglects the crude materiality of the imagery, which undermines Lowell's attempt at a traditional religious construct.

Bell calls this passage a "naively pictorial spectacle" that "evokes the chaste, childlike spirit of the devotional iconography of the Middle Ages" (*Lowell: Nihilist as Hero,* 27). This misrepresents both Lowell and the Middle Ages.

8. As evinced, for example, by Eliot's later social criticism, in which a regressive social definition of tradition displaces the sober literary definition propounded in "Tradition and the Individual Talent." Eliot offers a xenophobic view of traditional community: "What I mean by tradition involves all those habitual actions, habits, and customs, from the most significant religious rite to our conventional way of greeting a stranger, which represent the blood kinship of 'the same people living in the same place'" (*After Strange Gods: A Primer of Modern Heresy* [New York: Harcourt, 1934], 18). Tate, in essays published in the same decade (*Reactionary Essays on Poetry and Ideas* [New York: Scribners', 1936]) propounds a new agrarianism that is equally socially conservative and tinged with racism. Lowell in the 1940s sometimes expressed equally conservative social views, but later in life, contrary to the conventional view of political maturation, became much more liberal and progressive. The tension between progressive and reactionary social views is already present in *Lord Weary's Castle.*

9. The original title of the poem, under which it appeared in the *Partisan Review* in 1943, was *"The Capitalist's Meditation by the Civil War Monument."* The full title in *Land of Unlikeness* is "Christmas Eve in the Time of War," followed by (in italics) "A Capitalist Meditates by a Civil War Monument." Lowell revised the poem and published it in *Commonweal* in 1946 under the title "Christmas Eve under Hooker's Statue," this version identical to the *Lord Weary's Castle* version.

10. Melville's lines, from "The March into Virginia," read:

> All wars are boyish, and are fought by boys,
> The champions and enthusiasts of the state:
> Turbid ardors and vain joys
> Not barrenly abate—
> Stimulants to the power mature,
> Preparatives of fate.
>
> (Melville, *Collected Poems*
> [Chicago: Packard, 1947], 10)

11. Stéphane Mallarmé, "Poetry as Incantation," Bradford Cook, trans., in *The Modern Tradition*, Richard Ellmann and Charles Feidelson, eds. (New York: Oxford University Press, 1965), 112.

12. Eliot, "In Memoriam," *Selected Essays* (London: Faber & Faber, 1951), 328–38.

13. Some would add Kenneth Rexroth to this list, but I do not believe that his poetry of the 1940s deals with the complexities and challenges of modernism. Rather, it seems to take them for granted, and speaks in a voice that while of great clarity and often conspicuous beauty (as in much of *The Phoenix and the Tortoise* [New York: New Directions, 1944]) lacks the self-consciousness and reflexivity that engender the difficulties and rewards of Lowell's, Schwartz's, and Rukeyser's poetry. While Rexroth's earliest poetry, such as "A Prolegomenon to a Theodicy" (1927), is superficially modern in manner, I am not convinced that by tempera-

ment and sensibility he was a modernist, a postmodernist, or a critic of either mode. Rather, and perhaps to his credit, he seems to stand aside from that problematical dynamic, making possible calm and expansive poems like *The Heart's Garden, The Garden's Heart* (Cambridge, Mass.: Pym-Randall Press [1967]).

14. The objectivists cannot be considered merely ephebes of the high modernists Pound and Williams. In some cases, their more liberal or even radical political views separated them from the older poets, and in all cases their aesthetic concerns are too complex and individual to allow us to regard their objectivity as the only or even the main feature of their work. They did not, for the most part, see themselves as a school. As Rexroth notes, "Almost all the people that Zukofsky picked as Objectivists didn't agree with him" (*American Poetry in the Twentieth Century* [New York: Seabury, 1973], 111). They did, however, tend to favor an aloof and impersonal voice, though rarely one as ceremonial as Yeats's. Their preoccupation with formal problems sharply distinguishes them from Lowell, who in the 1940s, having temporarily abandoned free verse, favored conventional metrical structures and regularized end-rhyme schemes. Lowell was concerned with form, as he noted in 1960, looking back on this period: "[W]e believed in form, that was very important" (unpublished MS, Houghton Library). The objectivists, however, did not believe in form; that is, they did not take for granted its necessity or utility, but insisted on reinventing or rediscovering it with every poem. Their skepticism about form parallels Lowell's skepticism about language and prompts a different but comparable experimentation.

15. Auden had already gone much further than Lowell—or Williams for that matter—in developing alternative voices for contemporary poetry, but though Jarrell and other American poets admired him, his example had not and has not yet fully been absorbed.

16. Nine notebooks at Houghton Library, Harvard, filed as "Land of Unlikeness Notebooks," contain school notes and miscellaneous material, but largely consist of poems written from Lowell's years at St. Marks through his undergraduate years at Kenyon to the early 1940s. Most of the poems in *Land of Unlikeness* appear in these notebooks in rough-draft versions. The earliest poems are divided between rhymed and roughly metered formal poems and informal free-verse poems. Many are religious in topic; many others are humorous. For examples of this early verse, see Doreski, *The Years of Our Friendship*, 31–35, 43–45. Further cataloging of the contents of some of these notebooks may be found in Axelrod, *Robert Lowell: Life and Art,* appendix A.

17. Lowell stated that Edwards was one of his ancestors, but this claim may derive more from Lowell's sense of kinship with the religious enthusiast than from genealogical fact.

18. Lowell does not actually name the source, but in the "Note" at the front of *Lord Weary's Castle* says, "I hope that the source of 'After the Surprising Conversions' will be recognized" (vii). Lowell had at one time planned to write a biogra-

phy of Edwards. In 1942–43, while staying with the Tates in Tennessee, he "was heaping up books on Jonathan Edwards and taking notes and getting more and more numb on the subject, looking at old leather-bound volumes on freedom of the will and so on, and feeling less and less a calling" (interview, *Paris Review*, 64). During this same winter, he completed sixteen of the poems that would go into *Land of Unlikeness* (see Ian Hamilton, *Robert Lowell: A Biography* [New York: Random House, 1982], 82). At some point Lowell traveled to Northampton to inspect whatever Edwards relics he could find. He describes this "pilgrimage" in "Jonathan Edwards in Western Massachusetts" (*For the Union Dead*, 40–44). The most immediate products were, however, the poem under discussion here, and "Mr. Edwards and the Spider."

19. The most significant addition to Edwards's tale is Lowell's closure. Edwards ends the sad story by noting that "some pious persons . . . had it urged upon 'em, as if somebody had spoken to 'em, *Cut your own Throat, now is a good Opportunity. Now; Now!*" Lowell's added closing lines do a great deal to dissipate the gloom and general tenor of Edwards's tale of spiritual tragedy. Mazzaro argues that Lowell dated the poem 22 September because "it is the feast day of St. Thomas of Villanova, who sent the first Augustinians to the Americas as missionaries, and like Edwards' sermons, those of St. Thomas 'were followed by a wonderful change in the lives of men in all places he visited.'" (*The Poetic Themes of Robert Lowell*, 70). This seems to explain the specific date, but resetting the letter in the fall points to the larger strategy of secularizing the poem's motif of salvation. See Edwards's original letter in *Jonathan Edwards: Representative Selections*, Clarence H. Faust and Thomas H. Johnson, eds. (New York: Hill & Wang, 1962), 73–91; see also Patricia J. Tracy, *Jonathan Edwards, Pastor: Religion and Society in Eighteenth-Century Northampton* (New York: Hill & Wang, 1980), 109–18, Giovanni Giovannini's discussion of the source in "Lowell's 'After the Surprising Conversions,'" in the *Explicator* 9 ([June 1951], 53), Mazzaro's quotation of the relevant passage from Edwards's *Narrative* with comparable lines of the poem indicated parenthetically (*The Poetic Themes of Robert Lowell*, 69–70), and Marjorie Perloff's discussion of Lowell's revamping of Edwards's syntax (*The Poetic Art of Robert Lowell* [Ithaca: Cornell University Press, 1973], 120–23).

20. In one of the most fruitful discussions of this poem, Bruce Michelson in "Randall Jarrell and Robert Lowell: The Making of *Lord Weary's Castle*," in Bloom, *Modern Critical Views: Robert Lowell*, comments of Lowell's closure that "it saves him from one of those blind alleys of certainty that could make his voice intolerable, and further poetry in a sense impossible" (149).

21. Mazzaro, *The Poetic Themes of Robert Lowell*, 54. "Where the Rainbow Ends" did not appear in *Land of Unlikeness* (it was published in the *Nation* in 1946). Lowell revised it slightly, however, between the first and second printings of *Lord Weary's Castle*.

22. Staples, *Lowell: The First Twenty Years,* 107.

23. Phillip Cooper in *The Autobiographical Myth of Robert Lowell* (Chapel Hill: University of North Carolina Press, 1970) accurately if somewhat glibly characterizes the Pepperpot at the end of the rainbow as the place "where the sublime encounters the ridiculous" (85).

24. Yet even Harold Bloom, a decidedly skeptical critic, in his introduction mistakes the opening stanza of this poem as "an instance of . . . the poetry of belief" (4).

25. Lowell, *Collected Prose,* 45.

26. Lowell, "Epilogue," *Day by Day,* 127

27. This failure of mediation may signal the achievement of Lowell's mature postmodern style, one that accords with Fredric Jameson's observation that "perhaps the supreme formal feature of all the postmodernists" is "a new kind of flatness or depthlessness, a new kind of superficiality in the almost literal sense" (*Postmodernism, or the Cultural Logic of Late Capitalism* [Durham, N.C.: Duke University Press, 1991], 9). Certainly some reviewers of *Day by Day* found it disarmingly—or forbiddingly—flat and lacking in depth. Lowell's utter effacement of style—a truly postmodern style—and his final dropping of the mask seem to me the consequences of the process described in this essay.

28. Lowell, *Collected Prose,* 45.

29. *Lord Weary's Castle,* 8.

30. Staples, *Lowell: The First Twenty Years,* 45.

31. Ibid., 46.

32. *Lord Weary's Castle,* 9.

33. Ibid., 8.

34. Ibid., 10.

35. Staples, *Lowell: The First Twenty Years,* 52.

36. That the familiar colloquialism for sexual orgasm was current in Lowell's circle is made clear by this 1 November 1945 entry in Delmore Schwartz's journal: "Jean [Stafford Lowell] to Cal [Lowell]: May I tell Delmore? 'She was slow in coming, but when she came, she came like an alarm clock'" (*Portrait of Delmore: Journals and Notes of Delmore Schwartz, 1939–1959,* Elizabeth Pollet, ed. [New York: Farrar, Straus, 1986], 272).

37. Jarrell, "From the Kingdom of Necessity," 197.

38. Ibid., 188–89.

4. "Cut Down, We Flourish"

1. Gene Bardo, in reviewing the book for the *New York Herald Tribune Book Review* (22 April 1951), found the title poem a "rich achievement," but David Daiche's comment in *Yale Review* that the characters in the dramatic monologues

speak "with an odd mixture of casualness and hysteria" is more typical (*Yale Review* 61 [September 1951], 153).

2. Lowell to Randall Jarrell, 24 February 1952 (Berg Collection, New York Public Library).

3. Parker's account is paraphrased in Paul Mariani, *Lost Puritan: Robert Lowell* (New York: Norton, 1994), 130.

4. Randall Jarrell, "Three Books," *Poetry and the Age,* 234.

5. Much of the information about the Kavanaghs and St. Patrick's Church in this paragraph derives from a pamphlet entitled *A Self-Guided Tour: What to See in St. Patrick's Church.*

6. Mariani, *Lost Puritan,* 127.

7. *The Mills of the Kavanaughs* (New York: Harcourt, 1951), 2.

8. From a letter to Elizabeth Bishop, quoted in Mariani, *Lost Puritan,* 201.

9. See Staples, *Lowell: The First Twenty Years,* 58–62.

10. *Kenyon Review* 13: no. 1 (1951): 9.

11. *The Mills of the Kavanaughs,* 19.

12. Staples, *Lowell: The First Twenty Years,* 63–64.

13. Mazzaro, *The Poetic Themes of Robert Lowell,* 87.

14. Richard Fein, *Robert Lowell* (New York: Twayne, 1970), 37.

15. Yenser, *Circle to Circle,* 95.

5. The Corporate Fifties

1. Robert Lowell Papers, Houghton Library, Harvard University.

2. *Life Studies,* particularly the sequence of personal and family poems at its core, has commonly been read as a psychological exploration of the problem of self-individuation, a declaration of literary independence, a breakthrough into autobiography, and a protest against the stifling asexual and censorious atmosphere of the Boston of Lowell's childhood and youth. Nearly everyone has seized upon the obvious oedipal dimension of the depicted relationship between rebellious child-poet and uncomprehending parents and the contrast between that situation and the cool Jamesian perspective of the narrator. Further, because *Life Studies* is as much a product of twentieth-century aesthetic concerns as of Lowell's actual experiences, everyone—especially Lowell himself—has noted the shift from the heavily allusive, ruggedly metrical early work to lightly rhymed free or much-loosened verse, and various critics have credited William Carlos Williams with setting an appropriate example. Axelrod most fully makes the case for the influence of Williams in the third chapter of *Robert Lowell: Life and Art.* He also credits Bishop and Snodgrass with offering examples of formal and thematic breakthroughs, but dismisses, oddly enough, the continuing example of Allen Tate, whose autobiographical

poems of the early 1950s had strongly moved Lowell. For Lowell's own comments on the changes in his style represented by *Life Studies,* see his interview in *Paris Review,* 66–74.

3. William Gaddis, *The Recognitions* (New York: Harcourt, 1955), 299.

4. Allen Ginsberg, *Howl and Other Poems* (San Francisco: City Lights Books, 1956), 16.

5. R. V. Cassill, untitled statement, *Fiction of the Fifties,* Herbert Gold, ed. (New York: Doubleday, 1960), 21.

6. Kenneth Rexroth, "Disengagement: The Art of the Beat Generation," *World Outside the Window: Selected Essays* (New York: New Directions, 1987), 49. One might argue that poets have often felt alienated from society, especially since the romantic era. Rexroth complains with equal bitterness about the 1930s, for example. My point is that in the 1950s the complaints often focus on the particular issue of the abuse of language by government, corporation, and media, adding a fresh dimension to an old problem.

7. Perrin Stryker, "A Slight Case of Overcommunication," *Fortune* (March 1954): 116.

8. See Jürgen Habermas, *The Social Transformation of the Public Sphere* (Cambridge: MIT Press, 1989), esp. ch. 7. Though on page 245 Habermas adequately defines the sources of cultural hegemony that work to stifle discourse, his formalized conception of modern communication, however chilling, fails fully to factor in the pressure exerted by uncontrolled capitalism and a collapsing bourgeoisie to normalize the appearance of public opinion until even the mildest dissent has been erased. Of course, Habermas formulated his historical survey before the full consequences of the media-appropriation of the former public sphere became apparent. In the present situation, his concluding sentence (250) postulates a situation now overtaken by events. The function of the bourgeois public sphere has been almost entirely obliterated by electronic media control, most recently manifested through the commercial appropriation of the Internet, the intrusion of commercial TV into public schools, and the predatory technological coopting of education at all levels in the name of "computer literacy."

9. Herbert Block, *Herblock's Here and Now* (New York: Simon & Schuster, 1955), 3. Block focuses on the crisis in discourse, which he perceives as the product of superficiality and cowardice: "If it raps persistently, a phase may be taken in by the mind, and vice versa; and the notion that goes unchallenged brings along its trunk and settles down to become a cliché" (4). His convincing indictment of the McCarthy era as a breakdown in communication has been ignored by recent cultural historians, who tend to see the 1950s in revisionary terms as the "Golden Age" that Block mockingly describes. See William O'Neill, *American High* (New York: Free Press, 1986), x, for a recent rationalization of the policies that encouraged McCarthyism, and an eulogistic view of American domestic life in the period.

10. *Life Studies,* 85.

11. From a letter to Elizabeth Bishop, quoted in Mariani, *Lost Puritan,* 273.

12. Fein, *Robert Lowell,* 61.

13. *Life Studies,* 59.

14. Hart, *Robert Lowell and the Sublime,* xx.

15. Joseph Bennett, "Two Americans, a Brahmin, and the Bourgeoisie." *The Hudson Review* 12, no. 3 (1959), 431–39. Bennett's review may seem wrongheaded in most ways, but it marks the extreme but intelligible range of response generated by Lowell's remarkable book.

16. Bell presents an interesting discussion of the earth and lime imagery, arguing that because of Lowell's reversal of the "conventional associations [life represented by fertile soil, death represented by 'quicklime'] . . . the two conflicting directions in which this image moves makes it symbolically oxymoronic" (*Robert Lowell: Nihilist as Hero,* 57). However, this reading depends on the association of lime with "the caustic substance used to destroy dead bodies," which is actually quicklime. In the poem, however, the lime surely is not quicklime but merely harmless ground limestone, a very different substance. The child would hardly be placing his hands on quicklime, which is much too caustic for gardening.

17. Robert Penn Warren, "Pure and Impure Poetry," *Kenyon Review* 5, no. 2 (1943), 251.

18. This manic episode began in February, 1958. Hamilton points out that the earliest draft of "Waking in the Blue" was written at the beginning of the episode, while Lowell was still in a "locked ward"; it was worked on for three months. The first draft has the night attendant reading a "Social Relations text-book." Revising it to *The Meaning of Meaning* was only one of dozens of revisions of the diffuse early version, which Hamilton usefully reproduces. See Hamilton, *Robert Lowell: A Biography,* 244–46.

19. C. K. Ogden and I. A. Richards, *The Meaning of Meaning: A Study of the Influence of Language upon Thought and of the Science of Symbolism,* 8th edition (New York: Harcourt, 1959), ix–x.

20. Bell argues in *Lowell: Nihilist as Hero* that "*The Meaning of Meaning* is put before us . . . as a model of the brave human effort to achieve rational understanding of the relation between the mind and the wordless word. It is affiliated in the poem, therefore, with all the other more common visible signs of normalcy." (62). I believe it functions rather as a sign of the meaninglessness of attempting to assign meaning in an irrational world. If, as Bell argues, the poem demonstrates that "sanity and normalcy are the mind's defenses against itself and what it knows," (62) then I would point out that the poem also demonstrates that these defenses are pathetically ineffective.

21. Mazzaro identifies this poem as one "based on a comparison between the present and 'past forms of the state'"; he points out the relationships among Stuyvesant, Grant, and Eisenhower and the problem of public misadministration

and scandal (*The Poetic Themes of Robert Lowell*, 95). Dwight Eddins further remarks that while previous critics have noted the "Grant-Eisenhower parallel . . . they do not . . . seem to have emphasized the heroic criterion of a 'past form of the state,' which appears in Grant's victory at Cold Harbor and the self-sacrifice of the soldiers who died there for the preservation of 'the Republic.'" He then aptly links this poem to "For the Union Dead" as two examples of Lowell's obsession with "the theme of the decay of republics as evidence of the state's inability to exist for long on an ideal level" ("Poet and State in the Verse of Robert Lowell," in Bloom, *Modern Critical Views: Robert Lowell*, 48–49). This observation is wholly compatible with my argument that a crisis in communication and discourse occurs in *Life Studies* as a mutually binding public and private matter.

22. *Life Studies*, 7.

23. The version published in *Partisan Review* (20, no. 6 [1953], 631) has the Republic summoning Grant, not Eisenhower.

24. An editorial in *Fortune* in 1957 notes that "Mr. [note the resistance to "President"] Eisenhower himself has said that 'as long as the American people demand and, in my opinion, deserve the kind of services that this budget provides, we have got to spend this kind of money.'" The editorial is not entirely critical of Eisenhower, but notes the budgetary difficulties and contradictions in his economic and domestic principles and policies, and suggests that the president has departed from "the principles of individualism, of enterprise, and of limited government" ("The Retreat in Washington," *Fortune* (March 1957), 105–6).

25. As Mazzaro puts it in *The Poetic Themes of Robert Lowell*, "This 'sheepish' figure of Lepke turns on the earlier figures of Lowell and Lowell's father, recalling Lowell's own sense of being lobotomized and tranquilized and the Commander's loss of hope" (115). Gabriel Pearson compares Lepke in his cell "piling towels on a rack" with "Lowell's own situation, hogging a whole house, a thing also forbidden 'to the common man'" ("The Middle Years," in Bloom, *Modern Critical Views: Robert Lowell*, 32). However, I would insist that Lowell's perception of the man scavenging trash suggests that Lowell the householder imagines, at least for the moment, that everyone is as privileged as he.

26. *Life Studies*, 90.

27. From a letter to Bishop quoted in David Kalstone, *Becoming a Poet* (New York: Farrar, Straus, 1989), 185.

28. Having grown up in a grocery store in the 1950s I can attest to the popularity of sour cream and other delicacies among ordinary people. It was the ready availability of such items, difficult to obtain during the Great Depression and rare before the era of mechanical refrigeration, that helped define postwar prosperity.

29. Friedrich von Schiller, *On the Aesthetic Education of Man*, Elizabeth M. Wilkinson and L. A. Willoughby, trans. (Oxford: Oxford University Press, 1967), 171.

30. *Day by Day*, 46.

6. "One Gallant Rush"

1. Axelrod, *Robert Lowell, Life and Art,* 170.

2. At least fifty discussions of "For the Union Dead" have appeared in books or journal articles, making this one of Lowell's most discussed and most admired poems. None of these discussions, however, deals in any detail with the composition of the poem and nearly all find it a compelling example of the public voice in which Lowell writes. For example, Bell argues that the poem sets Shaw's public role against Lowell's, but he barely touches upon the poem's autobiographical complexity (*Lowell: Nihilist as Hero,* 95–96). Cooper claims that "the poem is a Northern counterpart to Allen Tate's 'Ode to the Confederate Dead'" (75). And Yenser argues that "For the Union Dead" is "the most comprehensive expression of the persona's renewed concern with the objective and historical world" (237). While this complex poem admits any number of readings, it is a less historical and objective poem than Tate's. While the parallel to "Ode to the Confederate Dead" is valid, since Lowell with his final choice of title clearly intended to respond to Tate, it describes only one dimension of Lowell's poem, and fails to explain why it seems so much more powerful than Tate's.

3. The crowd received the poem with enthusiasm, according to a *Boston Globe* article entitled "Poet on the Common Hushes Roar of the City" (6 June 1960). Nora Taylor, in *The Christian Science Monitor* (6 June 1960), referred to the poem as "a song of the city" and noted that Eleanor Roosevelt was in the crowd.

4. Lowell's "imitations" of odes by Horace in *Near the Ocean* (New York: Farrar, Straus, 1967) emphasize the autobiographical content of the originals.

5. Axelrod, *Robert Lowell: Life and Art,* 268. Other poems on Shaw include Phoebe Cary, "The Hero of Fort Wagner," William Vaughan Moody, "An Ode in Time of Hesitation," Robert Underwood Johnson, "Saint-Gaudens: An Ode," Benjamin Brawley, "My Hero, to Robert Gould Shaw," and Richard Watson Gilder, "Robert Gould Shaw." Of these serious, dignified, often skillfully written poems, none wholly escapes the stiff formalism Lowell feared. Perhaps, of these earlier tributes, James Russell Lowell's "Memoriae Positum," written the year of Shaw's death (1863), remains the most powerful and convincing.

6. The file of drafts of "For the Union Dead" at Houghton Library contains thirty-three pages of holograph or typescript, most with penciled or inked notations or corrections. The file includes four drafts entitled "One Gallant Rush" (or some variant); one entitled "The Old Aquarium"; five identified by Colonel Shaw's name in some variation ("Robert Shaw and his men," "Colonel Shaw and the Massachussetts [sic] Fifty-Fourth," etc.); and numerous pages carrying only ten or fifteen lines, variants of passages from the longer drafts. Lowell left no indication of the order of composition; my tracing of his writing process is therefore conjectural, but informed by his own comments and by internal evidence.

7. Peter Burchard, *One Gallant Rush: Robert Gould Shaw and His Brave Black Regiment* (New York: St. Martin's, 1965), 38–39.

8. Quoted by Burchard in *One Gallant Rush*, xii.

9. Thomas Wentworth Higginson, however, found Shaw a somewhat hesitant hero: "The young hero, Colonel Shaw, when I rode out to meet him, on his arrival with his Northern colored regiment, seriously asked me whether I felt perfectly sure that the negroes would stand fire in line of battle, and suggested that, at the worst, it would at least be possible to drive them forward by having a line of white soldiers advance in their rear, so that they would be between two lines of fire. He admitted that the mere matter of individual courage to have already been settled in their case, and only doubted whether they would do as well in line of battle as in skirmishing and on guard duty" (*Part of a Man's Life* [Boston: Houghton Mifflin, 1906], 131).

10. Struldbrugs, immortals in the kingdom of Luggnagg in *Gulliver's Travels*, struggled through eternity in decrepitude and, though they lived on, after a certain age were considered legally dead.

11. Burchard, *One Gallant Rush*, 12, 89.

12. After the fourth complete draft there are several pages of typescript discussing the poem's closure.

13. Statement for the Boston Arts Festival, June 1960 (Lowell Papers, Houghton Library).

7. Lowell in Maine

1. *The Review* 26 (summer 1971): 10.

2. *Near the Ocean*, 51–52.

3. Ibid., 15.

4. Discussing the ways in which details come into poetry, Lowell remarks that "you may feel the doorknob more strongly than some big personal event, and the doorknob will open into something that you can use as your own" (interview, *Paris Review*, 94). A few years later, the doorknob has found its place in an actual poem.

5. Richard Fein has pointed out that "whatever criticism will be made of Lowell's poetry for its insistence on measuring external scenes in terms of the poet's own 'Fierce, fireless mind,' his poetry, at least for some time, will have a strong appeal for those who find it impossible to look at worldly activities and not find some implicit correlation between their own secret fears and their culture" (*Robert Lowell*, 140).

6. Fein, *Robert Lowell*, 145.

7. *Day by Day*, 99.

8. *For Lizzie and Harriet* (New York: Farrar, Straus, 1973), 41.

9. Untitled statement in *Maine Lines,* Richard Aldridge, ed. (Philadelphia: Lippincott, 1970), 155.

10. *For the Union Dead,* 3.

11. Elizabeth Bishop, *One Art: Letters* (New York: Farrar, Straus, 1995), 408. In this same letter, Bishop suggests the phrases "lobster town" and "fish for bait," which Lowell used.

12. See Mariani, *Lost Puritan,* 166–68; Kalstone, *Becoming a Poet,* 139–45; Bishop, *One Art,* 164–65.

13. *For the Union Dead,* 63.

14. Perloff, *The Poetic Art of Robert Lowell,* 154.

15. Yenser, *Circle on Circle,* 260.

16. *Near the Ocean,* 30.

17. "New England and Further," in *Collected Prose,* 180.

18. Philip Booth, "Summers in Castine: Contact Prints: 1955–1965," *Salmagundi* 37 (spring 1977): 41.

19. Lowell papers, Houghton Library.

20. Alex Calder, "*Notebook 1967–68*: Writing the Process Poem," in *Robert Lowell: Essays on the Poetry,* Steven Axelrod, ed. (New York: Cambridge University Press, 1986), 124–26.

21. *Notebook 1967–68,* 5.

8. Vision, Landscape, and the Ineffable

1. Axelrod, *Robert Lowell: Life and Art,* 207.

2. See Hart, *Robert Lowell and the Sublime,* xx–xxi, and Jonathan Veitch, "'Moonlight in the Prowling Eye': The *History* Poems of Robert Lowell," *Contemporary Literature* 33 (1992): 458–79.

3. "After Enjoying Six or Seven Essays on Me," 114.

4. "Alexander," *History,* 39.

5. "After Enjoying Six or Seven Essays on Me," 113.

6. *History,* 184, 207.

7. "Romanoffs," *History,* 99.

8. "After the Democratic Convention," *History,* 177.

9. *History,* 108.

10. *Notebook*: Revised and expanded version, 262.

11. *History,* 24.

12. The relevant lines read: "Death is the mother of beauty; hence from her, / Alone, shall come fulfillment to our dreams / And our desires" (Stevens, *Collected Poems* [New York: Knopf, 1954], 68–69).

13. Ralph Waldo Emerson, "History," *Essays and Lectures* (New York: Library of America, 1983), 246.

14. *History*, 207.

15. Robert Pinsky, "The Conquered Kings of Robert Lowell," *Salmagundi* 37 (spring 1977): 105.

16. *History*, 206.

17. Ibid., 24.

18. Ibid., 25.

19. Ibid., 25.

20. Interview, *Paris Review*, 94.

21. *History*, 26.

22. Ibid., 198.

23. James McIntosh, *Thoreau as Romantic Naturalist* (Ithaca: Cornell University Press, 1974), 9.

24. Stevens, *The Letters of Wallace Stevens* (New York: Knopf, 1965), 274.

25. *History*, 141.

26. Bell, *Lowell: Nihilist as Hero*, 192.

27. *For the Union Dead*, 18.

28. *Robert Lowell, A Reading* (LP disk), Caedmon TC 1569 (1978).

29. McIntosh, *Thoreau*, 9.

30. The remark occurs in a 1943 letter to Robie Macauley quoted in Hamilton, *Robert Lowell: A Biography*, 81.

31. *History*, 123.

32. Ibid., 191.

33. R. K. Meiners, *Everything to Be Endured* (Columbia: University of Missouri Press, 1970), 32.

34. Yenser, *Circle on Circle*, 227.

35. *For the Union Dead*, 53.

36. *Robert Lowell: A Reading*.

37. *History*, 37, 32, 31.

38. Ibid., 111.

39. Ibid., 207.

40. Henry David Thoreau, *Walden* (Princeton: Princeton University Press, 1971), 3.

41. "After Enjoying Six or Seven Essays on Me," 114.

42. Hamilton, *Robert Lowell: A Biography*, 384.

9. Borrowed Visions

1. "After Enjoying Six or Seven Essays on Me," 112.

2. Cited in W. H. Auden, *The Enchafèd Flood* (New York: Random House, 1950), 58.

3. Ralph Waldo Emerson, "History," in *Essays and Lectures*, 250–51.

4. *History,* 90. This is revised from "The Abyss" in *Imitations* (New York: Farrar, Straus, 1961), 56.

5. *History,* 90. Revised from "Meditation," in *Imitations,* 54.

6. *Notebook,* 263.

7. John Baley, "Robert Lowell: the Poetry of Cancellation," in London and Boyers, *Robert Lowell: A Portrait of the Artist in His Time,* 197.

8. Ehrenpreis, "The Age of Lowell," 181–82.

9. Fein, *Robert Lowell,* 133.

10. John Simon, "Abuse of Privilege: Robert Lowell as Translator," in London and Bowers, *Robert Lowell: A Portrait of the Artist in His Time,* 197; Bishop, *One Art,* 395.

11. Robert Lowell papers, Houghton Library.

12. Perloff, "The Limits of Imitation: Robert Lowell's Rimbaud," *The Poetic Art of Robert Lowell,* 73.

13. See *Imitations,* 84–89, for the original versions.

14. *History,* 91. Revised from "At the Green Cabaret," in *Imitations,* 87.

15. *History,* 91. Revised from "A Malicious Girl," in *Imitations,* 88.

16. "After Enjoying Six or Seven Essays on Me," 112.

17. "Memories of West Street and Lepke," *Life Studies,* 85.

18. *History,* 92.

19. Ibid., 92. Revised from "Evil," in *Imitations,* 89.

20. *Lord Weary's Castle,* 6.

21. *History,* 93. Revised from "Napoleon After Sedan," in *Imitations,* 85.

22. *Land of Unlikeness* Notebook #3, Lowell papers, Houghton Library.

23. "The Downlook," *Day by Day,* 125.

24. *History,* 148.

25. *Preludes: Selected Poems from the Kathryn Irene Glascock Intercollegiate Poetry Contest 1924–1973* (South Hadley, Mass.: Mount Holyoke College, 1973), 55.

26. *History,* 177.

10. "Lightning on an Open Field"

1. *Day by Day,* 121.

2. William Carlos Williams, *Spring & All* (Paris: Contact Publishing, 1923), 82.

3. *Day by Day,* 90.

4. Harold Bloom, "Yeats and the Romantics," in *Modern Poetry: Essays in Criticism,* John Hollander, ed. (New York: Oxford University Press, 1968), 501.

5. M. H. Abrams, *Natural Supernaturalism* (New York: Norton, 1971), 8.

6. M. H. Abrams, "Structure and Style in the Greater Romantic Lyric," in *Romanticism and Consciousness,* Harold Bloom, ed. (New York: Norton, 1970), 201.

7. *For the Union Dead,* 24.

8. Ibid., 47.

9. *The Dolphin,* 28.

10. *Day by Day,* 125.

11. Ibid., 72.

12. *Day by Day,* 44.

13. Ibid., 126.

14. Ibid., 53.

15. Tillinghast, *Robert Lowell's Life and Work,* 113.

16. Robert Lowell Papers, Houghton Library.

17. *Day by Day,* 62.

18. *Imitations,* 148.

19. *Day by Day,* 66.

20. Ibid., 127.

21. Ibid., 6.

22. Ibid., 72.

23. *Notebook:* Revised and expanded version, 262.

24. Bell, *Lowell: Nihilist as Hero,* 209.

25. *Day by Day,* 96

26. Ibid., 3.

27. Helen Vendler, "Last Days and Last Poems," *Part of Nature, Part of Us* (Cambridge: Harvard University Press, 1980), 165.

28. Bell, *Lowell: Nihilist as Hero,* 210.

29. *Day by Day,* 121.

30. Priscilla Paton, "Saying What Happened: Robert Lowell's *Day by Day.*" (Ph.D. diss., Boston College, 1979), 154.

31. In the prose sketch that preceded the poem, the child has dropped down the register the Christus from a rosary. See "Antebellum Boston," *Collected Prose,* 302.

32. *For the Union Dead,* 10.

33. *Day by Day,* 120.

34. *The New Review* 4, no. 43 (1977): 3.

35. Ralph Waldo Emerson, "Nature," *Nature, Addresses, and Lectures* (Cambridge: Harvard University Press, 1971), 12.

Conclusion

1. Interview, *Paris Review,* 71.

2. James Olney, *Metaphors of Self* (Princeton: Princeton University Press, 1972), 3.

3. "After Enjoying Six or Seven Essays on Me," 112.

4. Though I have made little use of it, Hart's exploration of Lowell's readings in E. F. Carritt's *Philosophies of Beauty* (Oxford: Clarendon Press, 1931), his college textbook, is valuable for anyone exploring Lowell's aesthetic sense (*Robert Lowell and the Sublime*, 66–67).

5. "After Enjoying Six or Seven Essays on Me," 112.

6. Ibid., 112.

7. Ibid.

8. *History,* 194.

9. Lawrence Lipking, *The Life of the Poet* (Chicago: University of Chicago Press, 1981), 185.

10. Basil Bunting, *Collected Poems* (London: Fulcrum Press, 1968), 9.

11. "After Enjoying Six or Seven Essays on Me," 112.

12. Helen Flanzbaum, "Surviving the Marketplace: Robert Lowell and the Sixties," *New England Quarterly* 68, no. 1 (1995), 57.

13. *Day by Day,* 127.

14. Interview, *Paris Review,* 94.

15. "After Enjoying Six or Seven Essays on Me," 115.

Bibliography

Abrams, M. H. *Natural Supernaturalism.* New York: W. W. Norton, 1971.

———. "Structure and Style in the Greater Romantic Lyric." In *Romanticism and Consciousness,* edited by Harold Bloom. New York: W. W. Norton, 1970.

Auden, W. H. *The Enchafèd Flood.* New York: Random House, 1950.

Axelrod, Steven Gould. *Robert Lowell: Life and Art.* Princeton: Princeton University Press, 1978.

Baley, John. "Robert Lowell: The Poetry of Cancellation." In *Robert Lowell: A Portrait of the Artist in His Time,* 187–98.

Bardo, Gene. Review of *The Mills of the Kavanaughs. New York Herald Tribune Book Review,* April 22, 1951.

Bell, Vereen. *Robert Lowell: The Nihilist as Hero.* Cambridge: Harvard University Press, 1983.

Bennett, Joseph. "Two Americans, a Brahmin, and the Bourgeoisie." *Hudson Review* 12, no. 3 (1959): 431–39.

Berryman, John. *The Freedom of the Poet.* New York: Farrar, Straus, & Giroux, 1976.

Bishop, Elizabeth. *One Art: Letters,* edited by Robert Giroux. New York: Farrar, Straus, & Giroux, 1995.

Blackmur, R. P. "Nothing Loved." In *Robert Lowell: A Portrait of the Artist in His Time:* 3–4.

Block, Herbert. *Herblock's Here and Now.* New York: Simon & Schuster, 1955.

Bloom, Harold. Introduction to *Modern Critical Views: Robert Lowell,* edited by Harold Bloom. New York: Chelsea, 1987: 1–4.

———. "Yeats and the Romantics." In *Modern Poetry: Essays in Criticism,* edited by John Hollander. New York: Oxford University Press, 1968.

Booth, Philip. "Summers in Castine: Contact Prints: 1955–1965." *Salmagundi* 37 (spring 1977): 37–53.

Bromwich, David. "Notebook." In *Modern Critical Views: Robert Lowell:* 35–40.

Bunting, Basil. *Collected Poems.* London: Fulcrum Press, 1968.

Burchard, Peter. *One Gallant Rush: Robert Gould Shaw and His Brave Black Regiment.* New York: St. Martin's, 1965.

Calder, Alex. "*Notebook 1967–68*: Writing the Process Poem." In *Robert Lowell: Es-*

says on the Poetry, edited by Steven Axelrod. New York: Cambridge University Press, 1986: 124–26.

Carritt, E. F. *Philosophies of Beauty.* Oxford: Clarendon Press, 1931.

Cassill, R. V. Untitled statement. In *Fiction of the Fifties,* edited by Herbert Gold. New York: Doubleday, 1960: 21–22.

Cooper, Phillip. *The Autobiographical Myth of Robert Lowell.* Chapel Hill: University of North Carolina Press, 1970.

Corcoran, Neil. "Lowell Retiarius: Towards *The Dolphin.*" *Agenda* 18, no. 3 (1980): 75–85.

Daiche, David. Review of *The Mills of the Kavanaughs. Yale Review* 61 (September 1951): 153.

Dawson, Christopher. *Progress and Religion.* New York: Longmans, 1929.

Diehl, Joanne Feit. "In the Twilight of the Gods: Women Poets and the American Sublime." In *The American Sublime,* edited by Mary Arnesberg. Albany: SUNY Press, 1986: 173–214.

Doreski, William. *The Years of Our Friendship: Robert Lowell and Allen Tate.* Jackson: University of Mississippi Press, 1990.

———. *The Modern Voice in American Poetry.* Gainesville: University Press of Florida, 1995.

Eddins, Dwight. "Poet and State in the Verse of Robert Lowell." In *Modern Critical Views: Robert Lowell:* 41–58.

Edwards. Jonathan. *Jonathan Edwards: Representative Selections,* edited by Clarence H. Faust and Thomas H. Johnson. New York: Hill & Wang, 1962.

Ehrenpreis, Irvin. "The Age of Lowell." In *Robert Lowell: A Portrait of the Artist in His Time,* 155–86.

Eliot. T. S. *The Sacred Wood.* London: Methuen, 1920.

———. *After Strange Gods: A Primer of Modern Heresy.* New York: Harcourt, Brace, 1934.

———. "In Memorium." *Selected Essays.* London: Faber & Faber, 1951: 328–38.

———. *On Poetry and Poets.* New York: Harcourt, Brace, 1957.

Emerson, Ralph Waldo. *Nature, Addresses, and Lectures.* Cambridge: Harvard University Press, 1971.

———. *Essays and Lectures.* New York: Library of America, 1983.

Fein, Richard. *Robert Lowell.* New York: Twayne, 1970.

Flanzbaum, Helen. "Surviving the Marketplace: Robert Lowell and the Sixties." *New England Quarterly* 68, no. 1 (March 1995): 44–57.

Gaddis, William. *The Recognitions.* New York: Harcourt, Brace, 1955.

Ginsberg, Allen. *Howl and Other Poems.* San Francisco: City Lights Books, 1956.

Giovannini, Giovanni. "Lowell's 'After the Surprising Conversions.'" *The Explicator* 9 (June 1951): 53.

Habermas, Jürgen. *The Social Transformation of the Public Sphere.* Cambridge: MIT Press, 1989.

Hamilton, Ian. *Robert Lowell: A Biography.* New York: Random House, 1982.

Hart, Henry. *Robert Lowell and the Sublime.* Syracuse, N.Y.: Syracuse University Press, 1995.

Hecht, Anthony. "On Robert Lowell." Interview with Nancy Schoenberger. New York: New York Center for Visual History, 1987.

Higginson, Thomas Wentworth. *Part of a Man's Life.* Boston: Houghton Mifflin, 1906.

Jameson, Fredric. *Postmodernism, or the Cultural Logic of Late Capitalism.* Durham, N.C.: Duke University Press, 1991.

Jarrell, Randall. *Poetry and the Age.* New York: Alfred A. Knopf, 1953.

———. *Randall Jarrell's Letters,* edited by Mary Jarrell. Boston: Houghton Mifflin, 1985.

Kalstone, David. *Becoming a Poet.* New York: Farrar, Straus, & Giroux, 1989.

———. "The Uses of History." In *Modern Critical Views: Robert Lowell:* 81–100.

Kunitz, Stanley "Telling the Time." *Salmagundi* 1, no. 4 (1966–67): 22–24.

———. "The Sense of a Life." In *Robert Lowell: Interviews and Memoirs,* edited by Jeffrey Meyers. Ann Arbor: University of Michigan Press, 1988.

Lipking, Lawrence. *The Life of the Poet.* Chicago: University of Chicago Press, 1981.

Lowell, Robert. *Land of Unlikeness.* Cummington, Mass.: Cummington Press, 1944.

———. *Lord Weary's Castle.* New York: Harcourt, Brace, 1946.

———. *The Mills of the Kavanaughs.* New York: Harcourt, Brace, 1951.

———. *Life Studies.* New York: Farrar, Straus, & Giroux, 1959.

———. *Imitations.* New York: Farrar, Straus, & Giroux, 1961.

———. *For the Union Dead.* New York: Farrar, Straus, & Giroux, 1964.

———. *Near the Ocean.* New York: Farrar, Straus, & Giroux, 1967.

———. *Notebook 1967–1968.* New York: Farrar, Straus, & Giroux, 1969.

———. *Notebook:* Revised and expanded version. New York: Farrar, Straus, & Giroux, 1970.

———. *History.* New York: Farrar, Straus, & Giroux, 1973.

———. *For Lizzie and Harriet.* New York: Farrar, Straus, & Giroux, 1973.

———. *The Dolphin.* New York: Farrar, Straus, & Giroux, 1973.

———. *Day by Day.* New York: Farrar, Straus, & Giroux, 1977.

———. *Collected Prose,* edited by Robert Giroux. New York: Farrar, Straus, & Giroux, 1987.

———. "The True Light." *The Vindex* 59 (1935): 129–30.

———. "Dante's Inferno." *The Vindex* 59 (1935): 130–31.

———. "Aunt Hecuba." In *Preludes: Selected Poems from the Kathryn Irene Glascock Intercollegiate Poetry Contest, 1924–1973.* South Hadley, Mass.: Mount Holyoke College, 1973: 55.

———. Letter to Elizabeth Bishop, December 6, 1950, Bishop papers, Vassar College Library.

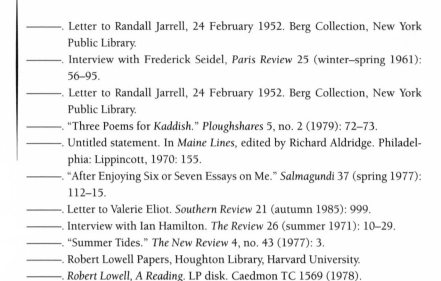

————. Letter to Randall Jarrell, 24 February 1952. Berg Collection, New York Public Library.

————. Interview with Frederick Seidel, *Paris Review* 25 (winter–spring 1961): 56–95.

————. Letter to Randall Jarrell, 24 February 1952. Berg Collection, New York Public Library.

————. "Three Poems for *Kaddish*." *Ploughshares* 5, no. 2 (1979): 72–73.

————. Untitled statement. In *Maine Lines*, edited by Richard Aldridge. Philadelphia: Lippincott, 1970: 155.

————. "After Enjoying Six or Seven Essays on Me." *Salmagundi* 37 (spring 1977): 112–15.

————. Letter to Valerie Eliot. *Southern Review* 21 (autumn 1985): 999.

————. Interview with Ian Hamilton. *The Review* 26 (summer 1971): 10–29.

————. "Summer Tides." *The New Review* 4, no. 43 (1977): 3.

————. Robert Lowell Papers, Houghton Library, Harvard University.

————. *Robert Lowell, A Reading*. LP disk. Caedmon TC 1569 (1978).

McIntosh, James. *Thoreau as Romantic Naturalist*. Ithaca: Cornell University Press, 1974.

Mailer, Norman. *The Armies of the Night*. New York: New American Library, 1968.

Mallarmé, Stéphane. "Poetry as Incantation," translated by Bradford Cook. In *The Modern Tradition*, edited by Richard Ellmann and Charles Feidelson. New York: Oxford University Press, 1965.

Mariani, Paul. *Lost Puritan: Robert Lowell*. New York: W. W. Norton, 1994.

Martz, William J., editor. *The Achievement of Robert Lowell: A Comprehensive Selection of His Poems with a Critical Introduction*. New York: Scott Foresman, 1966.

Mazzaro, Jerome. *The Achievement of Robert Lowell, 1939–1959*. Detroit: University of Detroit Press, 1960.

————. *The Poetic Themes of Robert Lowell*. Ann Arbor: University of Michigan Press, 1965.

Meiners, R. K. *Everything to Be Endured*. Columbia: University of Missouri Press, 1970.

Melville, Herman. *Collected Poems*. Chicago: Packard, 1947.

Meredith, William. Review of *Notebook 1967–1968, New York Times Book Review*, June 15, 1969: 1.

Michelson, Bruce. "Randall Jarrell and Robert Lowell: The Making of *Lord Weary's Castle*," in *Modern Critical Views: Robert Lowell*: 139–61.

Ogden, C. K., and I. A. Richards. *The Meaning of Meaning: A Study of the Influence of Language upon Thought and of the Science of Symbolism*. 8th edition. New York: Harcourt, Brace, 1959.

Olney, James. *Metaphors of Self: The Meaning of Autobiography.* Princeton: Princeton University Press, 1972.

O'Neill, William. *American High.* New York: Free Press, 1986.

Parkinson, Thomas. "For the Union Dead." *Salmagundi* 1, no. 4 (1966–67): 87–95.

Paton, Priscilla. "Saying What Happened: Robert Lowell's *Day by Day.*" Ph.D diss., Boston College, 1979.

Pearson, Gabriel. "The Middle Years." In *Modern Critical Views: Robert Lowell:* 19–34.

Perloff, Marjorie. *The Poetic Art of Robert Lowell.* Ithaca: Cornell University Press, 1973.

Pinsky, Robert. "The Conquered Kings of Robert Lowell." *Salmagundi* 37 (spring 1977): 102–5.

"Poets: The Second Chance." *Time,* 2 June 1967: 67–74.

"Poet on the Common Hushes Roar of the City." *Boston Globe,* 6 June 1960.

"The Retreat in Washington." *Fortune* (March 1957): 105–6.

Rexroth, Kenneth. *American Poetry in the Twentieth Century.* New York: Seabury, 1973.

———. *World Outside the Window: Selected Essays.* New York: New Directions, 1987.

Robert Lowell: A Portrait of the Artist in His Time, edited by Michael London and Robert Boyers. New York: David Lewis, 1970.

Rodman, Selden, editor. *A New Anthology of Modern Poetry.* New York: Modern Library, 1946.

Schiller, Friedrich von. *On the Aesthetic Education of Man,* translated by Elizabeth M. Wilkinson and L. A. Willoughby. Oxford: Oxford University Press, 1967.

Schwartz, Delmore. *Portrait of Delmore: Journals and Notes of Delmore Schwartz, 1939–1959,* edited by Elizabeth Pollet. New York: Farrar, Straus, & Giroux, 1986.

A Self-Guided Tour: What to See in St. Patrick's Church. Damariscotta Mills, Maine: St. Patrick's Church (n.d.).

Simon, John. "Abuse of Privilege: Robert Lowell as Translator." In *Robert Lowell: A Portrait of the Artist in His Time:* 130–51.

Singleton, Charles S., trans. *The Divine Comedy. Inferno: Text and Commentary.* Princeton: Princeton University Press, 1970.

Spears, Monroe. *Dionysus and the City.* New York: Oxford University Press, 1970.

Staples, Hugh. *Robert Lowell: The First Twenty Years.* London: Faber & Faber, 1962

Stevens, Wallace. *The Necessary Angel.* New York: Alfred A. Knopf, 1951.

———. *Collected Poems.* New York: Alfred A. Knopf, 1954.

———. *The Letters of Wallace Stevens,* edited by Holly Stevens. New York: Alfred A. Knopf, 1965.

Stryker, Perrin. "A Slight Case of Overcommunication." *Fortune* (March 1954): 116.

Tate, Allen. *Reactionary Essays on Poetry and Ideas.* New York: Scribners', 1936.

Taylor, Nora. Review of Boston Arts Festival. *Christian Science Monitor*, 6 June 1960.

Tracy, Patricia J. *Jonathan Edwards, Pastor: Religion and Society in Eighteenth-Century Northampton.* New York: Hill & Wang, 1980.

Thomas, Dylan. *Dylan Thomas: The Poems,* edited by Daniel Jones. London: J. M. Dent, 1971.

———. Letter to the editor. *Sunday Times* (London), September 1936.

Thoreau, Henry David. *Walden.* Princeton: Princeton University Press, 1971.

Tillinghast, Richard. *Robert Lowell's Life and Work: Damaged Grandeur.* Ann Arbor: University of Michigan Press, 1996.

Veitch, Jonathan. "'Moonlight in the Prowling Eye': The *History* Poems of Robert Lowell," *Contemporary Literature* 33 (1992): 458–79.

Vendler, Helen. *Part of Nature, Part of Us.* Cambridge: Harvard University Press, 1980.

Warren, Robert Penn. "Pure and Impure Poetry." *Kenyon Review* 5, no. 2 (1943): 251.

Williams, William Carlos. *Spring & All.* Paris: Contact Publishing, 1923.

Williamson, Alan. *Pity the Monsters: The Political Vision of Robert Lowell.* New Haven: Yale University Press, 1974.

Yenser, Stephen. *Circle to Circle: The Poetry of Robert Lowell.* Berkeley: University of California Press, 1975.

Index